ESSENTIAL ETHNOGRAPHIC METHODS

ETHNOGRAPHER'S TOOLKIT

Edited by Jean J. Schensul, *Institute for Community Research, Hartford*, and
Margaret D. LeCompte, *School of Education, University of Colorado, Boulder*

The **Ethnographer's Toolkit** is designed with you, the novice fieldworker, in mind. In a series
of seven brief books, the editors and authors of the **Toolkit** take you through the multiple,
complex steps of doing ethnographic research in simple, reader-friendly language. Case
studies, checklists, key points to remember, and additional resources to consult, are all included
to help the reader fully understand the ethnographic process. Eschewing a step-by-step
formula approach, the authors are able to explain the complicated tasks and relationships that
occur in the field in clear, helpful ways. Research designs, data collection techniques, analytical
strategies, research collaborations, and an array of uses for ethnographic work in policy,
programming, and practice, are described in the volumes. The **Toolkit** is the perfect starting
point for professionals in diverse professional fields including social welfare, education, health,
economic development, and the arts, as well as for advanced students and experienced researchers unfamiliar with the demands of conducting good ethnography.

Summer 1999/ 7 volumes/ paperback boxed set/ 0-7619-9042-9

BOOKS IN THE ETHNOGRAPHER'S TOOLKIT

1. **Designing and Conducting Ethnographic Research**, by Margaret D. LeCompte and
   Jean J. Schensul, 0-7619-8975-7 (paperback)

2. **Essential Ethnographic Methods: Observations, Interviews, and Questionnaires,**
   by Stephen L. Schensul, Jean J. Schensul, and Margaret D. LeCompte 0-7619-9144-1
   (paperback)

3. **Enhanced Ethnographic Methods: Audiovisual Techniques, Focused Group
   Interviews, and Elicitation Techniques,** by Jean J. Schensul, Margaret D. LeCompte,
   Bonnie K. Nastasi, and Stephen P. Borgatti, 0-7619-9129-8 (paperback)

4. **Mapping Social Networks, Spatial Data, and Hidden Populations,** by Jean J. Schensul,
   Margaret D. LeCompte, Robert T. Trotter II, Ellen K. Cromley, and Merrill Singer,
   0-7619-9112-3 (paperback)

5. **Analyzing and Interpreting Ethnographic Data,** by Margaret D. LeCompte and
   Jean J. Schensul, 0-7619-8974-9 (paperback)

6. **Researcher Roles and Research Partnerships,** by Margaret D. LeCompte,
   Jean J. Schensul, Margaret R. Weeks, and Merrill Singer, 0-7619-8973-0 (paperback)

7. **Using Ethnographic Data: Interventions, Public Programming, and Public Policy,**
   by Jean J. Schensul, Margaret D. LeCompte, G. Alfred Hess, Jr., Bonnie K. Nastasi,
   Marlene J. Berg, Lynne Williamson, Jeremy Brecher, and Ruth Glasser, 0-7619-8972-2
   (paperback)

ESSENTIAL ETHNOGRAPHIC METHODS

Observations,
Interviews,
and
Questionnaires

Kristyl Kepley

STEPHEN L. SCHENSUL
JEAN J. SCHENSUL
MARGARET D. LeCOMPTE

2 ETHNOGRAPHER'S
TOOLKIT

ALTAMIRA
P R E S S

A Division of Sage Publications, Inc.
Walnut Creek ◆ London ◆ New Delhi

For information:

AltaMira Press
A Division of Sage Publications, Inc.
1630 North Main Street, Suite 367
Walnut Creek, California 94596 USA
explore@altamira.sagepub.com
http://www.altamirapress.com

SAGE Publications, Ltd.
6 Bonhill Street
London, EC2A 4PU
United Kingdom

SAGE Publications India Pvt. Ltd.
M-32 Market
Greater Kailash I
New Delhi 110 048
India

Printed in the United States of America

Library of Congress Cataloging-in-Publication Data

Schensul, Stephen L.
    Essential ethnographic methods: Observations, interviews, and
questionnaires / by Stephen L. Schensul, Jean J. Schensul, and Margaret D. LeCompte
    p. cm. — (Ethnographer's toolkit; v. 2)
    Includes bibliographical references and index.
    ISBN 0-7619-9144-1 (pbk.: alk. paper)
    1. Ethnology—Methodology 2. Ethnology—Field work. I. Schensul,
Jean J. II. LeCompte, Margaret Diane. III. Title. IV. Series.
    GN345.S362 1999
    305.8'001—dc21   99-6359

This book is printed on acid-free paper.

99 00 01 02 03 10 9 8 7 6 5 4 3 2 1

Production Editor: Astrid Virding
Editorial Assistant: Nevair Kabakian
Designer/Typesetter: Janelle LeMaster
Cover Designer: Ravi Balasuriya
Cover Artists: Ed Johnetta Miller, Graciela Quiñones Rodriguez

CONTENTS

LIST OF TABLES AND FIGURES

LIST OF EXAMPLES

INTRODUCTION

The **Ethnographer's Toolkit** is a series of texts on how to plan, design, carry out, and use the results of applied ethnographic research. Ethnography, as an approach to research, may be unfamiliar to people accustomed to more traditional forms of research, but we believe that applied ethnography will prove not only congenial but also essential to many researchers and practitioners. Many kinds of evaluative or investigative questions that arise in the course of program planning and implementation cannot really be answered very well with standard research methods such as experiments or collection of quantifiable data. Often, there are no data yet to quantify nor any programs whose effectiveness needs to be assessed! Sometimes, the research problem to be addressed is not yet clearly identified and must be discovered. In such cases, ethnographic research provides a valid and important way to find out what *is* happening in programs and to help practitioners plan their activities.

This book series defines what ethnographic research is, when it should be used, and how it can be used to identify and solve complex social problems, especially those not readily amenable to traditional quantitative or experimental research methods alone. It is designed for educators; service professionals; professors of applied students in the fields of teaching, social and health services, communications, engineering, and business; and students working in applied field settings.

Ethnography is a peculiarly human endeavor; many of its practitioners have commented that, unlike other approaches to research, the *researcher* is the primary tool for collecting primary data. That is, as Books 1, 2, 3, and 4 of this series demonstrate, the ethnographer's principal database is amassed in the course of human interaction: direct observation; face-to-face interviewing and elicitation; audiovisual recording; and mapping the networks, times, and places in which human interactions occur. Thus, as Book 6 makes clear, the personal characteristics and activities of researchers as human beings and as scientists become salient in ways not applicable in research where the investigator can maintain more distance from the people and phenomena under study.

Book 1 of the **Ethnographer's Toolkit**, *Designing and Conducting Ethnographic Research,* defines what ethnographic research is and the predominant viewpoints or paradigms that guide ethnography. It provides the reader with an overview of research methods and design, including how to develop research questions, what to consider in setting up the mechanics of a research project, and how to devise a sampling plan. Ways of collecting and analyzing data and ethical considerations for which ethnographers must account conclude this overall introduction to the series.

In Book 3, *Enhanced Ethnographic Methods,* the reader adds to this basic inventory of ethnographic tools three different but important approaches to data collection, each one a complement to the essential methods presented in this book. These tools are audiovisual techniques, focused group interviews, and elicitation techniques. We have termed these data collection strategies "enhanced ethnographic methods" because each of them parallels and enhances a strategy first presented in this book.

Audiovisual techniques, which involve recording behavior and speech using electronic equipment, expand the capacity of ethnographers to observe and listen by creating a more complete and permanent record of events and speech. Focused group interviews permit ethnographers to interview more than one person at a time. Elicitation techniques allow ethnographers to quantify qualitative or perceptual data on how individuals and groups of people think about and organize perceptions of their cultural world.

It is important for the reader to recognize that, although the essential ethnographic methods described in this book can be used alone, the enhanced ethnographic methods covered in Book 3 cannot, by themselves, provide a fully rounded picture of cultural life in a community, organization, work group, school, or other setting. Instead, they must be used in combination with the essential methods outlined here. Doing so adds dimensions of depth and accuracy to the cultural portrait constructed by the ethnographer.

In Book 4, *Mapping Social Networks, Spatial Data, and Hidden Populations,* we add to the enhanced methods of data collection and analysis used by ethnographers. However, the approach taken in Book 4 is informed by a somewhat different perspective on the way social life is organized in communities. Whereas the previous books focus primarily on ways of understanding cultural patterns and the interactions of individuals and groups in cultural settings, Book 4 focuses on how social networks, patterns of interaction, and uses of what we term "sociogeographic space" influence human behavior and beliefs. The final chapter of Book 4 considers the concept of "hidden populations" and describes approaches to locating, entering, and collecting data from individuals who are invisible because there is nothing apparent to distinguish them from others, or because they are involved in behavior that they wish to hide.

Book 5, *Analyzing and Interpreting Ethnographic Data,* provides the reader with a variety of methods for transforming piles of fieldnotes, observations, audio- and videotapes, questionnaires, surveys, documents, maps, and other kinds of data into research results that help people to understand their world more fully and facilitate problem solving. Addressing both narrative and qualitative, as well as quantitative—or enumerated—data, Book 5 discusses methods for organizing, retrieving, rendering manageable, and interpreting the data collected in ethnographic research.

In Book 6, *Researcher Roles and Research Partnerships,* we discuss the special requirements that doing ethnographic research imposes on its practitioners. Throughout the **Toolkit**, we have argued that there is little difference between the exercise of ethnography as a systematic and scientific enterprise and applied ethnography as that same systematic and scientific enterprise used specifically for helping people identify and solve human problems. To that end, in Chapter 1, "Researcher Roles," we first describe how the work of ethnographers is inextricably tied to the type of person the ethnographer is, the particular social and cultural context of the research site, and the tasks and responsibilities that ethnographers assume in the field.

In the second chapter, "Building Research Partnerships," we recognize that ethnography seldom is done by lone researchers. We discuss how ethnographers assemble research teams, establish partnerships with individuals and institutions in the field, and work collaboratively with a wide range of people and organizations to solve mutually identified problems. The chapter concludes with ethical and procedural considerations, including developing social and managerial infrastructure, establishing and breaking contracts, negotiating different organizational cultures and values, and resolving conflicts.

Book 7, *Using Ethnographic Data: Interventions, Public Programming, and Public Policy,* consists of three chapters that present general guidelines and case studies illustrating how ethnographers have used ethnographic data in planning public programs, developing and evaluating interventions, and influencing public policy.

Throughout the series, authors give examples drawn from their own work and the work of their associates. These examples and case studies present ways in which ethnographers have coped with the kinds of problems and dilemmas found in the field—and described in the series—in the course of their work and over extended periods of time.

In this book, titled *Essential Ethnographic Methods,* we concentrate on what we consider to be the methodological foundations for the conduct of ethnographic research. The book is organized into 11 chapters. The first chapter discusses the importance of theory-driven research, triangulation through a mix of quantitative and qualitative methods, the local quality of ethnographic research, and the goal of applied ethnography—to generate innovative solutions to social issues and problems.

Chapter 2 offers an accessible approach to building formative theory as a conceptual guide and model for the conduct of ethnographic research. In this chapter, we describe what we mean by theory (the conceptual guidelines for a study), showing readers how they can move up and down the ladder of abstraction from "facts" observed in the field, to the paradigms or frameworks we outlined in Book 1.

In Chapter 3, we consider the concept of "operationalization," or defining how phenomena in the field are matched with concepts used to design the study. We address how we move from a concept or idea in the formative

Cross Reference: See Book 1, Chapter 3, for a discussion of paradigms used in social science research

theoretical model to observation in the field. Conversely, we also describe how we move from observation in the field to variables, factors, and domains in a research model. Operationalization is a critical step in ethnographic research. Without it, many researchers have found themselves at the end of their designated time in the research study site burdened with boxes of fieldnotes that are difficult to put together. The theme of operationalization will be revisited throughout the book as we move from unstructured to semistructured to structured methods of data collection. It is also revisited in those chapters of Book 5 that discuss identification of items, units, and patterns.

The next three chapters address entry into the research site and first or exploratory steps in conducting the planned research. Ethnographers must enter the research setting; identify contacts who can help them; make naturalistic observations; listen to conversations; and conduct open-ended, in-depth interviews. Methods for engagement in these activities are the focus of these chapters. The data gathered in the initial or exploratory stages of ethnography can

- Alter the concepts and relationships in the formative theoretical model
- Develop approaches for the operationalization of key concepts in this and the next stages of data collection
- Begin a process of description of the environment and social dynamics of the population under study

Cross Reference: See Book 5, Chapters 4 and 5, on analysis of ethnographic data, especially identifying items and units, as well as coding taxonomies

Cross Reference: See Book 6, Chapter 1, on researcher roles for details of the personal skills that facilitate these activities

Chapter 4 describes the process of entering the field, from seeking permission to enter a region, community, school, or hospital to locating key informants who can orient ethnographers to the field setting. Chapter 5 analyzes the meaning and the practice of open-ended or unstructured observation, including participant observation, in the field. Such unstructured data collection marks the beginning of all ethnographic studies. In Chapter 5, we discuss social happenings—events, rituals, and structures—that can be observed relatively unobtrusively. We also discuss what to look for and how to record observations accurately.

In Chapter 6, we focus on exploratory or unstructured, open-ended, in-depth interviews conducted with a relatively small number of individuals and groups. These interviews generally accompany unstructured observation in the initial stages of fieldwork. We will describe what they are, outline the preparation and skills needed to conduct them, discuss with whom they generally are conducted, and give examples of open-ended interview schedules and excerpts from interviews using elicitation techniques. Finally, we review some ways we have found useful for coding interviews and preparing them for analysis.

Chapter 7 on semistructured data collection moves researchers to the next—definitional—stage in data collection. At this point, researchers have identified the major domains in a study, as well as factors that need further elaboration across a larger number of respondents. Researchers still may have many unanswered questions about the meaning of what has been observed so far. In the definitional stage, ethnographers can focus on specific areas of investigation and identify the range of variation in responses in a population using semi-structured interviews with a more representative number of respondents. Semistructured interviewing combines the discovery capacity of unstructured interview schedules with the focus of the quantitative survey. The same principles apply to semistructured observations. First, we define what we mean by semistructured observational data collection techniques, and then we review the main reasons for selecting them, using case examples as illustrations.

The unstructured and semistructured qualitative methods we describe in Chapters 4 through 7 generate both an overall description of social settings and social dynamics in the research site and a set of hypotheses that seeks to explain and distinguish the attitudinal and behavioral characteristics of various subgroups among the population under study. The next step in the research process is to test these ethnographically informed hypotheses on a representative sample of the total population in the site with a survey instrument or observational scheme that obtains quantified data from structured, closed-ended questions and/or an observational coding system. Chapter 8 discusses the development of structured, quantitative data collection methods with population samples that emerge from and are built upon the qualitative data collected using methods described in the previous sections. These more structured methods are used with samples drawn from the study population.

To develop an ethnographic survey, closed-ended, quantitative items are created from those items, themes, or issues identified in the qualitative data. These variables are formatted into items that constitute the closed-ended responses amenable to quantitative analysis. These responses are, in turn, related to the subfactors, factors, and domains in the study's formative ethnographic theory.

Cross Reference: See Chapters 2 and 3 in this book on building formative ethnographic theories and operationalization, and Book 5, Chapters 4 and 5, on coding taxonomies

The ethnographic survey, unlike in-depth and open-ended interviews, is designed to obtain very specific information from a large, representative sample of individuals or situations in the local community. We first describe what we mean by structured data collection methods and introduce readers to different approaches to systematic and probability sampling. Next, we guide readers through steps in the development of an ethnographic survey instrument. Chapter 8 also includes a brief section on structured observation methods.

Chapter 9 discusses the collection and uses of secondary and archival data, including archival and secondary local and nonlocal informational resources and text databases. The final two chapters of *Essential Ethnographic Methods* review two issues critical to good ethnography: sampling methods and sampling bias, and issues of validity and reliability. Throughout, we will draw on examples from our own research in communities and organizations in the United States, as well as from the work of other researchers.

Readers less familiar with ethnographic research will gain an introduction to basic ethnographic principles, methods, and techniques by reading Books 1, 2, 5, and 6 first, followed by other books that explore more specialized areas of research and use. Those familiar with basic ethnographic methods will find Books 3, 4, and 7 valuable in enhancing their repertoires of research methods, data collection techniques, and ways of approaching the use of ethnographic data in policy and program settings.

—Jean J. Schensul and Margaret D. LeCompte

1

GUIDING PRINCIPLES

Ethnographic Research Is Guided by and Generates Theory
•
Ethnographic Research Is Both Qualitative and Quantitative
•
Ethnographic Research Is Conducted Locally
•
Ethnographic Research Is Applied

Ethnography is a scientific approach to discovering and investigating social and cultural patterns and meaning in communities, institutions, and other social settings. One primary difference between ethnography as science and other social and behavioral science methods of investigation is that ethnographers discover what people do and why before they assign meaning to behaviors and beliefs. People's perspectives then form the foundation for building local theories that can be tested, linked to scientific literature, and adapted for use elsewhere. Unlike other social sciences, ethnography depends on the researcher as the primary tool of data collection, so ethnographers pay special attention to issues of bias and ways of ensuring accuracy of data.

Methodologists take different positions with respect to what ethnography is and how to go about conducting ethnographic research. We base our approach to ethnography on four guiding principles:

- Ethnographic research is guided by and generates theory.
- Ethnographic research is both qualitative and quantitative.
- Ethnographic research is conducted locally.
- Ethnographic research is applied.

Cross Reference:
See Book 1, Chapter 1, for a general orientation to ethnography and ethnographic methods

ETHNOGRAPHIC RESEARCH IS GUIDED BY AND GENERATES THEORY

Definition: A formative theory includes an issue or problem central to the study, as well as ideas about which components of the physical, social, and institutional environment cause, predict, or are associated with the central problem

Definition: A research model is a diagrammatic representation of the relationships among these components

Cross Reference: See Book 5, Chapter 11, on interpretation of ethnographic research

Cross Reference: See Book 1, Chapter 7, and Book 5, Chapters 8-10, on ways of organizing and analyzing qualitative data

Consistent with other books in this series, we take the position that ethnographic theory is constructed recursively, that is, it begins with a set of connected ideas that undergoes continuous redefinition throughout the life of the study until the ideas are finalized and interpreted at the end. Researchers begin with an early or rudimentary version of a **formative theory** and a **research model** (cf. Pelto & Pelto, 1978; Trotter & Schensul, 1998). Formative theory may be generated from the following:

- Prexisting information on the research community and topic
- Literature on the study topic
- The researcher's experience
- Popular and media sources
- The experience of a local community

Theory development is the first step in the research process. Formative theory serves as a map that guides the research, providing an opportunity for generating initial hypotheses against which observations are made. Modifying theory is an ongoing process throughout the duration of the research. The research concludes with an interpretation of research results or findings and a revisiting of the initial theory, which provide starting points for the next study (cf. Schensul, 1985).

The researcher's initial theoretical or conceptual model helps to organize observations and interviews into units, patterns, and structures early in the research, thereby attributing meaning to otherwise disconnected social facts. A theoretically informed focus, then, helps ethnographers to concentrate their observations and interviews and to organize their information into a coherent framework.

Ethnographic research often begins with a question, such as, "What accounts for parental involvement in the Arts Focus program?" or "Who uses the Needle Exchange Program?" Based on prior work, researchers always know enough about a setting to move beyond the initial question and create at least a rudimentary formative theory. Researchers should attempt to develop a formative theory that is as accurate as possible and based on the most complete view of the available information. However, ethnography does not test the formative theory to determine whether it is right or wrong. Instead, it

- Expands and fills in the model
- Discovers the qualitative and quantitative associations among domains or variables
- Matches the expected results derived from the formative theory with the observed results that accrue from the data collection process

Glaser and Strauss (1967) refer to building theory as a process of constant comparison of concepts that emerge in the field. We add to Glaser and Strauss's formulation the idea that data collected are constantly compared against the initial or formative model. *The end result of this process is always a modification of the formative ethnographic theory.*

Key point

ETHNOGRAPHIC RESEARCH IS BOTH QUALITATIVE AND QUANTITATIVE

Ethnographers continue to debate whether or not ethnography includes quantitative research (cf. Bernard, 1995; Clifford, 1988; Pelto & Pelto, 1978). Many qualitative researchers consider it impossible to transform beliefs or behaviors into numbers, whereas others insist that only numerical data that are amenable to so-called objective

Key point

**Cross
Reference:**
See Book 1,
Chapter 1, for a
discussion on using
qualitative and
quantitative research
in ethnography, and
Book 1, Chapter 4,
for ways that
qualitative and
quantitative research
designs relate to
one another

statistical analysis are scientifically valid and reliable. Our approach to ethnography in general and to the essential ethnographic methods presented in this book rejects both of these positions. We argue for the *collection and integration of both forms of data. Both qualitative (defined as descriptions in words) and quantitative (numerical) data are vital parts of the ethnographic research endeavor.* Oral, written, and nonverbal communications using words, sentences, and signals utilize the capacity for complex linguistic and grammatical structures and meanings that is a unique property of the human brain. All communication between researchers and the members of a group under study must be based on the group's own linguistic structures and meanings. Entry into a research setting is always negotiated through presenting orally and/or in writing the goals and objectives of the study to participate in the research site. This is a qualitative process.

Ethnographers often work in communities where the languages and cultures are new and unfamiliar. Discovery depends to a great extent on learning the language used by members of the group to describe their beliefs, norms, behaviors, and motivations. This learning process also is qualitative.

To collect valid and reliable qualitative and quantitative data, ethnographers must frame questions carefully and in a culturally appropriate manner. Knowing how to frame quantitative questions so that they can be understood and can produce valid quantitative data requires antecedent qualitative research. Regardless of whether questions about knowledge, attitudes, and behaviors accumulate text data or numerical data, they must still be phrased in an appropriate manner, using words, sentences, and concepts that respondents can understand.

Whereas results may be expressed numerically through frequencies, percentages, correlations, and graphs, interpretation and communication of results always involves translation back into the qualitative language of ideas, concepts, and theories. Thus, numbers cannot be divorced from words either conceptually or practically.

Ethnographic research focuses on understanding a local population in a broader socioeconomic and political context. Understanding this broader or macrocontext is essential in order to situate local experience and cultural observations. Some aspects of the context (e.g., income, infant mortality rates, gross national product, exports) can be conveyed quantitatively. Much of the reader's understanding of the research setting derives not from numerical or statistical data but from detailed textual description that conveys a sense of history, culture, politics, and the social position of the group under study vis-à-vis the larger society and its institutions. Without descriptive context, numerical data have little meaning.

Numerical data, however, constitute an essential component of the description of human behavior. Numerical data convey more accurately than mere words the number of people in a meeting, the frequency of medication use, or the number of cars parked at an American Indian pow-wow in northern Minnesota at three points in time. Quantitative approaches require researchers to

- Select a representative sample
- Test statistically the relationships among numerically represented variables
- Understand the degree of *variance* accounted for by a set of independent variables in predicting the range of a dependent variable
- Perform a wide variety of *numerical operations.*

Cross Reference: See Book 5, Chapter 9, for a definition of variance

Cross Reference: See Book 5, Chapter 9, for a discussion of numerical operations

Both quantitative and qualitative data provide the cross-checks (*triangulation*) that ensure that the numerical data are a valid and effective representation of the phenomenon being measured. At the same time, quantitative data provide

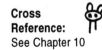

Cross Reference: See Chapter 10

Definition:
A cultural domain is a set of items, behaviors, beliefs, or events defined by a cultural group as belonging to the same category of things—a basic unit of meaning that shapes how people conceptually organize their worlds

Cross Reference:
See Book 3, Chapter 1, for an extensive discussion of cultural domains and the research methods utilized to obtain data on them

Definition:
A cognitive map is a display that illustrates how people organize their thinking about items in a cultural domain

Cross Reference:
See also Book 1, Chapter 4, and Book 5 for a discussion of the relationship between qualitative and quantitative data

the *external validity* that enables ethnographic researchers to generalize appropriately from their qualitative data.

As we noted in Book 1, the focus of ethnographic research is culture. Determining which **cultural domains** make up a particular culture and which ones are relevant to a particular research topic or question involves an innovative mix of qualitative and quantitative data (Lounsbury, 1964; Spradley, 1979; Weller & Romney, 1988). In a study of dietary practices, for example, ethnographers could use "free-listing," a research strategy used to elicit cultural domains. In it, respondents could be asked to list all "foods that help a person stay thin." The result would be a qualitative list of such foods. If the list were compared across respondents, the foods could be ranked in terms of the frequency with which they are mentioned and their mean rank (i.e., order of mention). Respondents then could be asked to sort the most frequently mentioned items into groups based on affinity (pile sorts). The analysis of these data would produce a quantitatively generated **cognitive map.** Data obtained through interviews and observations about people's eating patterns and choices would then help ethnographers to interpret the relationship of this quantitatively derived cognitive map of foods to body size of individual respondents or groups of respondents.

In this book, we describe the importance and utility of qualitative data collection and analysis as a stand-alone approach to data collection. We also show throughout how qualitative research can contribute to the formation of ethnographic survey instruments, as well as the interpretation of the results derived from quantitative data analysis.

ETHNOGRAPHIC RESEARCH IS CONDUCTED LOCALLY

When we use the term *local,* we mean the communities, organizations, workplaces, schools, and other population collectives that are spatially defined and within which ethnographers communicate face to face with research participants and collect primary data. Ethnographic research always involves face-to-face contact between the ethnographer and the community of study. Ethnographers must hear what community members have to say, observe them in action, and learn through participation in their daily lives. Thus, by definition, all ethnography is local. Ethnography effectively builds local theory—theories that explain events, beliefs, and behavior in the special site an ethnographer is studying. Local theories can then serve as the basis for understanding other local communities, as well as the changes in one community through time.[1]

Ethnographers also seek to understand the links between what happens locally and regional, national, and global events, policies, and political and economic structures. One of the unique strengths of ethnography is its ability to enhance understanding and interpretation of such varied global issues as increasing rates of unemployment, the new pressures associated with explicit sex in international media, and civil unrest as they are manifested in local communities or neighborhoods. Ethnographers can use research in local settings to generate local substantive (Kaplan, 1964) or midrange theories of culture (Merton, 1967; Pelto & Pelto, 1978; Trotter & Schensul, 1998) that can be tested through research and intervention in other local sites or in other locations in the world.

ETHNOGRAPHIC RESEARCH IS APPLIED

We conduct ethnographic research because we find that it can be an effective tool for both understanding and improving conditions faced by research participants and others in similar situations. Essential ethnographic methods and results can do the following:

- Describe a problem in a local population
- Assist in understanding the causes (and therefore the prevention) of a particular problem
- Assist members of the group under study to clarify and document their needs
- Provide information that can identify resources supportive of change
- Assist in formulating intervention program models
- Help to assess the efficacy of an intervention
- Modify interventions so that they will be more effective

Ethnography can decrease the turnaround time between the generation of knowledge and its translation into policy and program development. As a result, it is ideal for the development of pilot intervention programs, for process evaluation of these programs (in effect, a program-oriented ethnography), and for the development of further iterations of the program as it is applied in the local setting. These locally validated interventions can become the basis for the development of intervention models and policy guidelines or directives to be tested in other times and locations. This process is described in greater detail in Book 7. In the next chapter, we build on these principles to formulate the start of a theoretical framework for guiding the collection of basic ethnographic data in a specific field setting.

Cross Reference: See Book 7, Chapter 1, on research designed to change policy, and Chapter 2 on ethnographically informed

NOTE

1. These local theories are also called substantive or grounded theories (Glaser & Strauss, 1967; see also Book 5, and Chapters 2 and 3 of this book).

2

BUILDING FORMATIVE THEORETICAL MODELS

INTRODUCING THEORY

Ethnographers seek to generate useful information about culturally patterned beliefs and behaviors and reasons accounting for behavioral and other forms of diversity within groups. In contrast to the past when ethnographers could take a broader view, ethnographers now depict only selected cultural domains because they view those domains as related to some problem that a group of people agrees is in need of a solution.

In addition to the needs of their research partners, ethnographic researchers are required by funders, their colleagues or professors, and time and resource constraints to begin their research with a specific focus and research design (Johnson, 1998, p. 132). *Creating an initial focus calls for selecting one or more paradigms to organize the inquiry and for building a formative theory.* The process can be described as identifying a research problem; situating it in a research paradigm or "grand theory" (Miles & Huberman, 1994, p. 434); clearly formulating research questions; identifying a set of initial concepts, hunches, and hypotheses; and using this framework as a starting position for ethnographic research. As methodologist Thomas Schweitzer (1998) notes, research design or methodology:

Key point

Cross Reference: See Book 1, Chapter 3, for a review of paradigms used in the social sciences

includes discussion of method—How shall we proceed?—and of the principles of theory construction—What are the goals of inquiry? What shall the knowledge that we want to produce on our subject matter be like? What does the concept of theory mean? (p. 40)

THE ETHNOGRAPHER AS THEORIST

Many ethnographers are faced with the challenge of relating the dominant theoretical frameworks of their discipline to field situations in which their application is not readily apparent. Furthermore, they confront the notion that "only the leading figures in a discipline can generate theory"; the rest apply it. Finally, social scientists are expected to know the prevailing contemporary theories in their disciplines, but they are handicapped when not provided with the skills to enhance those theories or construct new ones. In our view, every researcher must be able to generate theory as well as formulate methodology if the data collection process is to be relevant to locally situated research, effectively organized, and readily interpreted.

The first job of an ethnographer is the organization of questions and hunches into an initial or formative theory that will guide the collection and, later, the analysis of data. However, the concept of theory has been so mystified that novice researchers shun theoretical discussions and argue that theory is neither practical nor comprehensible. It is the intent of this chapter to demystify theory and to begin the process of capacitating the reader-social scientist as theorist.

There are some straightforward and readily understandable definitions of theory that make its utility for both research and intervention obvious. Goode and Hatt (1952), for example, note that "theory refers to the relationships between facts" (p. 8), or to the ordering of facts in some meaningful way. In other words, theory is what makes sense of a series of observations, statements, events, values, perceptions, and correlations. It is the glue that aggregates facts into a hypothetical description of a given time and place, which then can be used to predict/explain events in another time and/or place. To the degree that it fails to predict events accurately for that next time and/or place, any initial formative theory will require modification and further testing. This occurs naturally during the ethnographic process.

➤•➤•➤ **EXAMPLE 2.1**

TRANSFORMING FACTS INTO THEORETICAL PROPOSITIONS

Researchers observed that more than half of the young people who participated in 1998's Summer Youth Research Institute at the Institute for Community Research enjoy and are skilled at some form of artistic expression (observable fact). They also noted that *their self-motivation is higher* when *performance, music, or drawing is integrated into the curriculum.* The preceding sentence is a low-level theoretical statement involving a hypothesized relationship between the two italicized ideas: *self-motivation* and *performance, music, or drawing in the curriculum.* We have created a preliminary or formative theory that hypothesizes that *school underachievers will do better at school if art is incorporated into their curriculum.* The preceding sentence is a mid-range intervention theory.

➤•➤•➤

Theory is no more and no less than description. Pelto and Pelto (1978) state that "description and theory are not different kinds of logical processes" (p. 7). Rather, *all description is* theory because it involves a selection and reorganization of observations of reality into a set of descriptions that seeks to predict future reality. Thus, a theory attempts to take text or quantitative data and organize them into a description or model of individual or group behavior in a specific time and place that predicts what people will do. This description or model can then be tested at another time or in another place.

Miles and Huberman (1994, p. 434) review other ways in which theory is described in the literature. Theory can consist of the following:

- A "map aiming to generalize the story or stories told about a case" (Rein & Schon, 1977, as cited in Miles & Huberman, 1994)
- A predicted pattern of events to be compared with what is actually observed (Yin, 1991)
- A network of nonhierarchical relationships expressed through statements defining linkages among concepts (Carley, 1991), an idea that is closely related to the idea of creating research models for discovery, discussed in Chapter 3 of this book on operationalizing
- A model consisting of "a series of connected propositions that [specifies] relations, often hierarchical among components" (Reed & Furman, 1992, as cited in Miles & Huberman, 1994), an idea that is related to modeling associations, described in Chapter 3 of this book

Key point

Theory is important because it helps us to determine what to consider and what to leave out of our observations. It is *never* possible to capture everything in our fieldnotes and records. For example, no matter how detailed the description of a community meeting, more will be left out than included simply because too much is happening at the same time for one or even several people to observe. Information left out of the description will probably include much verbal and nonverbal communication, behavior that appears to be idiosyncratic, interactions between dyads and in small groups, kinetics or body movements, and many aspects of the context. Sometimes, these elements may be observed or heard by the researcher but edited out as less relevant to the research topic; sometimes, they are missed (i.e., unseen or unheard); and on other occasions, they may be observed and noted but not recorded.

Cross Reference: See Book 2, Chapter 1, and Book 5, Chapter 2, on selectivity in recording data

Even if it were possible to record everything (and it never is, regardless of the recording medium), the facts of a single community meeting are useful only in terms of their ability to explain and predict future community meetings or events in the community. Thus, even the description of a single community meeting is theoretical to some degree because it edits out less relevant information in an attempt to describe how community meetings are conducted across time in a single place. This low-level theory must, of course, be tested against many community meetings in this place over time to provide an adequate test of the accuracy of the predictive statements.

Theory thus helps the ethnographer to select what to look for, ask about, and leave out in the process of data collection. Theory initiates the research process by helping the ethnographer to deal with the observation of real-world complexity in the field setting; it ends the research process by facilitating reorganization and elaboration of the initial formative theory through concepts that have been identified and verified by repeated observation in the field. This process may appear to be complicated at first, but in our experience, people from every walk of life can readily come to understand and use the process of theory building.

➤•➤•➤   EXAMPLE 2.2

THEORY-BUILDING IN THE NATIONAL TEEN
ACTION RESEARCH SUMMER TRAINING INSTITUTE

Youth aged 14-18 engaged in research training in the 1998 Summer Youth Research Institute of the Institute for Community Research determined that a variety of contextual and social factors predicted dropping out of school. To test these notions (mid-level theoretical statements), they collected data on self-esteem, pregnancy, and institutional racism (which they classified as major domains) in relation to dropping out. When they analyzed their data and discussed it in relation to the original model, they decided that two domains that were still missing were the effect of physical environment on attitude and behavior and the effect of a set of attitudes and feelings through which other factors were filtered so as to lead toward or away from dropping out. They thus modified their original model.

A similar group of youth studying factors associated with sex at an early age went through the same process, eliminating a number of unrelated domains and focusing mainly on self-esteem and the effects of the media on early initiation into sexual behavior.

➤•➤•➤

To summarize, theory is a tool of science. Theory

- Defines the kinds of data to be collected or narrows and helps to define the range of facts to be studied
- Offers a conceptual scheme by which relevant phenomena are systematized, classified, and interrelated
- Summarizes facts into empirical generalizations and systems of generalizations
- Predicts facts
- Points to gaps in our knowledge

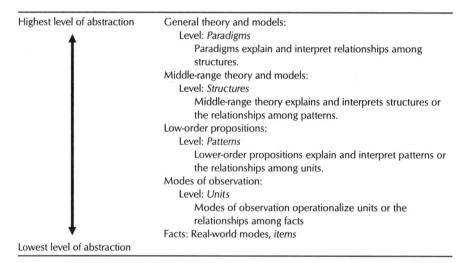

Highest level of abstraction

General theory and models:
    Level: *Paradigms*
        Paradigms explain and interpret relationships among structures.
Middle-range theory and models:
    Level: *Structures*
        Middle-range theory explains and interprets structures or the relationships among patterns.
Low-order propositions:
    Level: *Patterns*
        Lower-order propositions explain and interpret patterns or the relationships among units.
Modes of observation:
    Level: *Units*
        Modes of observation operationalize units or the relationships among facts
Facts: Real-world modes, *items*

Lowest level of abstraction

Figure 2.1. The continuum of levels of abstraction.

A number of philosophers of science and social science have provided schemata that deal with levels of abstraction, linking research paradigms (as broad lenses for viewing the world) at one end of the continuum with local "facts" sifted through the perspective of the researcher, the research topic, and the initial theoretical model or blueprint at the other (Harris, 1968; Kaplan, 1964; Kuhn, 1962/1970; LeCompte & Preissle, 1993). Figure 2.1 offers one way of thinking about this continuum. This figure combines the conceptual and analytic frameworks discussed in Book 1, Chapters 3 and 7, and Book 5, as well as that presented by Pelto and Pelto (1978).

In this scheme, Pelto and Pelto (1978, pp. 9-13) define *modes of observation* as operationalizing concepts; *propositions* as statements about the interrelationship among concepts, and *theories* as systems of interrelated propositions. LeCompte and Schensul define modes of operation as operationalizing *units* as organized patterns of association among observed facts or items; lower-order propositions as explaining or interpreting *patterns* or relationships among units; middle-range theories and models as explaining and interpreting *structures* characterized by relationships among patterns; and general theory as explaining and interpreting associations among structures linked to *paradigms*. As ethnographers, we can move up and down the ladder of abstraction when we collect data and generate preliminary hypotheses in the field—from facts to units, patterns, and structures, and the other way around.

Cross Reference: See Chapter 3, this volume, for a discussion of operationalizing

Cross Reference: See Book 1, Chapter 7, on data analysis and Book 5, Chapters 5 and 8, for a discussion of these relationships in data analysis

This scheme offers important guidelines for the conduct of ethnographically informed social science research, suggesting the following initial steps:

Initial Steps in the Conduct of Ethnographic Research

- Select a paradigm
- Build a formative or local theoretical model

SELECTING A PARADIGM

We recommend that ethnographers begin a study by choosing an initial paradigm such as those we outlined in Book 1, or other paradigms not mentioned here, for example, psychological or psychosocial frameworks such as social learning theory (Bandura, 1979) or behaviorism. It is im-

Cross Reference: See Book 1, Chapter 3, on paradigms

portant for ethnographers to think through the relationship of their research to these frameworks, as well as why the choice is appealing to them. Thinking about their reasons for choosing a research paradigm will reveal important personal values that can both guide and bias data collection.

The choice of research paradigm is just the beginning of sifting through the choices that ethnographers make with respect to the initial models that guide their research. The researcher's socioeconomic status, ethnic membership, gender, familial structure and dynamics, disabilities, neighborhood and residence, religion, and many other factors contribute to the selection of research question, paradigm, research model, and preference for data collection methods. We discuss this topic in greater detail in Book 1 and in Book 6, Chapter 1, on the researcher's role. We also discuss how self-reflection can be helpful with regard to the selection of paradigm and research model. We note that self-reflection helps researchers to

Cross Reference: See Book 1, Chapter 8, and Book 6, Chapter 1, on the researcher's role

- Make explicit (to themselves and the population under study) the underlying assumptions, ideas, and perspectives affecting the research design
- Locate, for users and funders, the intellectual traditions within which the research is situated
- Assist in the formulation of research blueprints, guides, and models that help to organize data collection

Once ethnographers have chosen an initial paradigm and clarified their reasons for doing so, they should select one or more guiding concepts. Guiding concepts form a link between the paradigm selected and the formulation of local or mid-range theory. The following are examples of paradigm and guiding concept choices that researchers have made:

Paradigm	Guiding Concept
Critical theory	Stigma
Phenomenological	Failed identity
Ecological	Cultural conflict
Network	Behavioral risk

The guiding concepts that researchers select should be consistent with their paradigm of preference. The next step in the process is creating a formative or local theoretical model.

BUILDING A FORMATIVE OR LOCAL THEORY

There are two main reasons for formulating initial ideas into a middle-range or substantive theory and a formative theoretical model. Doing so

- Makes explicit the nature of the research objectives
- Provides a set of ideas that can be compared to empirical results and systematically modified

What do we mean by the term *formative theory,* and why do we refer to it as "middle-range theory"? Formative or middle-range theory starts with a problem or question to be addressed in a localized population (one place, at multiple times) (Pelto & Pelto, 1978, pp. 2-7; Trotter & Schensul, 1998, pp. 696-698). We may call this starting point the "research topic" or the "research problem." We recommend that the research population be involved in identifying it.

EXAMPLE 2.3 ━•━•━•━

FINDING THE RESEARCH TOPIC

When Stephen Schensul joined the Department of Community Medicine at the University of Connecticut School of Medicine, he developed collaborative links with citizen groups in Hartford involved in health action, as the basis for initiating applied ethnographic research. One such group was the Tenants Rights Organization of a nearby public housing project. The general health problem they identified was rats, which they associated with fear of infant disease, damage to buildings, and threat to food supplies. Further analysis of the problem of rats led to questions about the extent of the problem (e.g., different domains of damage, greater or lesser damage, number of rats) and questions about rat behavior (rat holes, rat droppings, rat routes, and rat nests). Residents then proceeded to document both aspects or dimensions of the problem described above—"extent of problem" and "rat behavior." The formulation of this localized, low-level theory led tenants to begin to explore the factors that contributed to a wide range of health problems in the housing project, including poor health care access and environmental pollution. With these results, the group generated the middle-range theories which guided the development of several large research projects and the formation of a federally-funded community health center in the housing project.

There are a number of sources for the development of local or middle-range theory:

- The researcher's life experience, interests, attitudes, and values
- Popular, local, or "emic" conceptions of the phenomenon
- The literature documenting research results on comparable populations and issues
- The intervention, service, or policy needs of partner organizations
- The expressed views, needs, and interests of members of the local population

Cross Reference:
See Book 1, Chapter 1, and Book 5, Chapter 11, for discussions of the importance of local meaning and perceptions with reference to framing, analyzing, and interpreting the results of a study

The development of a research topic and an associated middle-range theory requires some prior knowledge of the community or setting within which the study is to be done, or of some other setting similar to it. This knowledge may be gained through reading relevant literature; reviewing media or of other popular conceptions of the topic; mulling over ideas generated through discussion with research partners, intervention organizations, or members of the research community in which the study is to be done; and prior personal experience of the researcher (cf. Stringer, 1996). *We do not recommend beginning an ethnographic study without going through the initial stages of the modeling process as we describe it in the following pages.*

Key point

Once we have identified the research topic, we may move in one of several directions:

- Description
- Association
- Evaluation

Description

First, we may wish to describe a research problem better, more deeply, or in a more comprehensive and systematic fashion (cf. Carley, 1991; Stringer, 1996, p. 93, fig. 5.1). Many ethnographic studies focus on obtaining a comprehensive qualitative understanding of a specific problem or question. For example, we may wish to understand variations in the ways in which parents, teachers, and students conceive of "growing up" in the preadolescent years between the ages of 9 and 12 and whether or not gender is associated with differences in their definitions, values, beliefs, and socializing practices related to growing up. *This descriptive approach is best suited for the very early stages of research in which the ethnographer is asking basic questions about the boundaries, characteristics, and component parts of a single cultural domain.* As the research proceeds, the ethnographer will want to know what connections this domain has with other domains in the group under study.

Key point

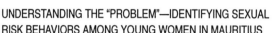
EXAMPLE 2.4

UNDERSTANDING THE "PROBLEM"—IDENTIFYING SEXUAL
RISK BEHAVIORS AMONG YOUNG WOMEN IN MAURITIUS

Researchers Schensul, Schensul, and Oodit focused their work in Mauritius on the increasing opportunities for sexual behavior and exposure to sexual risk of young, unmarried women who were working in the Export Processing Zone. As they began learning about sexuality, they identified two behaviors that they defined as involving risk, but that were not considered risky by the women. These behaviors were seen as not risky because they maintained virginity. The prevailing view among the young women workers was that neither of these behaviors produced pain or blood, the signs of loss of virginity. They believed that if virginity were maintained, any intimate behavior was safe. Therefore, although the study did not originally include virginity, its focus on sexual behavior in the context of risks related to contracting sexually transmitted diseases required the research team to obtain more information on the concept of virginity in understanding sexual behavior and risk (Schensul, Oodit, et al., 1994).

Association

Second, in addition to learning more about the problem or topic, we may wish to identify what leads to or is associated with it (cf. Reed & Furman, 1992). Association is especially important when ethnographic work is done with education and other forms of experimental or intervention programs and in research in general, because it is a sign of understanding the study problem and in determining the most important targets for intervention and prevention designed to impact on the problems. For example, if adolescent pregnancy or parental involvement in early education programs is the topic of interest, a researcher may be concerned with what leads to or is associated with either one of them.

The work of a University of Connecticut medical student researcher is typical of this approach. During the summer

Cross Reference:
See Book 7, Chapter 2, for more information on ethnographic contributions to intervention programming

of 1998, she was interested in exploring the relationship between adolescents' previous experience with the resolution of familial conflict through verbal or physical means and their current strategies for resolving conflict with their friends (Wilson, 1998).

Another way of approaching association is to consider the influence of the problem on potential consequences for the study community (Stringer, 1996, p. 95, fig. 5.2). For example, researchers may wish to investigate the proposition that teen pregnancy influences or even predicts positive consequences, such as higher levels of self-esteem and school performance. In the Institute for Community Research Summer Youth Research Institute, high school students examined the relationship between age of initiation of sex (which they termed "sex at an early age") and future life outcomes, which they predicted would include low self-esteem, dropping out of school, and the probability of having children early (Schensul, 1998).

Evaluation

Many ethnographers are asked to conduct ethnographic descriptions or assessments of programs. Sometimes, these programs are guided by middle-range theories that program developers have selected from those available in the literature. More often than not, programs are guided by unarticulated local theories of "how things work" that produce program goals and objectives. The program goals and objectives constitute the standard or baseline against which ethnographers are asked to collect and compare their data. But the theoretical underpinnings are not clear. One major contribution that ethnographers can make to program evaluation is to work with program staff to generate their own program theory (cf. Guba & Lincoln, 1989).

EXAMPLE 2.5 ━●━●━●━

FINDING AN INTERVENTION THEORY THROUGH EVALUATION

In an ethnographic and quantitative outcome evaluation of a fourth-grade diet, nutrition, and gardening program in a working-class town in the northeastern United States, interventionists introduced classroom and summer outdoor garden projects, as well as a nutrition curriculum with interactive classroom exercises and homework. The curriculum was introduced to four treatment classrooms, and the results were compared to those obtained from four control classrooms that received the standard fourth-grade didactic nutrition and diet curriculum.

As ethnographer and outcome evaluator, Jean Schensul collected data on program events, classroom process, teacher instructional style, student products, and pre- and posttest scores on a knowledge-based assessment instrument. The study design called for demonstration of better outcomes on posttests administered to children in the treatment classrooms. The results of quantitative analysis of test scores using ANOVA demonstrated that the anticipated improvements in the treatment classrooms as a group were significantly higher than in the comparison classrooms. In comparing the results from the four treatment classrooms, however, Schensul showed that performance outcomes improved in two classrooms but did not change in the other two. A review of the ethnographic data collected through process evaluation in treatment classrooms showed that instructors in the two high-achieving classrooms used interactive, cooperative learning techniques; small group work; and facilitated learning; whereas teachers in the other two classrooms favored didactic instruction and lectures. When Schensul presented these findings to the program directors, they used the findings to revise their original curriculum "theory," which involved the belief that children would learn more effectively, and would demonstrate better performance outcomes, if instruction were based on material interesting to them and include cooperative learning instrumental methods.

━●━●━●━

It is not important at this stage in the development of the research to decide which qualitative and quantitative research methods should be used in the research design. What is important is the framing of the question as a formative or middle-range theory.

GENERATING A FORMATIVE RESEARCH MODEL

Research is conducted to describe particular phenomena, delineate their variability, document their distribution in time and place, understand their associations with other phenomena, and attempt to predict and influence these phenomena through intervention. The starting point for all research is having a clear sense of the phenomena to be researched. In applied research, these phenomena are usually perceived to be a problem in the society, such as teenage sexuality, school dropouts, drug abuse, poor nutrition, smoking, low agricultural productivity, unemployment, or access to health care.

A formative research model is a diagram that represents the initial relationships among elements or concepts with regard to the topic you want to study. Each of the types of models identified in the previous section (description, association, and evaluation) produces a different type of visual model (see Figures 2.2, 2.3, 2.4, and 2.5). The ability to develop, use, and modify such a representational diagram or model is an important first step in conceptualizing essential data collection.

Figure 2.2 illustrates description: factors important in describing "school success." The next two figures display different ways of viewing association. Figure 2.3 illustrates influences on the issue or problem of school success; Figure 2.4 illustrates the issue or problem of school success as an influence on a variety of consequences. The last figure (Figure 2.5) illustrates an ethnographic evaluation model in which the outcomes (school success) are anticipated, but the influences are not known fully.

Both the construction of a research model and the subsequent operations associated with the data collection require a series of logical transformations. The challenge is to move from abstract concepts (e.g., happiness, self-esteem, sexual risk) to **valid** and **reliable** operations for data collection.

Definition: Validity refers to the idea that the procedure to collect the data is a good operational measure of the abstract concept; reliability refers to the idea that the measurement is consistent (replicable or repeatable) from one time or person to the next

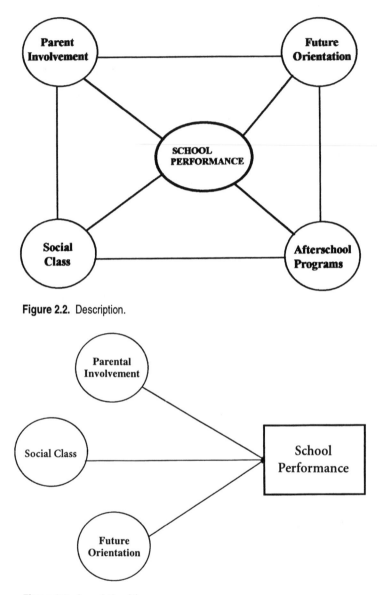

Figure 2.2. Description.

Figure 2.3. Association (1).

In Books 1 and 5, and earlier in this book (see Figure 2.1), we use the transformative and relational terms: *paradigm, structure, pattern, unit,* and *fact* to denote such levels. In this

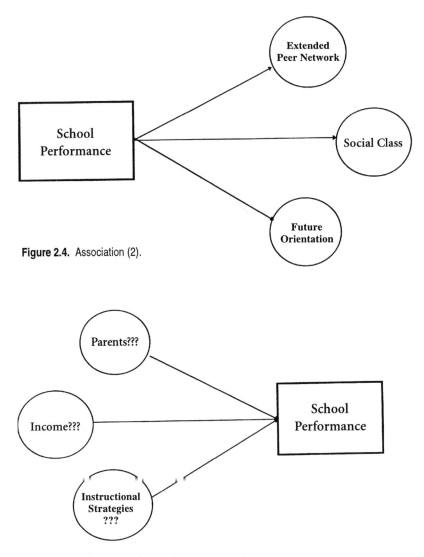

Figure 2.4. Association (2).

Figure 2.5. Evaluation: Finding the theoretical model.

book, we also use an analogous set of four terms—*domain, factor, variable,* and *item*—as the basic building blocks for the development of theory. These eight terms establish a vocabulary for describing movement from abstract to operational levels. Table 2.1 illustrates the intersection of these

TABLE 2.1 Linking Theoretical and Operational Levels in Ethnographic Research

	Structure	*Pattern*	*Unit*	*Item or Fact*
Domain	Family dynamics; and relationship to life achievement			
Factor		Parental discipline; and job performance		
Subfactor			Modes of parental punishment; and ability to supervise employees	
Variable				Frequency of spanking, and frequency of evaluative feedback to employees

terms as we will refer to them throughout this book and Book 5.

What is important here is that the researcher should understand and visualize the linkage between the levels and make appropriate transformations, no matter which terms are used to indicate the intervening levels (i.e., it is the trip that is important, regardless of the language of the signposts en route).

STEPS IN CONSTRUCTING MODELS

The formation of a model is not a unilinear and unidirectional process. The human brain is a complex instrument; it can receive information about phenomena in one place and one time and generate "grounded theory" (Glaser & Strauss, 1967); it also can imagine a grand scheme for human behavioral motivation (cf. Skinner and "behaviorism" or biological development as framed by Darwin's conception of evolution); it can enter the fray at a midpoint (middle-range theory), suggesting that two cultural domains seem to be linked, and generate ideas about them both inductively and deductively. We can even start with a single domain, factor, or variable and rapidly expand our thinking horizontally and vertically. It is difficult to match the set of guidelines described here for theory construction with the human capacity for complex conceptualization. However, we hope that these guidelines provide a system of thinking that can be an effective starting point. Suffice it to say that we can think of theory generation as a complex matrix that gives us the following conceptual and cognitive options:

- Moving horizontally from a single phenomenon to include related phenomena at the same level of complexity
- Moving vertically (inductively) from lower- to higher-order concepts (from the top down)
- Moving vertically (deductively) from higher- to lower-order concepts (from the top down)

Cross Reference: See Book 5, Chapter 5, on analysis from the bottom up

Cross Reference: See Book 5 on analysis from the top down

EXAMPLE 2.6 ━●━●━

MOVING HORIZONTALLY TO DEFINE DOMAINS AT THE SAME CONCEPTUAL LEVEL

In a study conducted by Oodit, Bhowan, and S. Schensul of women in Mauritius who were admitted to the hospital with complications due to abortion, the dependent domain was "type of service sought for abortion" (self-induced, "back-street," and private medical practitioner). Domains at the same level of complexity or abstraction that researchers believed influenced choice of service included family composition and contraceptive history (Oodit, Bhowan, & Schensul, 1993).

━●━●━

EXAMPLE 2.7 ━●━●━

AN EXAMPLE OF VERTICAL MODELING FROM THE BOTTOM UP

Stephen Schensul consulted on a study conducted in 1996-1998 by Professor Tilak Hettiarachchy at the University of Colombo, Sri Lanka, on sexual risk among young women working in the free trade zone factories in that city. A major question in this study related to the ways in which women were exposed to risk. The factories were isolated behind high security walls and barbed wire fences. Women workers lived in dormitories housing up to 10 women in each room. Large numbers of young women, estimated at close to 60,000, primarily from rural areas, moved from work to the dormitories in large groups to avoid the dangers lurking between the safety zones of the dormitory and the worksite. These dangers included groups of young and older men who attempt to engage and gain access to the earnings of young women, and jewelry and frock shops seeking to relieve women of disposable and nondisposable income.

When the research team observed women moving quickly through the "danger zone," weaving their way with varying degrees of success among the groups of men, shops, restaurants, and other stands, they developed the domain "exposure." This domain was subdivided into three factors: "relationships," "activities," and "time spent outside the factories and outside the residences" (i.e., in unprotected zones). Variables identified within the factor "relationships" were "having a boyfriend" and "having friends involved in risky behaviors"; in the factor "activities," "going to musical evenings"; and in the factor "time spent outside safety zones," "amount of time taken in the commute between work and home." The "exposure" domain proved to be a strong predictor of sexual risk.

EXAMPLE 2.8 ━●━●━

AN EXAMPLE OF VERTICAL MODELING FROM THE TOP DOWN

Motivated by the global HIV/AIDS pandemic, the notion of sexual risk has been a driving force in the research of Schensul and Schensul since 1991. As we delved more deeply into this domain among young people in Mauritius, we learned that there was far more to sexual risk than risk of HIV/AIDS or other STDs. In fact, these infections were last on the list of priorities for Mauritian youth. Young women in Mauritius added to the list of negative outcomes premarital pregnancy, loss of boyfriend, loss of virginity, loss of reputation, emotional and psychological problems, physical pain, reduced marriageability, negative feeling about men, abortion, other STDs, and alienation from the family. In this study, we began with the factor "risk of HIV/AIDS," moved up to the domain "sex risk," and back to other risks as listed above. This list eventually was reorganized into the subfactors "medical risks," "social risks," and "psychological risks," under which each of the specific risk catgories listed above was located (Schensul, Oodit, et al., 1994).

Now we will describe the process of model construction from the top down, focusing on the construction of a research model at the domain level. The model will consist of three classes of domains: the dependent domain, independent domains, and mediating or modifying domains. Note that each domain is composed of two or more factors and that each factor is composed of two or more **variables**. The term **dependent domain** refers to a domain that changes in response to variations in other domains. Another way of stating this definition is to suggest that a change in the dependent domain is "caused" or influenced by changes in the independent domains. For example, tutoring programs (independent domain) are believed to improve school performance (dependent domain); however, the obverse is not likely to be as obviously true.

Definition: A variable is a logical grouping of attributes or items; items or attributes are characteristics or qualities that describe a person, place, thing, attitude, belief, or behavior

Definition: A dependent domain is one that changes in response to changes in other domains

Definition:
An independent domain logically precedes a dependent domain, and change in it is not in response to changes in the dependent domain

Independent domains precede dependent domains in terms of presumed causality; change in the independent domains is independent of or unaffected by change in the dependent domain. For example, exposure to media through television and movies (the independent domain) is believed to have a negative influence on adolescent drinking behavior (the dependent domain) because it portrays positive images associated with the use of alcohol. Changes in exposure to the media, however, are not likely to occur because of changes in adolescent drinking. Instead, other factors, such as parental control over use of television or movie attendance (or an increase in the cost of videos and movies), are likely to change adolescent media exposure.

Mediating domains modify, come between, or intervene in the normal or direct relationship between independent and dependent domains. For example, mothers' health status prior to pregnancy (the independent domain) affects the health of the infant in the first year (dependent variable). Pre-pregnancy health status may be defined as consisting of many variables, including weight or height, age, and blood pressure. Health of the infant in the first year may be defined by such variables as birth weight, sickness, and weight for age. We propose—or theorize—(with good evidence from experience and prior studies) that the better the mother's pre-pregnancy health status, the better the child's health in the first year of life will be, as illustrated in Figure 2.6.

But prenatal care may be available for at least some mothers and may improve the health of these mothers and the fetus during pregnancy. We can, in fact, hypothesize that adequate involvement in prenatal care will result in better infant health despite pre-pregnancy health status. In this case, we can say that prenatal care is a mediating/modifying domain, intervening in or changing the relationship between mother's prepregnancy health status and the health of the child in the first year. This relationship could be diagrammed as shown in Figure 2.7.

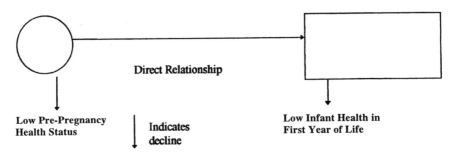

Figure 2.6. A direct relationship between independent and dependent domains: Pre-pregnancy health status and infant health.

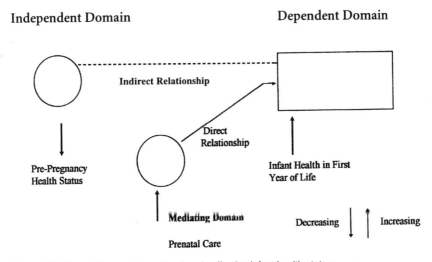

Figure 2.7. Prenatal care: Intervening domain affecting infant health status.

The diagram in Figure 2.6 depicts a predictive relationship between the independent and the dependent domains; as mother's prepregnancy health improves, infant health improves. This relationship is described as *direct*. With the addition of the mediating domain "prenatal care," we can represent the relationships as shown in Figure 2.7.

In Figure 2.7, the addition of the prenatal care domain influences or mediates the direct relationship between the independent and dependent domains, reducing or eliminating the effect of mother's pre-pregnancy health status on the health of the child. This diagram shows the relationship of prenatal care to infant health as a direct one. The hypothesis now depicts the idea that the more the mother is involved in prenatal care, the better the health of the infant will be.

THE DEPENDENT DOMAIN

The construction of a research model at the domain level starts with delineation of the dependent domain. For example, we may be interested in sexual risk among adolescents in urban communities in the United States. The domain of sexual risk could include a large number of behaviors. However, at this point, we are looking for a domain definition that corresponds to societal concerns, delimits the phenomenon to be studied, and includes multiple manifestations. Thus, we define the domain of sexual risk as any intimate contact between two people that can result in transmission of sexually transmitted disease and/or pregnancy. Whereas this definition would include kissing as an element in sexual risk, it would specifically exclude transmission of flu virus as a result of close contact because flu is not a sexually transmitted disease. Knowing what is or is not within the dependent domain will be crucial to both measurement and theory development.

The problem or phenomenon that constitutes the dependent domain should be one that demonstrates variability, as the following example illustrates.

 **EXAMPLE 2.9**

IDENTIFYING VARIABILITY IN THE DEPENDENT DOMAIN

Researchers Schensul, Schensul, and Zegarra were interested in factors associated with household development in evolving shantytowns in the northwest quadrant of the city of Lima, Peru. However, there was no point in using variations in household development as a dependent domain shortly after a group of people invaded public land, squatted on it, and took it for their own, because all households were identical temporary residences, each consisting of four straw-matted walls roofed with a straw mat supported by bamboo poles. However, after the city of Lima and the urban municipality granted the residents title to the land, and individual households had possession of their homesteads, families gained residential stability and household construction flourished. What emerged over time was a **wide range of variability** in household development (i.e., there were many differences among households) as measured by the presence or absence of electricity, piped-in water, latrines, glass windows, and durable (concrete and brick) construction of walls and roof (Schensul, Schensul, & Zegarra, 1985).

The selection of the dependent domain determines the study's research topic. It should be congruent with the interests of the researcher, with the concerns of the population under study, and with the funders or the potential funders of the study. Figure 2.8 is the first step in developing a diagram that illustrates the model for the study in which the dependent domain is located on the right-hand margin of the page.

INDEPENDENT DOMAINS

Our next task is to identify independent domains that are associated with, or predict the variation in the dependent domain. The first step in identifying an independent domain is to construct a series of **hypotheses**. In a study of human reproductive health, an associate hypothesis might be the following:

Definition:
Hypotheses are statements that propose a relationship between two variables such that by knowing the value of one of the variables, the value of the other is predicted

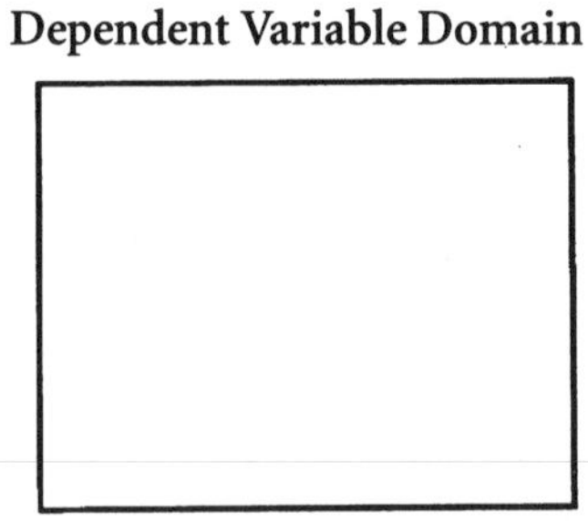

Dependent Variable Domain

Figure 2.8. A diagram illustrating the placement of the dependent domain in a formative research model.

> The amount of formal education a woman has (independent variable domain) is related to the number of children she will have (dependent variable domain).

This hypothesis does not indicate the direction of the relationship; it merely specifies that there is an association between the two domains. This hypothesis is illustrated in Figure 2.9.

The hypothesis can be stated in another form, illustrating the direction of the relationship, as follows:

> The higher the education level (as measured by number of years of formal education) of women in the community (independent domain), the fewer children they will have (dependent domain).

Figure 2.10 illustrates this inverse relationship between the independent and dependent domains.

In this example, an inverse relationship between the number of children a woman will have throughout her reproductive career and her level of education predicts that the *lower* her education, the *greater* will be her number of children, and the *higher* her education, the *lower* will be the number of children over her reproductive career.

We know, however, that complex societal issues are the product of multiple forces and not simply a product of

Independent Variable Domain   Dependent Variable Domain

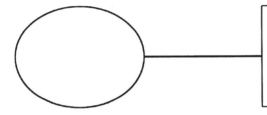

Figure 2.9. An association between an independent and a dependent variable domain.

Independent Variable Domain   Dependent Variable Domain

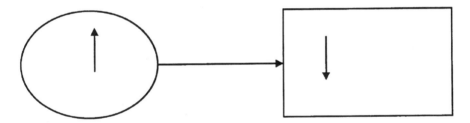

Figure 2.10. An inverse relationship between an independent and a dependent variable domain.

single variables. This complexity suggests an additional hypothesis reflecting a supposed *inverse* relationship between income (a second independent variable domain) and fertility level as defined by number of children (the dependent variable domain):

> The higher the income of a woman and her family, the lower her fertility.

This can be diagrammed as shown in Figure 2.11.

Independent Variable Domain (1)   Dependent Variable Domain

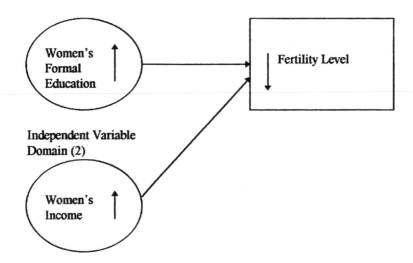

Figure 2.11. Another inverse relationship introducing a second independent variable domain.

Social researchers have conceptualized the link among variables as a web of interrelationships in which independent variables are not just related to the dependent variable but have relationships with other independent variables. In line with this concept, we might posit the following hypothesis showing a *direct* relationship between education and income:

The higher a woman's education, the higher her income.

The diagram that would result from the hypothesized interrelationships among these variables is represented in Figure 2.12.

We now have the beginnings of a research model. It is important to keep in mind that cultural domains are "packed" with (or include) many variables. We do not always know the direction of the relationships among variable domains at first. Thus, it is sufficient simply to hy-

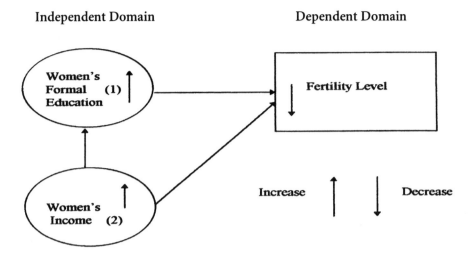

Figure 2.12. Relationships among independent variable domains.

pothesize associations or relationships without predicting their direction. In a more elaborate design, with a larger number of independent variable domains, the associations might resemble Figure 2.13, which illustrates the actual research model with which researchers Schensul, Silva, Schensul, and de Silva began their work on AIDS risk in Sri Lanka.

In the model represented in Figure 2.13, the single lines indicate predicted significant relationships among domains; the dotted lines indicate anticipated weak or nonexistent relationships among domains. In the Sri Lanka formative research model, the hypothesized associations are numbered and were the following:

1. Peer relationships have a *significant* effect on adolescent participation in sexually risky behavior.
2. Family variables have a *significant* effect on adolescent peer relationships.
3. Family variables have *little relationship* to adolescent sexual behavior.

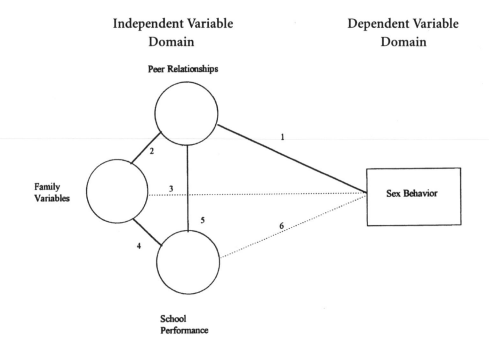

Figure 2.13. A formative research model showing hypothesized strong and weak relationships among independent and dependent variable domains.

4. Family variables have an *important effect* on adolescent performance in school.

5. School performance is *significantly related* to peer relationships.

6. School performance has *little or no relationship* to participation in sexually risky behavior.

In a more narrative form, both the diagram and the set of six hypothesized relationships describe a multifactoral model involving the three sectors of an adolescent's world: family, school, and peer relationships. Families affect both the nature of adolescent participation in school and the people with whom their children socialize. School performance also contributes to and interacts with peer relationships among young people. However, the model shows that researchers anticipated that peer relationships would play the most significant role in sexually risky behavior; the other domains are indirectly related or not related at all.

The narrative, the hypotheses, and the diagram are each important components of the conceptual framework for any research. They can, however, be generated in any order that is comfortable and responds to the complexities of the research process. In other words, domains, factors, and variables can be added at any time. For example, the researcher may have an opportunity beforehand to conduct focus groups or in-depth interviews with a number of adolescents, leading to a narrative description of the situation. Later, this description can be transformed into a series of hypotheses that is then incorporated into a model such as the one portrayed above.

Cross Reference:
See Book 3, Chapter 2, for more information on focused group interviews

Searching for Independent Domains

One of the strengths of ethnographic research lies in the ability of ethnographers to identify independent domains that have not been previously recognized as associated with the dependent domain. Steps in the process of identifying these domains are the following:

Cross Reference:
See Chapters 4 to 6 of this book for more information on these steps

- The initial phases of unstructured observation and interviewing
- Review of previous research related to the dependent domain
- Development of guidelines that help the researcher examine sectors likely to be overlooked in more quantitative designs

The process of searching for independent domains and diagramming a theory-informed model has two components:

- Antecedent demographic characteristics or conditions, including socioeconomic status, family dynamics, the nature of the residential community, and the characteristics of the school and the workplace

■ Knowledge, attitudes, and behaviors such as knowledge of contraception, attitudes toward premarital sexuality, and contraception behavior, which may be directly related to both root causes and the dependent domain

The search for independent domains in either category is a strength of the ethnographic approach. The following example illustrates the locating of new independent domains.

EXAMPLE 2.10 ━●━●━●━━

LOCATING NEW INDEPENDENT DOMAINS

Dr. M. W. Amarasiri de Silva, of the Department of Sociology of the University of Peradeniya, Sri Lanka, was evaluating the *impact of mosquito repellent-impregnated bed nets* (the independent variable) in an endemic malarial area in southern Sri Lanka. The project recorded little reduction in the *incidence of malaria* (the dependent variable).

Unstructured observation and interviewing led him to examination of sleeping patterns in this area. Most of the houses consisted of one room, with mother sleeping with young children and father sleeping on his own. In order to have some privacy, the couple were required to leave their bed nets and go outside into the garden, frequently at a time when the mosquitoes were at their most active. In this case, observation revealed that *household crowding* (independent variable) that forced people to seek privacy in malaria-infested outdoor locations was a more important factor in exposing people to malaria than not using bednets inside the house.

Casting a "broad net" is a real advantage in finding important independent domains!

The following example, drawn from Margaret Le-Compte's study of an arts program in a middle school, shows how various sectors of the school community offered theoretical propositions that helped to guide the formulation of the research design for an evaluation study.

EXAMPLE 2.11

SHOWING HOW STUDY PARTICIPANTS CAN HELP
TO IDENTIFY THEORETICAL PROPOSITIONS

LeCompte and her associates began meeting in April with teachers, the principal of Centerline Middle School, and parents in the community to identify research questions and problems in which the various constituencies involved in the program were interested, and to see if they had developed any theories about why the program upon which they were embarking would be effective.

Independent	Dependent

Parents had ideas about the relationship between student achievement and student attitudes toward school; they supported the arts program because they thought it would increase their children's enthusiasm for school and, consequently, their achievement.

Domain: Arts program	Children's enthusiasm for school Children's achievement

The *teachers* firmly believed that the arts provided a kind of discipline in both thought and practice that would help the students do better in their regular schoolwork.

Domain: Arts discipline *Factor:* Cognitive discipline Behavioral discipline	Improved schoolwork performance

Both the principal and the parent group supported the program because they hoped it would increase enrollment at the school and fend off efforts by the school district to close it.

Domain: Arts program	Increase student enrollment School preservation

The *principal and key non-arts teachers* also were concerned that the arts program enhance the climate of the school as a whole and that it not interfere with what they perceived to be an already effective academic program.

Domain: Arts program	Improve school climate Retain effective academic program

LeCompte and her research team used these ideas to develop an evaluation design that considered the effect of the Arts Focus program on Centerline Middle School as a whole, as well as a set of research questions that focused both on the characteristics of the instruction offered by the arts teachers and on the links between specific arts instructional practices and attitudes that the students had about school, themselves, and how they engaged with intellectual ideas.

Another approach that facilitates identifying independent domains involves classifying all independent domains into two groups: (a) those related to "organized services" and (b) those related to a target population or community. For example, domains in the organizational group may include

- Governmental laws
- Regulations
- Services
- Nongovernmental organizations at any level
- Local health or educational service systems

Thus, for example, when considering research on health care access, it is useful to focus not only on institutions providing services (e.g., hospitals, community health centers, health maintenance organizations, group and private practices), but also on other institutions that may affect how they deliver those services (e.g., Social Security, Medicare/Medicaid or other public funding guidelines, insurance companies, and provider advocacy groups). They are *all* important components or domains in a study of health care accessibility.

Focusing on populations or communities suggests the following possibilities:

- Those who have a specific educational or health problem
- Those at greater risk of acquiring the problem
- Those directly affected by the problem
- All those with a common health or education problem
- Those cohorts or groups defined by demographic characteristics such as age and ethnicity
- Occupational groups (e.g., unions, tanners)
- Employees at a common worksite (e.g., urban industrial workers in Port Louis, Mauritius)
- Individuals and families who reside in the same geographic area

Readers will find a broader discussion of ways of identifying study populations in Book 1.

Domains of relevance to populations could include any number of arenas of knowledge, attitudes, behaviors, social relationships, psychological states, sports or other types of activities, dietary patterns, food preparation, and material lifestyle, among others.

Many ethnographers and other social scientists focus on those independent domains that have to do with the target population or community, forgetting about broader social, structural, or policy issues that could be important in a study. Categorizing independent domains into two sectors —institutional or organizational and community—forces researchers to consider both in developing a theoretical and a formative research model.

Cross Reference: See Book 1, Chapter 5, for a discussion of ways to identify populations

➤●➤●➤ **EXAMPLE 2.12**

CONSIDERING ORGANIZATIONAL AND POPULATION DOMAINS IN A STUDY OF ADOLESCENT HEALTH AND SEXUAL RISK

In the Sri Lanka study, conducted by researchers Stephen and Jean Schensul, K. Tudor Silva, M. W. A. de Silva, and others (Silva et al., 1997), independent organizational domains with potential for contributing to sexual risk in adolescents came to include the following:

- Access to adolescent-oriented health services
- Level of service provider training on adolescent needs and approaches
- National policies on sex education and fertility
- Policies influencing the distribution of contraceptives and sex education in schools
- School attitudes toward sex education

➤●➤●➤

Without considering the organizational sector, researchers might have forgotten about these domains in considering what might affect sexual risk attitudes and behavior in youth.

Among the youth population—the target population for the study—domains believed to be relevant to influencing risky sexual behavior and exposure to AIDS included the following:

- Youth knowledge of protective behavior
- Youth knowledge of sexuality
- Youth attitudes and values toward sexuality
- Boy-girlfriend relationships
- Types of peers among youth
- Youth activities with peers

The selection of the independent and the dependent domains underpin the study's formative theory and guide the process of exploratory data collection discussed in Chapters 4, 5, and 6 of this book. At the same time, the results of unstructured interviewing and observation allow ethnographers to identify new domains, eliminate domains originally included in the formative research model, and identify and refine the variables that are included in the domains. Through these means, the ethnographer discovers and examines realms that others are not likely to consider.

By now, it should be obvious that the development of formative theory is an interactive process that identifies the most valid and locally appropriate domains through using methods that extend the opportunity to do so.

Diagramming and Modeling the Formative Research Model

The next step is to organize these domains into a formative research model in which relationships can be expressed as a function of closeness of association. The following are guidelines for locating independent and mediating domains in relation to one another in a diagram.

- Independent domains with closer and more direct relation-ships (in time or logical linkage) to the dependent domain should be located closer to it.

- Independent domains with closer associations with one an-other should be clustered together.

- Only some independent domains should be directly related to the dependent domain; others should be related indirectly or not at all.

- Only some independent domains should be directly related to each other.

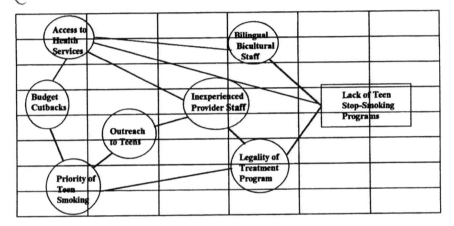

Figure 2.14. Constructing a model using organizational domains believed to be associated with the dependent domain: Lack of teen stop-smoking programs.

The variables can be located in a two-dimensional grid in which the dependent domain is placed in the far right column(s), the far left column contains background and antecedent domains, and the middle columns include di-rect precursors to the dependent variable. Clusters of do-mains can cross-cut these columns. The template for the organization of the initial model on a two-dimensional surface could be represented by the diagram in Figure 2.14, which includes the primary organizational domains asso-ciated with the lack of smoking cessation programs for teenagers.

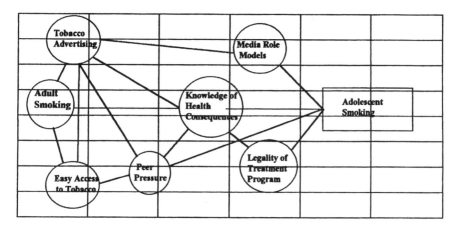

Figure 2.15. Constructing a model using community- or population-level domains believed to be associated with the dependent domain: Adolescent smoking.

The objective of this first stage of modeling is to identify as many independent domains as the researcher can hypothesize to be directly or indirectly related to the dependent domain. Researchers should conduct the same exercise with respect to community- or population-level domains. One such result is portrayed in Figure 2.15.

The next step in the generation of the research model is to consider both of these models and identify the dependent variable that is the focus of investigation. It might be either of the two identified in Figures 2.14 and 2.15 (stop-smoking programs or adolescent smoking), or a composite domain. Subsequently, a process of prioritization and inclusion/exclusion will produce the best set of independent domains possible early in the study. *Researchers should limit the number of independent domains in a study to between two and five.*

External factors that should be taken into consideration when selecting the most relevant independent domains include the following:

- Domains identified in previous studies
- Domains listed by key informants

Key point

Cross Reference: See Chapter 4 in this book; see also Book 1 for more information on the discovery of cultural domains

- Domains identified through researchers' firsthand experience
- Domains that are compatible with the researcher's disciplinary background and resources

Internal factors to be considered when prioritizing the selection of independent domains include the following:

- Selecting different domains that vary in proximity to the dependent variable
- Whether or not an independent domain is central, i.e., to what extent it is viewed as directly related to several other independent domains as well as to the dependent domain
- Selecting a balance of independent domains identified from both organization and population analyses

The result of this process is a formative research model that represents the following:

- An initial theoretical paradigm for how things work that is to be tested and modified based on primary data collection
- The criteria for comparing between the expected (or what the researcher hypothesizes will occur) and the observed (or what the researcher actually verifies)
- A map or research design that guides data collection
- A set of criteria for establishing valid and reliable research and measurement instruments

Cross Reference: See Book 1, Chapters 2 and 4, and Book 5 for a discussion of research design in ethnographic research

SUMMARY

The process of conceptualizing research, including the development of paradigms, theories, and models, has always been shrouded in an aura of mystery. For some, the process involves sitting in an armchair and staring at a blank wall; for others, every observed act and heard phrase leads to the discovery of theory. This serendipitous process is made even more difficult by the fact that although students take classes and seminars in theory, they rarely take a class called theory construction.

In this chapter, we have tried to shed some light on this process, recognizing that what we have described is a linear process, but that what occurs in the process of generating models is simultaneously both vertical and horizontal. It is also, to some degree, idiosyncratic.

Nevertheless, we have attempted to outline a set of guidelines that can be applied to most situations and that will generate successfully useful local formative theories and research models. The key elements of these guidelines are the following:

Theory Construction

Guidelines for Generating Local Theories and Research Models

- Establishing the focus of the study—the dependent domain
- Identifying independent and modifying domains that are believed to influence the dependent domain
- Diagramming the model on a two-dimensional surface to clarify conceptual thinking and make the conceptualization process accessible to others
- Explaining the reasons behind the hypothetical relationships among the independent and dependent domains in the model
- Eliminating domains on the basis of priority, centrality to the study, available time, and human resources
- Finalizing the model as a proposal for research funding and the conceptual starting point for the study
- Altering the model as data are collected and throughout the data collection and analysis process

We have described this process as deductive. However, we have shown in this chapter that it can also be inductive; ethnographers can start in the middle and work both up and down the conceptual ladder of abstraction. Theory and model building are skills to be developed. The more they are practiced, the easier they become. We hope that this approach stimulates ethnographers to view themselves as theoreticians and to improve on existing descriptions of ways in which local and middle-range theories can be generated.

3 ━●━●━●━

OPERATIONALIZATION

The function of social science research is to explain **social phenomena**. The first step in ethnography is to define which social phenomena are to be studied. For example, researchers must decide whether they wish to study the factors contributing to high levels of infant mortality (death) or high levels of infant morbidity (disease), or whether to combine them (morbidity leading to mortality vs. morbidity leading to survival). Or, they could distinguish between teachers' instructional techniques and children's behaviors in cooperative learning settings, or try to consider the relationship between the two.

Next, they must decide how to measure the phenomenon, that is, how to identify it consistently in the social setting. Measurement appears simple when the topic is mortality: death. Measurement becomes more complex when information on the actual number of deaths and the households in which death occurs is not readily available. In some places, deaths are not recorded. In others, certain types of deaths may be neither reported nor recorded. Many homes do not have addresses, so even if there were a record

Definition: 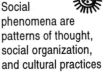 Social phenomena are patterns of thought, social organization, and cultural practices

Definition: Measuring a phenomenon means defining it clearly and identifying it consistently in a social setting

49

of all deaths, the location might not be available. Measuring cause of death is always a problem because there may be multiple causes, records may be absent or inaccurate, and, if there are no records, and the study depends on symptom recall, the recall is very likely to be faulty. Assessment of instructional techniques that teachers use in cooperative learning programs is even more challenging. Researchers must observe teachers' behavior over time, determine which behaviors relate to cooperative learning, define these behaviors, and apply the definitions to observations of behavioral streams in the classroom. Recognizing and attending to measurement problems such as these are central components in the conduct of ethnographic research on

Key point

social phenomena. *It is important for researchers to realize that measurement as we discuss it here does not require mechanical devices, and that many measurements are not expressed in terms of scores or numbers. Measurement simply permits the researchers to assess the variation in a particular variable.*

Determining which phenomena are to be studied therefore requires the following:

Cross Reference:
See Book 1 for a discussion of establishing boundaries for populations, phenomena, and units of analysis

- *Definition:* Establishing boundaries to distinguish this particular phenomenon from others and to communicate that distinction to other researchers
- *Measurement:* Describing or measuring the phenomenon
- *Establishing validity:* Assessing the adequacy of the measurements in representing the phenomenon
- *Establishing reliability:* Ensuring consistency in the measurement process over time and among the researchers carrying out the measurement activities

These processes are referred to as *operationalization.*

Pelto and Pelto (1978) define operationalization as

the striving for . . . better and better research operations in order to generate more accurate observations, hence more

effective theory building and testing. Specification of operations enhances control of extraneous variables, increases the
precision of basic measurements . . . and provides the framework for information that permits the researcher to trace his
or her steps mentally in order to understand both predicted
and unpredicted results. (p. 39)

Through operationalization, primary elements (terms) of
researcher descriptions and theoretical propositions are
structured or phrased in language that makes it possible for
researchers and research participants to understand each
other, and to locate what they are talking about in the field.

Bernard (1995) makes the distinction between *conceptual* definitions and *operational* definitions: "Conceptual
definitions are abstractions, articulated in words, that facilitate understanding. [They are] the sort of definitions we see
in dictionaries. . . . Operational definitions consist *of a set
of instructions on how to measure a variable* [italics added]
that has been conceptually defined" (p. 6).

Operationalization involves processes of logic and observation. As we have seen in the development of formative
theory, the process of operationalization can start from the

- Ground up (inductive)
- Top down (deductive)
- Middle—working both up and down from the start point

By "ground up" (see (1) in Figure 3.1), we mean the
process of first identifying phenomena at the variable level
and then situating them within the proper subfactor, factor,
and domain (in that order).

By "top down" (see (2) in Figure 3.1), we mean disaggre-
gating, unpacking, or breaking down a domain into its
component factors, factors into subfactors (if appropriate),
and subfactors into variables.

By "midpoint" (see (3) in Figure 3.1), we mean identifying factors or subfactors, situating them within a domain,

**Cross
Reference:**
See Book 1 and
Book 5, Chapters 4
and 5, for additional
descriptions of how
to operationalize

**Cross
Reference:**
See Table 2.1, this
book, and Book 5,
Chapters 4 and 5,
for a discussion of
top down and bottom
up approaches to
defining units; and
Chapter 6 for how to
organize units into
patterns or factors
during analysis

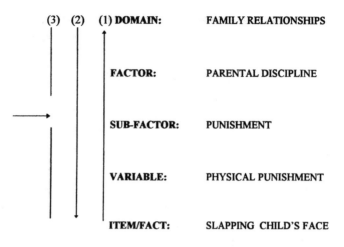

(3)	(2)	(1) DOMAIN:	FAMILY RELATIONSHIPS
		FACTOR:	PARENTAL DISCIPLINE
		SUB-FACTOR:	PUNISHMENT
		VARIABLE:	PHYSICAL PUNISHMENT
		ITEM/FACT:	SLAPPING CHILD'S FACE

Figure 3.1. Operationalizing—Transforming information from one level of abstraction to another.

and at the same time identifying and measuring the variables associated with them. Figure 3.1 depicts what we mean by this transformation process.

One approach to making these transformations is to locate items or observations at an appropriate level of abstraction based on the researcher's judgment. Researcher judgment about where to place an item conceptually comes from a variety of different sources:

- Prior personal experience
- General knowledge of the phenomenon obtained through field observations
- Instruments developed by other researchers that measure the phenomenon
- Logic
- Feedback from others

A second approach to transformation is based upon insider perspectives, or the hierarchical classification systems and sets of meanings that the study participants them- selves use. Elsewhere, we have referred to this approach as an "emic" perspective. These systems can be derived using elicitation techniques that have been variously described as "componential analysis" (Goodenough, 1956), "folk taxon- omy" (Frake, 1964) and freelisting and other systematic data collection methods (Weller & Romney, 1989; Werner & Schoepfle, 1987). Using these inductive or bottom-up approaches to the development of taxonomies, we can ask informants where concepts or behaviors identified at the variable level fit (e.g., where does "a father slaps a child" fit in a taxonomy in which the domain is family relationships, as in Figure 3.1 or Table 2.1), or we can ask respondents to sort a series of items (e.g. yell, slap rear end, slap face, punch, stop speaking, send to room, add chores) into groups (pile sorting) and then interpret, name, and class the groupings as factors or domains. We can also ask our informants to "list all types of ways parents discipline a child" (freelisting). These classificatory systems also emerge less formally through the analysis of qualitative fieldnotes.

Cross Reference: See Book 1, Chapter 1, for "emic perspective"

Cross Reference: See Book 3, Chapter 3, for a discussion of elicitation techniques including listing and pile sorting

Our next challenge is to locate the item or observation in an appropriate place on the continuum of abstraction, a task that is easier to do than to describe. It is easiest to situate items properly at the variable level. To do so, we can ask: Is the procedure for accurate identification reliable, that is, can it be replicated? Would two observers watching a par- ent's hand meeting a child's cheek agree that this behavior is "slapping the child" (an item) and that it is a component of the subfactor "physical punishment"? At the subfactor and factor levels, researchers must ask whether the concept has enough breadth and inclusion to be located at a higher (i.e., more inclusive) level of abstraction than a variable. To situate a concept at the domain or most abstract level, researchers should be able to generate a full taxonomic structure, including factors, subfactors, and variables.

Cross Reference: See Book 5, Chapters 2-7, for a detailed discussion of the ways in which researchers elicit classificatory systems from text data

Ethnographers use operationalization for organizing, understanding, and analyzing qualitative data; improving the precision of their data collection; and organizing hierarchical coding systems for their qualitative data. This approach also facilitates the organization of items into variables that can be quantified into indexes and scales for use in the construction of an ethnographic survey.

Cross Reference: See Book 5, Chapter 8, for a discussion of constructing indexes and scales

We now describe operationalization from the top down, recognizing that ethnographers use both deductive and inductive processes to weave a rich fabric of description and analysis. The formative research theory provides the first step in operationalization by directing the researcher's attention to the domains of interest and their potential interrelationships. The next task is to move down the levels of abstraction in each of the domains in the research model to define factors, subfactors (if necessary), and variables that are valid measures of those domains. To accomplish this task, we have found it most useful to use the technique of **tree diagramming** (cf. Weller, 1998). A tree diagram must have two or more levels. This method of categorization is represented in Figure 3.2.

Definition: Tree diagramming involves organizing information into hierarchical taxonomies in which items are subsumed under broader categories

The method calls for returning to the research model to select the domain (see Chapter 2) and then "unpacking" the domain into component parts at each level in the hierarchy of abstraction—factor, subfactor, and variable. This process represents a transformation from more abstract (factor and subfactor) to more concrete (variable) levels. The end product of the transformation is a set of operationalized or measurable variables. Difficulties encountered at any stage in the operationalization process are an indication that further transformations need to be made. This is especially the case at the variable level. Figure 3.2 suggests that transformations from the domain to the variable level can be made in three steps, but many concepts require four or five levels to become fully operationalized.

Abstract

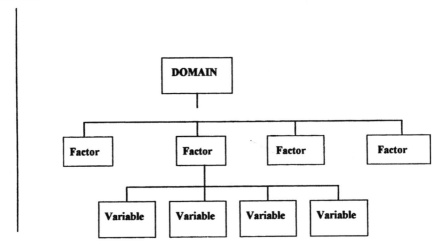

Operationalized

Figure 3.2. Operationalizing—Organizing information into hierarchical taxonomies by degree of abstraction or inclusion of the concept.

Making the transformation from the domain to the variable level is based on many things:

- Intuition (personal experience)
- Prior research studies
- Data gathered from each stage of the ethnographic research process
- Logical reasoning

To illustrate, if the domain "family" arises in the course of a discussion with a key informant, an ethnographer can follow logically with the question: "Can you tell me more about families in this community?" Answers to this question and observation of families in the course of fieldwork will lead to identification of the constituent components of the domain "family" from the point of view of the population under study. Generally, ethnographers try to induce informants to provide information at the level of "factors" because the informants may or may not think and speak in terms of the logical taxonomies that are required to fully understand the content of a domain. Usually, it is the researcher's task to reorganize the information provided by study participants into factors, subfactors, and even variables.

Cross Reference: See Chapter 7, in this book, for detailed instructions on how to conduct semistructured data collection

Semistructured interviews and observations are useful for further operationalizing factors. For example, the factor "discipline" may emerge as important in the "family" domain. A semistructured interview that asks the respondent to describe her experiences with parental discipline will identify initial subfactors and variables that are important as the researcher goes about measuring and collecting data on the domain of discipline. The identification of variables may be concrete enough to allow these variables to be transformed into closed-ended items on a survey instrument. If we learn that one subfactor associated with the factor "discipline" is corporal punishment, and one variable within corporal punishment is beating with a cane, we may want to ask a structured or closed-ended question, "Have you ever been beaten with a cane?"—the answer to which is "yes" or "no." Each level of abstraction in the operationalization process produces useful and valid information on the phenomenon being studied, but it also provides the basis for further operationalization down the ladder of abstraction.

This approach to operationalization also permits movement from the concrete back to the abstract. Thus, "caning" may be discovered first. It can be recorded and, on the basis of additional ethnographic data collection, located in the more inclusive category or subfactor called "corporal punishment." Once the subfactor "corporal punishment" is identified as valid and important in the study, "caning" becomes one item in a scale measuring this broader concept. Further investigation using semistructured or even key informant interviews would lead researchers to identify other behaviors comparable to "caning" that are indicators of the subfactor or concept "corporal punishment." Depending on the ethnographic context, "corporal punishment," a subfactor, may be situated within "family discipline," a factor, or it may equally well be situated within another factor termed "family relationships." Working up the ladder of abstraction, the factor location for the subfactor "corporal punishment" will depend on the questions raised in the original study and the ways in which behaviors are conceptualized and categorized in the local setting. Thus, in this approach, each datum has a conceptual home, allowing the researcher to avoid orphaned facts and isolated information.

Finally, this approach to operationalization establishes categories for the coding of textual data.

━●━●━ **EXAMPLE 3.1**

OPERATIONALIZING THE "FAMILY" DOMAIN AMONG YOUNG MAURITIAN WOMEN IN THE WORKFORCE

We felt that the family played a crucial role in the lives of the young women whom we studied in the project that examined AIDS-related risk behaviors among unmarried young women working in the industrial zone in Mauritius. Having identified the domain "family" as important, the research team began to delineate its component factors. Our objective in this task was not to identify every possible factor associated with the domain "family." Instead, it was to locate and focus on those components hypothesized to be related to the dependent domain: AIDS-related risk behaviors.

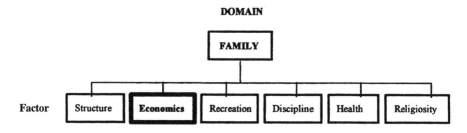

Figure 3.3. Identifying factors associated with the domain "family."

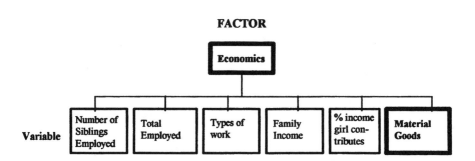

Figure 3.4. Operationalizing the factor "economics."

Our first attempt at identifying family factors associated with AIDS-related risk behaviors is illustrated in Figure 3.3.

Our next task was to operationalize further each of the factors identified as components of the domain "family." Figure 3.4 shows how the factor "economics" (meaning "household economic characteristics") is disaggregated into a number of variables, one of which is material goods. "Material goods" refers to material items or possessions owned by the household.

Some of these variables already are sufficiently concrete or operationalized. For example, we could ask the young woman in the industrial zone to respond to the question: "What percentage of your monthly income do you contribute to the household?" Others require further operationalization, such as material goods owned by the household. Figure 3.5 shows how we operationalized this variable. The figure illustrates a series of items that can be further defined by their presence or absence

VARIABLE

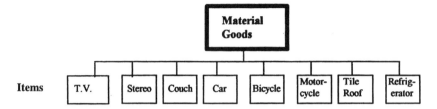

Figure 3.5. Operationalizing the variable "material goods."

in a household. In the analysis stage, it is possible to combine these items into a "material style of life (MSL)" scale by summing the number of items present in each household to create a household score.

The research model we discussed in the previous chapter, based on domains, can be defined as a "horizontal" model. We term the process of creating this formative research model "horizontal modeling" because it proposes relationships at *only* one level—the level of the domain. We refer to the tree diagram that we have been describing in Figures 3.3-3.5 as a "vertical model" because it uses logic, empirical observation, and inquiry to generate linkages or relationships along the continuum from the most abstract level (domain) to the most concrete level (variables and items or attributes).

The delineation of taxonomies (or tree diagrams) in the formation and the conduct of an ethnographic study gives researchers tools to begin to construct units, patterns, and structures. In Figure 3.6, we can see that the relationships among domains can be explored at the variable, subfactor, and factor levels. It also demonstrates how relationships among subfactors and factors can be explored by linking

Cross Reference: See Book 5, Chapter 8, for a discussion of scales and indexes and an example of a Material Style of Life scale

Cross Reference: See Book 1, Chapter 7, this book, Table 2.1, and Book 5, Chapters 5, 7, and 10, on units, patterns, and structures

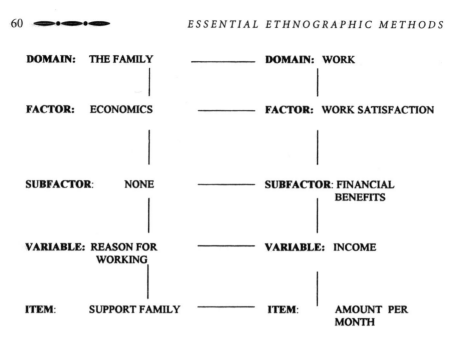

Figure 3.6. Locating concepts at the domain, factor, and variable levels of abstraction.

appropriately coded blocks of qualitative or text data, or quantitative data analysis.

The conceptual work completed to this point provides the basis for creating a clear formative research model. The model acts as the basis for developing a research design and writing a research proposal or prospectus that can be reviewed by colleagues, supervisors, review committees, and potential funders.

Cross Reference:
See Book 1, Chapters 4 and 5, on elements of good research design

USING THE RESEARCH MODEL TO CLARIFY RESEARCH GOALS, OBJECTIVES, AND HYPOTHESES

The first step in establishing a research design using a research model is to generate a statement of research purpose. This statement should be based on the dependent domain or the research problem. Table 3.1 illustrates some examples of problem statements focusing on the dependent

TABLE 3.1 Purpose Statements Based on a Theoretical Research Model

Purpose	Dependent Domain	Independent Domains
The purpose of this research is to understand how older Latina women interpret, report, and manage symptoms of diabetes	Symptoms of diabetes	
The purpose of this research is to identify factors associated with variations in children's performance in math-related activities	Children's performance in math-related activities	
The purpose of this research is to describe the diffusion of an agricultural innovation (dependent variable) among farmers in rural Iowa	Diffusion of an agricultural innovation	
The purpose of this research is to identify peer, community, and family factors influencing conflict resolution skills in young adults	Conflict resolution skills	Peer Community Family
The purpose of this research is to examine the association of self-esteem, social influences, and the media on running away from home among adolescents	Running away from home	Self-esteem Social influences Media

variable alone, or on relationships between independent and dependent variables.

The next step is to develop a series of research objectives directed toward clarifying or explaining the relationship between the independent and dependent domains. These are stated using terms or concepts generated from the tree diagram, such as the one in Figure 3.7, taken from research on AIDS risk in Sri Lanka where a dependent domain is "sex behaviors." An example of a relationship between family (independent domain) and sex risk (dependent domain) is: "Family problems is associated with risky sex behaviors."

The next step in designing the research is to generate a specific set of questions or hypotheses that can be tested or explored by considering the relationships among domains at the factor and variable level, as illustrated in Example 3.2 from research conducted in Mauritius.

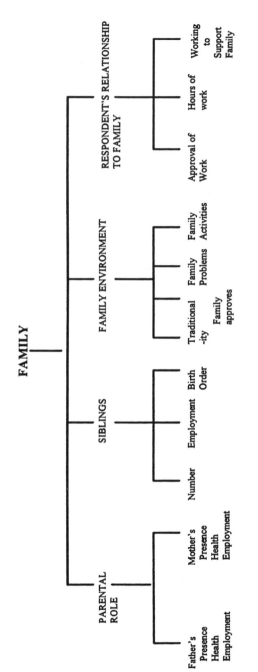

Figure 3.7. A tree dagram: Conceptual taxonomy for the domain "family."

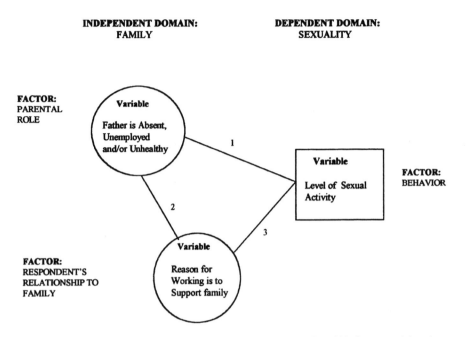

Figure 3.8. Generating hypotheses about relationships among variables within factors and domains: Mauritius study, family domain.

━●━●━ **EXAMPLE 3.2**

CONSTRUCTING A RESEARCH DESIGN USING THE "DOMAIN, FACTOR, AND VARIABLE" FRAMEWORK: AN EXAMPLE FROM MAURITIUS

Title: Young Women, Work, and AIDS-Related Risk Behavior in Mauritius

Purpose: To identify factors associated with sexual attitudes, behavior, and risk (pregnancy, abortion, STDs, and AIDS) among young women working in the Mauritius Export Processing Zone (EPZ)

Objective: To describe and understand the relationship between social/contextual domains (family, peer, and work) and factors, sexual risk, and sexual attitudes of young women aged 15 to 25 in the EPZ

Figure 3.8 draws from the conceptual taxonomy of domains, factors, and variables illustrated in Table 3.2. It selects two critical domains in the study (family and sexuality), two factors drawn from the family domain (parental role and respondent's relationship to the family), and one factor from the sexuality domain (sex behavior). After reviewing the variables included in each of the factors, researchers selected one from each of the two family factors and one from the sex behavior factor (see variable column in Table 3.2). Variables are located in the circles in Figure 3.8.

TABLE 3.2   Conceptual Taxonomy (Tree Diagram) for "Family" Domain: Mauritius Study

Domain	Factor	Variable
Family	Parental role	Father's presence, health, employment
		Mother's presence, health, employment
	Siblings	Number
		Employment
		Birth order
	Family environment	Scale of traditionality
		Family approval of work
		Scale of family violence
		Family problems
		Family activities
	Respondent's relationship to the family	Approval of work
		Hours of housework
		Working to support family
Sexuality	Behavior	Participation in behaviors ranging from holding hands to oral sex
		Condom use
	Values	Premarital sex
		Virginity
		Men
	Knowledge	AIDS transmission
		Condoms
	Risk perception	Loss of virginity
		Becoming pregnant
		Acquiring STD
		Acquiring AIDS

Having chosen the variables, researchers then speculated as to what the relationships among them might be. The directional hypotheses as stated in the study are as follows:

Hypothesis 1: The loss of the father as a wage earner will mean that young women are forced (rather than choose) to enter the EPZ to support their families

Hypothesis 2: The loss of the father will be associated with greater levels of sexual behavior for young women

Hypothesis 3: Women who are working in the EPZ to support the family will show higher levels of sexual activity

━●━●━●

Table 3.3 summarizes the links between elements of research design and their conceptual source or inspiration using the modeling process that we have described.

TABLE 3.3   Links Between Components of Research Design and Conceptual Source Using Tree Diagrams

Elements of Research Design	Conceptual Source
Purpose	The dependent domain *Retention of Create*
Objectives	The relationship between the independent and dependent domains
Research concepts	Tree diagrams
Hypotheses	Relationships among factors and variables

LINKING STAGES IN RESEARCH DESIGN WITH STAGES IN DATA COLLECTION

Two of the greatest challenges facing ethnographic researchers are how to mesh qualitative (text) data with quantitative (numerical data) and how to know when in the sequencing of a study to choose one approach to data collection over another. The approach we have outlined in this chapter provides the basis for both by linking stages in conceptual development and modeling with specific research methods. Table 3.4 summarizes these stages.

The objective of Stage 1 is to use personal/professional experience, prior research, and a review of secondary and archival data to develop the formative research model. This stage involves identifying a set of independent and dependent domains and constructing hypotheses that link them. Researchers should remember that the formative research model is just that and is subject to modification, refinement, and improvement at any point throughout the life of the study.

Stage 2 focuses on the development of the domains in the formative research model. Exploratory data collection techniques are most useful in elaborating on the definition and unpacking of domains. During Stage 2, new domains

Cross Reference: See Book 2, Chapter 9, on secondary and archival data

Cross Reference: See this book, Chapters 4, 5, and 6, on exploratory research methods

Cross Reference: See Book 5, Chapter 5, for a discussion on identification of items in a conceptual taxonomy from the bottom up

TABLE 3.4   Stages in Research Design, Selection of Research Methods, and
Study Objectives

Conceptual Component	Research Method (Books 2, 3, and 4) and Sampling Approach (Book 1; Book 2, Chapter 10)	Research Objectives
Stage 1: Research model	Reviewing secondary data (Book 2, Chapter 9) • Secondary databases • Prior experience in study site • Researcher experience	• Development of initial domains • Selection of domains • Construction of hypotheses
Stage 2: Domain	Exploratory data collection (Book 2, Chapters 4, 5, 6, 10) • Key informant interviews • Unstructured observation • Participant observation Sampling: Unique cases; extreme cases	• Discovery of new domains • Testing of domain selection • Beginning operationalization at all levels
Stage 3: Factor	Semistructured data collection (Book 2, Chapters 7, 10; Book 3, Chapters 2, 3) • Semistructured interviews • Semistructured observation • Focus groups • Elicitation: Freelisting and pile sorts Sampling: Quota sampling	• Operationalization of factors and variables • Identifying language and terminology for study • Identifying cultural consensus
Stage 4: Variable	Structured data collection (Book 2, Chapters 8, 10; Book 3, Chapter 1; Book 4, Chapters 1, 2, 3) • Structured interviewing • Questionnaires, surveys • Structured observation Sampling: Probability or systematic	• Operationalization of variables • Obtaining representative sample of responses • Testing hypotheses

are discovered as researchers find that units do not logically fall into initially identified domains. During this stage, the first steps in operationalization also take place. As items emerge, they are identified as factors, subfactors, or variables in a developing conceptual taxonomy.

 Cross Reference: See Chapter 7 for more detail on the conduct and uses of semistructured interview schedules

Stage 3 focuses primarily on exploration at the factor level through semistructured data collection techniques. Researchers create a list of open-ended questions about factors and ask the same questions of a number of people, seeking variations in the responses. The variations are at the variable or unit level. For example, a researcher might ask 15 people their opinions about public versus private schools in a series of questions. Altogether, they might provide a list of 10 different opinions, such as "public schools have limited resources," "students can get a quality education in both schools," and "private schools restrict entry." The list provides the alternative responses for closed-ended survey questions and ideas for additional interviewing. Johnson (1998), in a recent discussion of research design and research strategy, presents a similar argument. Differentiating between exploratory and explanatory approaches to research, he notes:

Cross Reference: See Chapter 8 of this book for information on the construction of ethnographic surveys

> Exploratory approaches [our Stages 1-3] are used to develop hypotheses and more generally to make probes for circumscription, description and interpretation of less well understood typics. . . . Exploratory research can be the primary focus of a given design or just one of many components. (p. 139)

In Stage 4, researchers explore the range of variation in a representative sample of the target population often, though not always, through the use of ethnographically informed surveys. Analysis explores and tests hypotheses based on the original conceptual framework as well as emerging ideas. Johnson (1998) refers to Stage 4 as explanatory research, suggesting that "explanatory approaches generally involve testing elements of theory that may already have been proposed in the literature or that have been informed by exploratory research" (p. 139).

Many social science researchers now readily accept the idea that ethnography includes both qualitative and quantitative approaches to data collection. Having formulated their initial model (Stage 1), researchers should begin their work with methods of data collection that emphasize discovery (Stage 2). Discovery is useful in

- Determining the utility, appropriateness, importance, and definition of the dependent domain
- Identifying and selecting the independent domains
- Beginning to operationalize domains (deconstructing or unpacking them into their respective factors and variables)

Cross Reference: See Book 5, Chapter 8, for the definitions of variables and their attributes

Cross Reference: See Book 5, Chapters 9-11, for a detailed discussion of the analysis and integration of qualitative and quantitative data using this strategy

In the third stage, semistructured qualitative interviews and observations provide information that helps to confirm factors and identify variables. These forms of data collection allow us to explore the range of possible responses or options that could be included as variables or as attributes of a variable as well as the broader meaning of variables, factors, and domains. These data will be useful in interpreting survey results at the end of the study.

Stage 4 involves testing ideas or hunches about relationships among variables, factors, and domains in a representative (preferably random) sample of people. As we will see in Chapter 8, proceeding in this manner allows us to approach the analysis of qualitative (in-depth and semistructured text data) and quantitative (survey) data in much the same way: by describing variables and exploring the relationships among them.

SUMMARY

In this chapter, we have reviewed the basic steps in the operationalization of a formative research model. Most researchers begin with a question that is elaborated as they move through the stages of research outlined in Table 3.4. The initial research question rapidly becomes transformed into a dependent variable domain or a problem or topic for research. However, the domains and factors associated with it may not fully emerge until later in Stage 3 of the research process. Many researchers will be satisfied to collect and analyze in-depth and semistructured interviews and other forms of exploratory data to test their research model and answer their research questions. Others will choose to test their model quantitatively with a larger and more representative sample. Researchers may choose either strategy, knowing that both the qualitative and the quantitative data they have so painstakingly collected will apply directly to the dimensions they have identified in their theoretical model.

4 ━●━●━

ENTERING THE FIELD

*Fieldwork
and the Field*

•

*The Ethnographer
as Self-Reflective
Tool of Inquiry*

•

*Establishing
Relationships to
Facilitate Entry*

In the first three chapters, we discussed the steps in preparing conceptually for ethnographic field research.

> ### Conceptual Steps in Preparation for Fieldwork
>
> - Developing the main research questions
> - Reviewing ideas drawn from the previous studies reported in the literature
> - Looking at available secondary data
> - Talking with other people who have had research experience in the chosen setting
> - Building an initial conceptual framework for guiding the research
> - Identifying initial domains and factors for further exploration and analysis

Having completed these steps, ethnographers are ready for entry into the field. In this chapter, we discuss the process of entry, or how to enter the field setting where the research is to take place in ways that build relationships conducive to implementation of the research plan over time.

Definition:
Entry is the process of developing presence and relationships in the designated research setting that make it possible for the researcher to collect data

FIELDWORK AND THE FIELD

Definition:
The field is the natural, nonlaboratory setting or location where the activities in which a researcher is interested take place

The concepts of "field" and "fieldwork" have been the hallmarks of ethnography. Fieldwork involves the actual research tasks carried out in a chosen setting or location. The field is a physical setting, the boundaries of which are defined by the researcher in terms of institutions and people of interest, as well as their associated activities in geographic space. For ethnographers, the field can be any naturalistic geographic/social setting or location where a selected research problem is to be studied. Some examples of field settings described in this book series include a shooting gallery in Hartford, a classroom or school in Colorado, a school district in Phoenix, Arizona, or in the Navajo Nation in the United States, a university campus in Sri Lanka, a shantytown in Lima, a psychiatric ward in an urban hospital, or a factory production floor in Mauritius.

When we say that ethnographic researchers go to the field, we mean that they leave their own communities, institutional settings, and familiar behavioral and cognitive patterns to enter another social world—the world in which the research is to be conducted. In the process, they must learn what residents of the field already know—the language of the setting; the rules guiding social relationships; and the cultural patterns, expectations, and meanings that people in the setting share. Learning these rules, norms, boundaries, and behaviors is the task of ethnography. The first step in learning is establishing the relationships through which this learning process can take place.

The entry process is complicated because researchers must learn a number of things at the same time:

- How to function in a new setting where the language, rules of behavior, norms, beliefs, social relationships, dietary patterns, and other aspects of life in a community may be very different

- How to locate and build relationships with the people who have access to important information and other resources relevant to the study
- How to collect and record information in the setting in a way that is both unobtrusive and efficient
- How to begin to sort out what information is new, interesting, and likely to be useful for study purposes, especially in situations where everything the researcher encounters is new and different

Constant self-conscious reflection is called for to work through these issues in a systematic way.

Most ethnographic researchers, at least initially, choose to do their research in field settings unfamiliar to them, or in communities to which they do not belong. But, as we have said in Book 1, some researchers choose to study communities or settings within which they hold some form of membership. They may have grown up in the community, or they may belong to the ethnic group they wish to study. They may self-define as members of the group of research interest, in terms of sexual preference, religious choice, or personal interest. However, regardless of their group membership or identification, no researcher can be fully identified with members of the group under study.

Cross Reference: See Book 1, Chapters 1 and 8, for a discussion on the challenges of conducting research in the researcher's community of origin

No single researcher, for example, can be both male and female, old and young, poor and middle class, educated and not educated—that is, no one is ever fully representative of every potentially important constituency or sector of a given community. *Ethnographic researchers hold an identity that is never fully coterminous with the individuals who are members of the community or research setting in question.*

Key point

Whether or not researchers view themselves as holding membership in the community of study. They are always marginal to some degree while they are conducting research. The process of ethnographic research demands that the researcher learn how it is to "not be me" in a physical setting that is "not mine" with rules and guidelines for verbal and physical behavior that "I do not know" and may understand only in a limited way. Ethnographers are simultaneously members and nonmembers of the study group and must struggle continuously with framing and reframing their identity. This struggle has ethical implications because the more integrated researchers become in the field setting, the easier it is for local residents to forget that they are collecting data. Ethnographers must always remember that they are researchers and remind study participants of their identity as researchers, even at times when they may be acting as friends, counselors, providers of information, helpers, and cultural brokers.

Cross Reference: See Book 6, Chapter 1, on the researcher's role and ethical responsibilities

THE ETHNOGRAPHER AS SELF-REFLECTIVE TOOL OF INQUIRY

Ethnographic research is never autobiographical. It requires that the researcher separate stereotypes, opinions, and judgments from accurate observation and effective recording of the words, meanings, and opinions of research participants. Thus, entry means more than *going into* a medical clinic, a crackhouse, or a school; it also requires that researchers transform themselves into the primary instrument of data collection. Ethnographic research calls for engagement in direct learning through physical and social involvement in the field setting. Knowing, for ethnographers, is first and foremost experiencing by observing, participating in conversations and daily activities of members of the community under study, and recording these observations.

For the ethnographer, however, recording the observations is only one component of a more elaborate task that includes the following elements:

- Careful and ongoing reflection on the meaning of the experiences
- Understanding the setting
- Reflecting on the personality and behavioral transformations that the researcher is required to make because of his or her experience

Taking these activities seriously helps an ethnographer to function increasingly effectively as a member of the group under study. The ability to function unobtrusively (in other words, in a culturally competent manner) is critically important to doing good ethnography in the field because it minimizes the influence of the researcher on the setting. The less obtrusive the observer, the more likely the people are to behave as they normally would. The renowned anthropologist Bronislaw Malinowski was one of the first social scientists to make this point about the effect of his presence in a Trobriand Island community over time, noting,

> It must be remembered that the [local people] saw me constantly every day, they ceased to be interested or alarmed or made selfconscious by my presence and I ceased to be a disturbing element in the tribal life which I was to study, altering it by my very approach as always happens with a newcomer to every . . . community. (Malinowski, 1922, p. 8)

This approach places a great deal of responsibility on ethnographic researchers as they shift from familiar settings in which they can behave in ways that are unconscious, unreflective, and automatic to unfamiliar settings that call for self-conscious reflection and careful selection of appropriate new behaviors. The task is at once complex and overwhelming. It involves the following activities:

- Listening
- Recording and understanding the meaning of the language used in the field setting

- Observing, recording, and interpreting behavior
- Organizing information and understanding so that they increasingly predict future observed events
- Reflecting on the ways that what is heard and seen affects behavior, attitudes, and values including their own

Thus, ethnographers voluntarily expose themselves to a process of enculturation or socialization, while at the same time studying their own transformation as it occurs.

Definition: Building rapport means developing good personal relationships with people in the research setting that facilitate access to activities and information necessary for conducting the study

Another unique feature of ethnographic entry is the fact that ethnographers generally bring with them few inducements for local people to cooperate with them other than the opportunity to build a trusting relationship and talk about topics of mutual interest. This process of establishing personal relationships in the field built upon trust is referred to as **building rapport**. Good ethnographers build relationships easily. Although sensitive to their surroundings, they have few reservations about asking questions that enable them to learn new things.

Definition: Key informants are people with recognized special expertise in a topic of interest to the researcher; cultural experts are people who have special cultural expertise

There have been occasions when ethnographers have used incentives including paying their **key informants** or **cultural experts** for the time it takes to participate in an interview. Others have found different kinds of incentives or material exchanges to be useful. For example, ethnographers involved in AIDS research generally carry bleach kits, condoms, and other materials that they can pass out or leave behind to assist respondents to protect themselves against AIDS. Educational ethnographers may carry out evaluations or construct data collection instruments needed by school staff, which are not part of the study design. Researchers who invite young people to participate in focus groups often find that offering them food they enjoy makes the experience more appealing.

All ethnographers should understand the importance of reciprocity in building relationships. Thus, they may share their time, transportation, knowledge, relationships with service providers, or other resources valuable to research participants and communities. For the most part, however, when ethnographers enter the field, they do so armed only with their social skills, their intellectual persistence, commitment to the research topic, and personal good will.

Ethnographers undergoing the discomforts of the entry process should be encouraged by the knowledge that most people in a community or institutional setting pay little attention to the *cover story* or explanation of the project. What is more important in the end is not how the research is explained initially, or even the organizational base and reputation of the researcher. Rapport ultimately rests on the connections through which ethnographers have been introduced to the community setting, how comfortable researchers are with the people in the field, how well they maintain confidentiality, and how fast they learn local customs and norms. The researcher's appearance, use of language (including humor), perceived comfort level, growing knowledge of the setting, and reactions to difficult or challenging new situations are all important in building the personal relationships that mark the entry process in ethnography.

Cross Reference: See Book 6, Chapter 1, for a discussion of the cover story

Initially, local people give researchers a fair amount of latitude in the field. It is usually quite acceptable for unsuspecting researchers to shake hands when bowing is more appropriate, but eventually, participants will come to expect that the researcher will learn the more culturally appropriate behavior. For example, handshaking between western men and Sri Lankan women is tolerated (although hugging and cheek kissing is not), but the Buddhist greeting that involves placing hands together at chest level, bowing slightly, and saying *ayubowan* is more appropriate. Learning the appropriate greeting in the first few weeks in the field will be viewed as an important sign of social integration.

Cross Reference: See Book 1, Chapter 9, on the ethics of field research, and Book 6, Chapter 1, on the researcher's ethical responsibilities in conducting field research

The purpose of quickly learning to blend in is that it minimizes the degree to which the ethnographer disrupts the normal, ongoing process of interaction within the group. Ethnographic researchers must establish rapport and trust based on their personal characteristics, not on their status and their promises. In this sense, entry for the field researcher is not very different from a nonresearcher's entry into a new social situation. The difference lies in the researcher's need to make the process and the product of ethnography explicit by indicating that he or she will be recording conversations, conducting interviews and observations, and undergoing personal transformations (acquiring new knowledge, perspectives, sensitivities, and desensitivities) during the rapport-building and acceptance process.

ESTABLISHING RELATIONSHIPS TO FACILITATE ENTRY

Key point

The researcher begins to develop interpersonal relationships during the entry phase of field research. *Often, some of the first members of the group to be attracted to the new outsider will be those more marginal members who hope to promote their own interests or enhance their personal status by befriending the researcher.* While these individuals may be most receptive and forthcoming initially, they may also be the least well informed. Members of the group who are more reserved, ask more probing questions about the researcher's work, and are initially more reluctant to offer information may later become important members of the researcher's network of key informants.

Cross Reference: See Book 6, Chapter 2, on building research partnerships for more information on how to build relationships for conducting field research

For any researcher who is perceived to be an outsider or who becomes the observer in his or her own social group, gaining access to important social events and settings is a complex process. Because the length of the research period usually is limited by time and money, entry must proceed relatively smoothly and rapidly, building strong and appropriate relationships in a short period of time. Researchers seeking full access to the ideas, behaviors, and social activities of research participants must find ways of truncating the process of becoming fully integrated into the group. The discussion to follow outlines in detail some steps that researchers can take to build relationships so that successful ethnographic inquiry can take place.

Steps in Entering a Research Setting

- Obtain formal permission
- Establish contact with people knowledgeable about the local setting
- Identify and conduct interviews with local gatekeepers
- Carry out observation from a distance
- Obtain introductions through local gatekeepers and key informants to others in the research site
- Gain direct involvement in the research setting with the assistance of gatekeepers or key informants

Obtaining Official Permission

Some field situations are so open that there are no obvious officials or **gatekeepers** from whom to obtain permission to enter. But most situations are not so fluid, and the researcher's professional and personal security require that senior officials or stakeholders be identified and contacted and their formal approval obtained prior to beginning a study. Some examples of senior officials from whom formal permission for entry must be sought are union or company presidents or vice presidents, heads of social service agencies and immigration offices, mayors or other senior political officials, ministry heads, and in-country heads of international agencies with regional offices.

Definition: Gatekeepers are those who control access to information, other individuals, and settings

Key point   *Researchers who wish to conduct research in locations outside their own country must obtain the necessary formal entry permits.* To do so, it is advisable to gain the support of an incountry or local sponsor, such as the following:

- A national university or department head (Makerere University in Uganda or the Department of Pediatrics, University of Peradeniya, Sri Lanka);
- The regional office of a bilateral or international agency (the U.S. Agency for International Development (USAID), the United Nations Development Program (UNDP), or the World Health Organization (WHO))
- A large nongovernmental or voluntary organization (e.g., the Mauritius Family Planning Organization in Port Louis, Mauritius; CARE-Sri Lanka; the Ndugu Society in Nairobi, Kenya; or Peru Mujer in Lima, Peru)

At the same time, it is always helpful to make contact with local/on-site researchers who are familiar with your topic and who may be able to contribute to it.

The following example illustrates protocols followed in gaining access to a local field research site in rural Mexico.

EXAMPLE 4.1   ▬•▬•◂▬

ACCESSING FIELDWORK SITES IN RURAL MEXICO

When Jean Schensul wanted to conduct research on changes in elementary educational curriculum content and school-community-industry relationships in rural Mexico, she could not simply arrive in the municipality she had selected as the base for her research and begin work. She first needed to contact applied researchers in Mexico City who had been involved in linking other North American anthropology students to rural sites in the state of Hidalgo. Next, she made contact with the senior official responsible for industrial development in the area, as suggested by Mexican anthropologists who had been conducting field research in the target area. Her third step, with the assistance of other researchers who had been conducting ethnographic research on educational change in the area, was to meet the principals of public/governmental regional high schools and elementary schools to explain the purpose

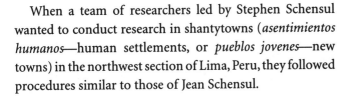

of her work. Next, she met important families in the market town near her research site, who provided her with a "family" base. Finally, she sought permission from the local educational administrator in the market town to conduct research in an elementary school in the town she had identified as her research site.

When a team of researchers led by Stephen Schensul wanted to conduct research in shantytowns (*asentimientos humanos*—human settlements, or *pueblos jovenes*—new towns) in the northwest section of Lima, Peru, they followed procedures similar to those of Jean Schensul.

EXAMPLE 4.2

**ACCESSING SHANTYTOWNS IN A FIELD SITE
IN THE NORTHWEST SECTOR OF LIMA**

To conduct research on the relationship between pediatric morbidity and the evolution of community infrastructure, Stephen Schensul established a relationship between his home university—the University of Connecticut—and a private medical school in Lima with a history of commitment to community and public health research and service. He arranged for the University of Connecticut Health Center to extend an invitation to the rector (provost) of the medical school to visit Connecticut. The visit was designed to show the rector community health research as practiced in Hartford and to establish contacts with Connecticut medical school faculty. The visit involved a series of formal and informal dinners with university officials and community researchers and the signing of a *Convenio,* or an agreement to explore joint research and training ventures.

Several months later, the team of Connecticut researchers arrived in Lima, and Stephen Schensul, as head of the Connecticut research team, immediately contacted the rector. The rector invited the team to a formal meeting at the university to discuss the study with department heads and interested community medicine faculty. The rector's endorsement of the project signaled to the Lima faculty as well as to the project *la luz verde* (the green light)—an authorization to develop the first joint project between the Universidad Cayetano Heredia and the University of Connecticut Medical School.

At the same time, the meeting resulted in the identification of faculty interested in the project. These faculty included members of the departments of community medicine and pediatrics who were working in the area of Lima identified as a potential location for the study and who could provide entry to community leaders and health professionals in that area.

━━•━━•━━━

Individuals such as other researchers, senior officials, university administrators and department heads, and key community members hold power and influence over the research setting. They control the researcher's access to the setting and the resources needed to support a study. If they understand the nature of the project, the reasons for the research, and the ways in which it will benefit their constituencies (as well as avoiding harm to these same constituencies), they can be valuable allies and assets to the study. If they do not understand the project's goals and objectives and are not personally familiar with the researcher, they may become suspicious of the project and find ways to interfere with its success.

Establishing Contact With People Knowledgeable About the Local Setting

Once in the country or the geographic area where the research is to be conducted, ethnographers must identify and gain access to the community or institutional settings where the study is to take place. Researchers should contact local officials to obtain their approval and support in entering the settings that have been selected for the research. Local researchers and other professionals familiar with potential study sites also are very important in helping to select schools, clinics, hospitals, communities, or other locations suitable for the proposed research.

Some of the types of people and the locations in which they can be found (and where research is likely to be conducted) are listed in Table 4.1.

Individuals such as these can identify such critical characteristics as the following:

- Demographic characteristics of the people who are the focus of the study
- Background information relevant to the study
- Political constraints, including individuals or circumstances that might facilitate or hinder the study
- Specific people who might facilitate the introduction of the study into the community or institutional setting
- Cultural problems in introducing or carrying out the study
- Relevant protocols for sampling
- Potential key informants or local experts with knowledge of the topic and the communities in which the research is to be conducted

In addition, researchers can seek help and information in a variety of other places. In a study of commercial sex workers in Hainan, for example, researcher Su-Su Liao wished to visit and interview young women involved in the sex trade, and then to introduce an AIDS prevention intervention in rural restaurants and dance halls. For this purpose she sought help from the provincial ministry health educators, family planning personnel, and town officials (Laio, 1997).

Interviews With Local Gatekeepers

Local gatekeepers are people who control access to resources, whether human, geographic, social, or informational. The best strategy for any researcher is to attempt to find out whom they must meet to gain access to a specific research environment in order to study it. Some gatekeepers are obvious and easy to identify, and others are less so. In a

Definition: Local gatekeepers are people who control access to resources or information researchers need

TABLE 4.1 Local Resources, Gatekeepers, and Key Informants

Roles	Locations	Types of Information and Other Resources Provided
Teachers	Schools, meetings, union offices	School census data, children's school performance, health and family problems, access to children
Factory floor supervisors	Factory settings	Production schedules, employee characteristics, factory and floor organization
Local politicians	At home, municipal meeting locations, community meetings	Community access, community issues, organizations, sectors and factions, key contacts and other gatekeepers
Taxi drivers	At taxi stands	Clients, routes, areas where specific activities occur
Hotel receptionists and other personnel	In hotels, motels, rooming houses	Information on types of clients, clients' communities of origin, and patterns of use
Agency heads and program directors	In communities	Community issues, program or agency issues, program access, client/user access, information about organizations, sectors and factions, information about key contacts and other gatekeepers, client records
Leaders of blocks or other formal social units	In communities	Information on membership lifestyle, concerns, level of organization, needs, resident records
Informal leaders	In communities, by referral	Information on community residents' lifestyles, issues, needs, locations of activities, key informants
Community health workers	Clinics and health outposts, hospital outpatient departments, local Ministries of Health, public health departments	Information on community health needs, access to homes and home visits, village geography, patterns of health maintenance and health care use
Union leaders	Union offices, factory shop floors, at home by referral	Information on workers, work availability, work and workers' health conditions, employment, salaries and wages, organization of work

school, the principal may be an official gatekeeper, but a coach, secretary, counselor, or hall monitor may be an unofficial gatekeeper important in accessing students or gaining information about a specific topic, such as dropping out of school or violence in the building. In a hospital setting, official gatekeepers may be the ward chief, the head of nursing, or the hospital director, whereas an unofficial gatekeeper may be the head nurse at the nursing station. A personnel director, a union steward, or a supervisor may be primary gatekeepers in an industrial setting. Other examples based on our personal experience include a village chief in Ankole in southwestern Uganda; the mayor of Lakewood, a small community in northern Minnesota; and the director of a settlement house in Chicago's West Side Mexican community. These individuals may or may not be useful sources of information, but like the senior officials mentioned earlier, they too can facilitate or block access.

Depending on their characteristics, gatekeepers may become excellent research partners and key informants for ethnographic researchers. Building relationships with gatekeepers calls for the same patience and openness as does building relationships with other people who are likely to be important sources of information in the field. Gatekeepers can be helpful if researchers:

- Describe the project to them
- Ask for their opinions and support
- Interview them about the community, their own role, their contacts, and their views on topics related to the subject of the research
- Ask for their help in identifying others in the community who might be able to provide information on the research topic
- Maintain regular communication with them to ensure continued rapport and support

Identifying Key Informants

Effective key informants are individuals who have broad knowledge of the research setting or deep knowledge of an important aspect of the research. According to Gilchrist, "Key informants differ from other informants by the nature of their position in a culture and by their relationship to the researcher which is generally one of longer duration, occurs in varied settings and is more intimate" (Gilchrist, 1992, p. 71).

Key informants are articulate in their ability to communicate their knowledge to researchers. Most often, they have gained their knowledge by virtue of their position and experience in the community, their established network of relationships, their ability to express themselves orally, and their broad understanding of their community. Such informants know a great deal about the topic of interest and have more information than most other people who could be interviewed. With their ability to conceptualize and express their opinions, they are able to convey useful and important perspectives relevant to the research topic and the domains included in the formative theoretical model.

As with gatekeepers, key informants cannot be expected to know everything there is to know about a topic. Furthermore, their own exposure to information or their personal experience may be limited by their gender, age, social class, ethnicity, or geographic accessibility. Although the primary purpose for interviewing key informants is to gain deeper knowledge about one or more specific topics, it is always better to interview several key informants on the same topic to ensure validity and reliability. In this way, data obtained from several different key informants can be accumulated and cross-checked. Ethnographers can be more convinced that what they are learning from a key informant has validity when they hear the same information from several

Cross Reference:
See Book 1 and Chapter 11 in this book on validity and reliability in ethnographic research

people and/or observe the same phenomenon in the field
several times in different settings.

➤•➤•➤ **EXAMPLE 4.3**

CONFIRMING PERCEPTIONS OF RACISM IN AN URBAN HIGH SCHOOL

Researchers at the Institute for Community Research (ICR) have been involved in a
long-term investigation of ethnic and racial barriers to the formation of cross-ethnic
and cross-generational relationships among urban teenagers. Some teenagers and a
number of adult research staff and facilitators in the ICR's Summer Youth Research
Institute made the initial assumption that racism was an important component of
school environment in one urban high school and a significant factor in dropping
out of school. Youth-conducted interviews with key informants (three vice principals) at the school produced information to the contrary. This multiethnic (Puerto
Rican, Irish-American, and West Indian) team of vice principals disagreed that racism
(discriminating against students or faculty because of their African origin, physical
features, and linguistic and cultural practices) was a significant element at the school.
They pointed out through the use of examples that for them, gender differences were
more important. Several student leaders, including several African American students interviewed from the same school, confirmed that from their point of view,
racism was not a problem, but other "isms" were. Still convinced that racism was a
problem, student researchers included questions about harassment based on racist
attitudes in a survey on factors related to dropping out of school. Once again, the
results were negative. Information from two different groups of key informants and
a survey led both adult and youth researchers to conclude that racism, at least as
defined in the study and by key informants, was, indeed, not a problem at this urban
high school.

➤•➤•➤

Key informants come from different sectors and have
knowledge specific to cultural domains of interest to researchers. They are selected because of their ability to provide exploratory information and because they can connect
researchers to other possible key informants and sources of

information. Because they can never fully represent every important demographic category or cultural domain, however, interviews with key informants should never be treated as representative of an entire population. Furthermore, their knowledge base is generally specific—that is, they cannot know everything and may know little about any other aspect of culture except the domain in which they have special expertise.

Cross Reference: See Book 6, Chapter 1, on problems associated with identification with specific segments of the population, and Chapter 2 for ways of broadening the spectrum of key informants for building research

Key informants can be chosen for exploratory reasons (to discover a topic or new domains associated with an already identified topic) or for theoretical reasons (to explore relationships among elements in an already formulated theoretical model) (Johnson, 1990). Regardless, they should be chosen from as broad a spectrum of the population as possible to ensure representativeness. This strategy is also important in terms of ensuring the neutral position of the researcher in the community. It is a disadvantage for researchers to be associated with any one specific sector of the community, especially during the early months of a study.

Spradley notes that "although almost anyone can become an informant, not everyone makes a good informant" (1979, p. 45). In general, good key informants are the following:

- Natural researchers, interested in the purpose of the research and in exploring the topic in their own settings, together with, as well as in the absence of, the ethnographer
- "Boundary spanners," able to relate to a variety of different settings, sectors, networks, and individuals, and prepared to link the ethnographer with these informational resources
- Self-critical, able to recognize that they may not know everything about their own setting or a topic in which they are viewed as having expertise, and prepared to admit their own knowledge gaps to the ethnographer

- Risk-takers, willing to associate with the ethnographer despite questions about the research and the identity and intentions of the researcher
- Able to perceive and understand a variety of perspectives on a subject
- Experienced, with a number of years of involvement in the research setting or with the topic of interest to the ethnographer

Observation From a Distance

Observation from a distance is a form of observation that is spectator-like; not participatory; it is designed to orient the researcher, at least superficially, to places, people, social interaction, clothing, language, and other aspects of the community setting with which he or she should become familiar. Researchers can observe from a distance some workers on a production line, couples walking in a "lover's lane" or park, or mothers and teachers playing with young children in an outdoor playground. Observation from a distance is only possible when it can be conducted unobtrusively, in such a way that participants do not notice the researcher. Furthermore, the behavior observed must occur in public settings, where observations pose no threat or consequence either to the observer or the observed. These observations help researchers to gain geographic bearing; learn what is commonly worn, and discover age, gender, and class differences in clothing, appearance, and use of space. In general, these unobtrusive observations orient the researcher to the community environment and provide a backdrop to more systematic inquiry (Bernard, 1995).

Definition: Observation from a distance refers to the researcher's long-distance observation of activities related to the topic of interest

Gaining an Introduction Into the Research Site

At some point, ethnographic researchers will feel ready to engage in social interactions and inquiry in the study site. This may happen immediately, or it may happen later in the entry process. Often, a gatekeeper or local key informant will perform introductions. Sometimes, the presentation process involves describing the project to many different people and sectors at the same time. For example, in 1998, Jean Schensul and a team of researchers began a study of progression from gateway drugs such as marijuana to heroin and cocaine use in young adults. Researchers introduced the project to coordinators of youth programs, maternal outreach programs, and instructors in alternative education programs to seek their help in referring participants to the study. It is always useful to develop a script or cover story for the project; this will ensure that the basic description of the study is consistent from location to location, even though the presentation style and the responses to questions about the project will change from one presentation to the next.

Usually, when someone who is well thought of in the community introduces the researcher, only a limited cover story is necessary. This is because in most communities, relationships are based on trust. Introduction by a trusted acquaintance or friend is an endorsement of the person. However, to maintain a neutral position in the community, researchers should make sure that representatives from more than one sector of the community introduce them. In this way, researchers can avoid being identified with any single faction.

Once introduced to the site, researchers should maintain visibility through regular visits; informal interviews with people at the site or in the community; and willingness to visit people's homes, eat meals with them, shop with them, and attend community events.

In ethnographic research, the boundaries between the entry process and formal initiation of the study are not very clearly defined, because ethnographers begin collecting information from the very first moment they step into the field. Nevertheless, the first month or so of fieldwork produces many impressions that are not accurate or relevant to the study. As researchers become more comfortable with the field setting and their eyes and ears become attuned to what is going on around them, they can begin to focus more clearly on what elements of culture are relevant to their study. The first stage of focused ethnographic research—unstructured or open-ended interviewing and observation—is the topic of the next two chapters.

5 ━●━●━

EXPLORATORY OR OPEN-ENDED OBSERVATION

Participant observation refers to a process of learning through exposure to or involvement in the day-to-day or routine activities of participants in the research setting. Participant observation represents the starting point in ethnographic research for the following reasons:

- It is central to identifying and building relationships important to the future of the research endeavor.
- It gives the researcher an intuitive as well as an intellectual grasp of the way things are organized and prioritized, how people relate to one another, and the ways in which social and physical boundaries are defined.
- It demonstrates—and, over time, can confirm—patterns of etiquette, political organization and leadership, social competitition and cooperation, socioeconomic status and hierarchies in practice, and other cultural patterns that are not easily addressed or about which discussions are forbidden.
- It endorses the presence of the researcher in the community.
- It provides the researcher with cultural experiences that can be discussed with key informants or participants in the study site and treated as data.

According to Bogdewic, participant observation offers other advantages, including the opportunity to witness

Definition:
Participant observation is a data collection technique that requires the researcher to be present at, involved in, and recording the routine daily activities with people in the field setting

91

events that outsiders would not be invited to attend, and to access situations that might be hidden from the public, such as certain religious rituals, illegal or socially stigmatized activities, or activities that groups use to maintain a special identity (Bogdewic, 1992).

PARTICIPATION

Definition: Participation refers to presence in and interaction with a site when an activity or event is occurring

We begin our discussion regarding tools of observation with definitions of observation and participation. **Participation** is always defined by researcher presence at the event being observed. Participation means near-total immersion when ethnographers live in unfamiliar communities where they have little or no knowledge of local culture and study life in those communities through their own participation as full-time residents and members. The traditional definition of participant observation refers to this immersion experience. Even in these circumstances, however, researchers must retreat from the field from time to time, even if retreating is only to their room or private space to write up their notes. Otherwise, their unrecorded experiences will never be transformed into documents that can be read and interpreted by them, as well as others, as scientific data.

Ethnographers and other researchers still can identify opportunities for immersion experiences. But for the most part, observers are not full participants in community life. In some instances, such as ethnography conducted with drug users or others engaged in illegal activity, it is not ethically or professionally acceptable for ethnographers to become fully involved. The range of opportunities, from "nonparticipation to active participation to complete participation," has often been expressed as a continuum (De Walt & De Walt, 1998, pp. 262-263; also see Spradley, 1980).

In Book 6, we describe some of the personal characteristics that influence the degree of ease with which ethnographic researchers may be accepted into a situation. These include appearance, language, class background, manner, ease of interaction style, age, size, gender, race, and ethnicity. Structural characteristics, such as rules regulating the behavior and interaction of men and women, or rules of hospitality, also may affect possibilities for interaction. In rural Mexico or in Senegal, for example, it is not culturally acceptable for researchers to live alone or in a hotel. A researcher must live with a family and experience social life in the context of that family's position and role in the community. Families or community members may even give researchers a local, family, or clan name. In Mexico, Jean Schensul's Spanish name was Juanita. In Senegal, she first was given the Wolof version of her first name—Jenoba; later, when leaders of a traditional women's group raised the question of to which family she belonged, she was informally assigned the clan name of the family with whom she was living at the time.

Becoming incorporated into a family brings with it many personal, social, and scientific advantages. On the other hand, finding private time to work or travel alone becomes a challenge when researchers are expected to participate in family events. Furthermore, the position of the family in the community may limit researcher access to information and opportunities. In contrast to the previous examples, in China, a researcher may be treated as an official visitor whose residence is confined to a hotel or housing for foreigners and whose opportunities for learning are limited in other ways.

As Werner and Schoepfle (1987) note, how much participation is possible or feasible is influenced by the setting

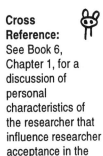

Cross Reference: See Book 6, Chapter 1, for a discussion of personal characteristics of the researcher that influence researcher acceptance in the field

and the research question: "Studying a Polynesian village while living in it requires full-time participation; commuting daily to a fire station to study firemen while living at home requires only part-time participation" (pp. 258-259).

Participation also varies in terms of the activities in which the researcher is expected to or can participate. Sometimes, researchers are present in a community or at an activity and need do nothing but accompany others, observe, and ask questions. At other times, they may be expected to participate more actively. Sometimes, researchers can find ways of making themselves useful—for example, by watching children, shopping for food, fixing a broken car, playing a game with youth or adults, or working with public health officials and teachers on a public health campaign. Traditionally, ethnographers were expected to learn by doing (i.e., participating), but even in immersion settings, there are situations, such as religious ceremonies, to which outsiders are not invited or are forbidden to participate.

Ethnographers may be excluded from participation for a variety of reasons. These may include lack of trust, the community's discomfort with an outsider, community members' anticipation that a situation might be dangerous, or the community's reluctance or inability because of poverty or civil war to provide continuing support for a stranger. Some exclusionary techniques include the following:

■ Using a standard language unfamiliar to the researcher
■ Code switching (changing from a language familiar to the researcher to one not understood)
■ Changing the subject of a conversation when the ethnographer approaches
■ Refusing to answer questions
■ Positioning so that the ethnographer cannot hear what is being said
■ Not inviting researchers to attend social events

Every researcher can expect to experience exclusion. Recognizing whether or not one is intentionally excluded and determining what exclusion means for the success of the research is an important component of any field study, especially in the early stages. Setting boundaries and limits around one's participation during the first months of ethnographic fieldwork, establishing a routine, and taking regular breaks from the field are ways of coping with the stresses and ambiguities of long-term immersion in a research setting.

After a period of participation and observation, researchers are likely to come to the realization that they have become recognized and accepted in the study community. Often, this occurs after an unusual incident, such as helping a family or a group in a crisis, during which they are perceived as behaving in a manner that demonstrates serious commitment to the community (DeWalt & DeWalt, 1998, p. 269).

OBSERVATION

Observation is always filtered through the researcher's interpretive frames. The most accurate observations are shaped by formative theoretical frameworks and scrupulous attention to detail. Other influences on observation, such as personal biases and values and other tacit, implicit, or unarticulated theories, are less helpful. Ethnographers should be scrupulous in their understanding of the research problem and its formative theoretical framework, as well as their own biases—attempting to strengthen the effects of the former and minimize the effects of the latter. The quality and importance of the facts that an ethnographer observes and records depend on the observational, documentation, and interpretation skills of the observer and the opportunities he or she has for observing.

Definition: Observation refers to what can be seen through the eyes of the ethnographer

Cross Reference: See Books 1, 5, and 6 for discussions of how these frames affect data collection and fieldnotes

In the remainder of this chapter, we will discuss what ethnographers observe, when and where they observe it, what tools are available to improve observational skills and data quality, and how observational data are recorded.

WHAT DO ETHNOGRAPHERS OBSERVE?

What ethnographers observe in the field will differ during a field stay. Researchers spend the first days and months of a field experience getting oriented. The need to learn how to function in a new situation as well as curiosity about it will drive observation. Later on, observation will become more selective.

When they first enter the field, ethnographers will not know exactly what they are observing, especially if the setting is unfamiliar. During the early stages, it is very important to document observations accurately and in concrete detail without prematurely imposing categories derived from a preestablished external theory or conceptual framework external to the community or cultural context being studied. Local formative theory assists researchers to direct their observations and to find out what to look at. Over time, and with repeated observation and questioning, the meanings of items, articles, patterns of behavior, and social relationships and events become clearer. At this point, it becomes possible to associate behaviors observed in the field with domains in the formative theoretical model, or to create new domains, because their meanings are now known.

To make sense of the bewildering array of new visual, aural, olfactory, and social stimuli in the field, ethnographers usually start by doing the following:

- Observing settings
- Observing and tracking events and event sequences
- Counting, census-taking, and ethnographic mapping

■ Searching for indicators of socioeconomic difference

These observational activities orient researchers to the field and enable them to begin to sort out major social and cultural dimensions in the field setting.

Observing Settings

Settings are locations identified as potentially important to a study, where behaviors and activities relevant to understanding the context of the study may occur. Settings and locations can be identified either through discussions with key informants or by working with local research partners who know the research community well. When they are public or quasi-public, researchers can conduct observations in these settings in an unobtrusive manner. Identifying, locating, and mapping settings for more systematic semistructured or structured observation can take place early in a study and are useful in identifying important behaviors, events, and people for further investigation through interviewing and observation.

Definition:
Research settings are locations where behaviors and activities relevant to a study take place

Cross Reference:
See this book, Chapters 7 and 8, for more information on semistructured and structured observation and interviewing

➤•➤•➤ **EXAMPLE 5.1**

IDENTIFYING STREET SITES WHERE TEENAGERS GATHER

To identify locations for recruitment of youth into a study of transitions to cocaine and heroin in youth in Hartford, researchers Jean Schensul, Lorie Broomhall, and Raul Pino conducted interviews with older adolescents familiar with the streets and neighborhoods of the city. They first asked adolescents to list the types of places where teens gathered either after school or during school when they skipped classes. Youth listed basketball courts, designated areas of city parks, street corners, streets, package stores, pool halls, and clubs. The young people then worked with large street maps of the city, using markers to identify the locations they knew about, the kinds of activities that usually took place there, and the types of young people who hung out in those settings. This information enabled young ethnographer/outreach staff on the project to visit these sites, confirm the reports of teenagers with their own observations, and recruit them for the study.

➤•➤•➤

The following example illustrates how working with local key informants or experts simplified the process of spatially situating health care locations in Lima.

EXAMPLE 5.2 ◄●◄●◄●

LOCATING HEALTH CARE SITES IN *PUEBLOS JOVENES*
(NEW COMMUNITIES) IN LIMA, PERU

In a study of the relationships among health care institutions, community organizations, physical infrastructure, and pediatric diseases in Lima, ethnographers first worked with local pediatricians to identify the communities and the locations in those communities where the delivery of health care was occurring. The list included larger health clinics; health care outposts; hospitals; community dining rooms (*comedores,* locations where women prepared meals for a group of community residents who paid a minimum fee for them in advance); locations where milk was distributed; and pharmacies. The research team was able to visit examples of each of these sites and to document spatial arrangements, staffing patterns, types of health problems treated there, perceived problems in health care delivery, links with other health care facilities, types of patients, community health education programs, the presence of community health workers, and community ties. These data were recorded by hand and transformed into fieldnotes.

◄●◄●◄●

The following example illustrates how researchers can work with health educators to identify targeted locations for exploratory observation.

PLACES IN PORT LOUIS WHERE YOUNG ADULTS SOCIALIZE

Stephen and Jean Schensul, Geeta Oodit, and colleagues conducted a study of sexual risk among young, unmarried women in the industrial workforce in Mauritius. In Mauritius, female virginity is still believed important, but sexual values and norms are changing. In recent years, young women have joined the industrial workforce in large numbers, gaining exposure to male companionship outside the confines of familial supervision.

One of the first steps the research team undertook was to ask younger members of the health education team of the Mauritius Family Planning Association to list and describe types of locations where young couples could meet one another and could go to have romantic experiences. The research team generated a list of locations based on local knowledge, which included clubs, beach parties, beach hotels, local parks, and bus stops where young workers waited for bus transportation home. Key informant interviews with taxi drivers, club managers, receptionists at beach hotels, and industrial floor managers confirmed this list and added several other locations. Members of the research team were then able to station themselves unobtrusively in these public locations to observe interactions between young men and women.

➤•➤•➤

Events

Events are activity sequences that are larger, longer, and more complex than single activities. They take place in a specific location and have a specific purpose and meaning about which most people agree, although individual renditions of the meaning of the event may differ somewhat depending on differences among informants. They usually

Definition:  Events are activity sequences that can be bounded in time and space

- Involve more than one person
- Have history and consequence
- Are repeated

Some examples of events are a community meeting to discuss school reform; a gathering of community health workers to learn new information about preventing diarrhea; the opening of a gallery exhibit on Franco-Canadian wood carvings; a drive-by shooting in an urban neighborhood; a "ragging" session (hazing of new students) at a Sri Lankan university; or a public theatrical performance given by a middle school arts program.

Each of these has time duration. For example, the community meeting may begin at 6:00 p.m. and end at 7:30 p.m. The gallery exhibit opening reception begins at 4:00 p.m. and ends at 8:00 p.m. The ragging session begins on a weekend day and ends 6 weeks later. The event surrounding the drive-by shooting may last only 15 minutes.

The classic journalist's questions expressed by the interrogatory terms "who, what happened, where, when, why, for whom" should be answered in describing an event. One such event is described in Example 5.4.

EXAMPLE 5.4　　　　　━●━━●━━●

TREATMENT FOR ABUSIVE ALCOHOL USE AT A SPIRITUALIST CENTER

For a number of years, a spiritualist center [where] provided a variety of spiritual, consultative, and educational services on a main street in the heart of Hartford's Puerto Rican community [where]. Each January, around the time of Three Kings Day [when], the Center sponsored a community gathering at which the Madrina (godmother) or lead spiritualist healer [who] went into a trance, took on the persona of the Spirit of San Lazaro, and conducted healing sessions [what happened] with members of the congregation [with whom]. The sequence of activities involved [what happened] the following:

- The gathering of the community
- Formal introduction of spiritualist trainees
- A period during which they practiced entry into and exit from a trance in front of the audience
- The blessing of the food, flower, and candle offerings
- The entrance of the spirit of San Lazaro through the Madrina, marked by the presence of cigar smoke

Members of the congregation either volunteered to be blessed by San Lazaro, acting through the Madrina, or were identified by the spirit as needing healing. The healing process [what happened], which took place in front of the entire community of attendees and mediums-in-training [with whom], involved a variety of strategies, ranging from a blessing alone to an interpretation of a problem and a remedy for healing, which usually involved spiritual, family, and community support.

On one occasion, San Lazaro selected for attention one of the spiritualists-in-training who was known to use alcohol as an excuse to abuse his family physically [for whom]. San Lazaro described these behaviors in great detail before the audience, noting that the traditional Latino male role required providing support and income to the household, and that abuse as a result of alcohol use was inconsistent with that role. The spirit told the audience of the unhappy contradiction between the helping role of the spiritualist-in-training and that of an abusive husband. San Lazaro then extracted a public promise [what happened] from the trainee to stop drinking and to perform in a manner consistent with the traditional definition of machismo—care of self, family, and community. Following this sequence, the spiritualists-in-training went into a trance, and the spirit departed the body of the Madrina. The congregation then shifted to talking with one another, eating, and talking with the mediums.

➤•➤•➤

The above description illustrates how the guiding elements "who, what happened, where, when, why, for whom" can be incorporated into a description of an event. A more complete description of the event would include the following:

- A count of attendees by gender, age, and any other distinguishing features
- A portrayal of the layout of the center
- A description of the furnishings of the center
- A description of how people were arranged in space over time
- A description of the mediums-in-training and their activities
- A full description of the Madrina's behavior from prior to taking on the spirit of San Lazaro to the end of the healing session
- The details of each healing event

Eventually, this description of a single event would be supplemented with accounts of other events taking place at the center, a history of the spiritual center, a full exploration of the material items in the center, a schedule of activities taking place there, and an explanation for each activity. These data would form the basis of an ethnograhic description of the role of the "centro" in the community.

Counting, Census-Taking, and Mapping

Definition: Cross-sectional refers to the collection of data at a single point in time, whereas longitudinal refers to the collection of the same data from the same population at two or more points in time

Counting, census-taking, and mapping are all ways of obtaining a more accurate picture of the presence of people, places, and things in social space in the early stages of fieldwork when researchers' capacity in the local language and access to local assistance are limited. These data can be collected **cross-sectionally** or **longitudinally** to show change over time.

Counting. Counting refers to listing and enumerating types of people, material items, locations, or other things that are important in situating the event, location, or activity more accurately in the context of the community. For example, accurately reporting that "the block between Hillside and McDonough streets" includes seven three-story flats, one 25-unit brick apartment building with three vacancies, a 150-bed nursing home, and a small corner grocery on the northwest corner allows researchers to compare structures on this block with those on other blocks along the same avenue, and to document more accurately changes over time in that block.

One of the first things experienced ethnographers do whenever they enter a social event is to identify and count the social categories of people attending the event (e.g., artists, students, young people, etc.). They also estimate how many people are there, and where they are sitting or standing in relation to one another. When ethnicity, gender, and age are important dimensions of social difference, as they often are, well-trained ethnographers scan the setting to count:

- Numbers of men and women
- Their approximate ages
- Whether the event is ethnically mixed (by obtaining an approximate count of those whose appearance suggests specific ethnic membership)

Ethnographers observing at bars, beach hotels, and parks in Mauritius counted the number of young couples who entered and left on a Saturday evening over a designated (usually 2-hour) period of time, compared to older couples. By repeating their observations over a month-long period, they were able to enhance their observations with actual numbers of couples and to determine consistency of use over time (Schensul, Oodit, et al., 1994).

Experienced ethnographers in Hartford counted the number of heroin addicts on two main avenues on several occasions at three points during the day—morning, noon, and evening. By doing so, they were able to judge the best times for distributing bleach kits and recruiting injection drug users into intervention studies.

Census-taking. A **census** lists every person, household unit, or other unit (e.g., reindeer, latrines, water pumps, public telephone booths, garbage dump sites) in the research setting of interest to the researcher. Conducting a census is a useful activity in any setting, although in large urban areas, where taking a complete census is usually neither possible nor cost-effective, census enumeration is conducted only in the designated areas of the city where the research will take place. Census enumeration provides ethnographers with a general picture of how a population or material items are distributed, as well as an accurate count of research units for sampling purposes later. Thus, only a small amount of information is collected in a census.

Cross Reference:
See Book 4, Chapter 3, on conducting research with hidden populations

Definition: A census is a 100% sample or count of a specific unit in the research setting of interest to the researcher

TABLE 5.1   Household Enumeration Form

1. Street Address _____

2. Number of people in household _____

3. No. of rooms in household _____

4. Rental _____   Owned _____

5. Is there anyone between the ages of 16 and 24 living in this household? List names and ages (by birthdate):

   (a) _____   _____

   (b) _____   _____

   (c) _____   _____

   (d) _____   _____

6. Is there anyone between the ages of 16 and 24 who is a family member but living outside the household? List all names, ages, current addresses, and ways of contacting

	Names	Other names	Ages	Current Addresses	Contacts
(a)	_____	_____	_____	_____	_____
(b)	_____	_____	_____	_____	_____
(c)	_____	_____	_____	_____	_____
(d)	_____	_____	_____	_____	_____

Cross Reference: See Cromley's chapter in Book 4 for a detailed discussion on the uses of spatial mapping in ethnographic research

Where street addresses are known, household census data are generally collected with a brief survey form or enumeration sheet (see Table 5.1). Where there are no street addresses (e.g., in emerging shantytowns ringing urban areas in developing countries, or in rural areas of Sri Lanka or Senegal), census enumerations may be conducted by placing households on a geographic map. Maps are also useful tools for enumerating other infrastructural or environmental characteristics.

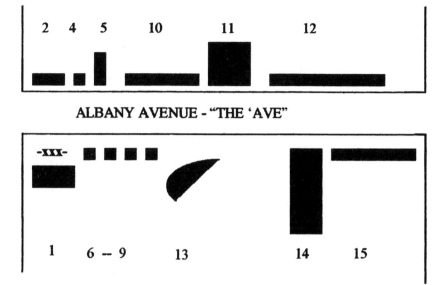

Figure 5.1. A map of one block in Hartford's North End.

Ethnographic mapping. Pelto and Pelto (1978) noted that

> it is a source of constant surprise that many ethnographic
> reports do not contain maps of the physical setting within
> which social behavior takes place. Such maps should locate
> major action settings (e.g., ball fields, religious places, market-
> places), social divisions of the community, agricultural areas,
> directions and distances of neighboring communities and ma-
> jor natural features such as rivers, mountains and swamps.
> (p. 193)

Ethnographic mapping is still underutilized and constitutes
an important first activity in getting to know a city neighborhood, a rural community, or any other sociogeographic
area.

Figure 5.1 shows a street map. Any observer can construct such a map by walking down a main or residential

street in a neighborhood and noting the location and approximate size of buildings, their function, appearance, whether or not they appear to be residences or businesses, and anything else about them seemingly relevant to the research topic. An easy way to do this is to number the buildings on the drawing itself and to keep a set of observations for each of the buildings.

For example, ethnographers walking down the main avenue (the "Ave") in North Hartford, Connecticut would note that the map in Figure 5.1 refers to the block between Blue Hills and Homestead. The first building (1) is an office building that houses the Urban League of Greater Hartford and some other businesses. Opposite is an elementary school (2). Beside the elementary school is a branch of the public library (4), and beside it is a three-story flat (5). Buildings 6-9 are single-family homes; residents of (6) and (7) are small groups of three and four men who know each other. Area 13 is a small park where male teens gather to shoot baskets and mothers bring their small children to play on the swings on the street side. Buildings 10-12 together constitute North Hartford's middle school complex; the remainder of the buildings on the block (14, 15) are boarded up and may be marked for demolition by the city.

The symbol "-XXX-" marks the street location where a car, chased by the police, bounced into and wrapped itself around a telephone pole. A crowd gathered while the driver and passenger extricated themselves and ran down a side street chased by the police, leaving observers to wonder what was happening. This map records the context of the event. The event occurred as ethnographers were observing the block, so both were recorded on the ethnographers' map. These data constitute an important descriptive backdrop to additional events that may eventually be observed on the street.

We could go on to indicate sites where young mothers shop or stop to talk with each other; where empty syringes can be found; other locations where teenagers hang out and play basketball; places where alcohol is purchased by under-age teens; locations where members of the diverse ethnic groups that reside in this part of the city (West Indian/Caribbeans, Haitians, African Americans, Cubans and Puerto Ricans, Dominicans, and other groups) gather; routes taken by mothers accompanying their children to school; and so on. All of these bits of data, collected and accumulated over time, provide the building blocks for a constructed history and description of life on one of the 15 blocks that constitutes the heart of the North End's commercial strip.

In the maps in Figures 5.2a and 5.2b, the ethnographer has located groupings of individuals in clusters in a community park where a health fair is occurring. The clusters are numbered by group (GP) and number (1-5). Each grouping consists of a booth or table, with people gathered around it. Readers can note a dramatic increase in number of participants attending the fair (as indicated by the x's) from the point in time at which the map in Figure 5.2a was drawn—9:30 a.m.—to the time at which the map in Figure 5.2b was drawn—1:30 p.m. The maps also give a rough indication of which booths were most popular at each point in time, as suggested by the relative number of x's from one time point to another and from one booth to another. The fieldnotes associated with this map identify the possible reasons for the groupings; what differentiates the members of each cluster, if anything; how many people altogether are present; and any observed relationships between individuals in clusters and among the clusters themselves.

Classrooms also can be mapped. Different arrangements of desks and chairs; boards; type, array, location, and acces-

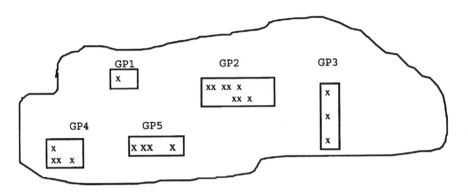

Figure 5.2a. Community Health Fair, 9:30 a.m.

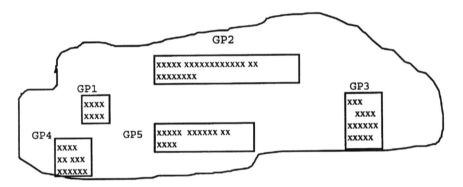

Figure 5.2b. Community Health Fair, 1:30 p.m.

sibility of educational materials; and the placement of a teacher's desk are all important pieces of evidence in interpreting the story of social relations in the classroom, the teacher's choice of instructional techniques, and the degree to which multiple learning styles are considered.

EXAMPLE 5.5

USING A GEOGRAPHIC INFORMATION SYSTEM (GIS)
TO INTRODUCE CHILDREN TO SOCIAL MAPPING

In an interesting experiment designed to introduce children to social mapping and the use of **GIS,** a group of fourth graders decided to consider the interaction of ethnicity and gender among classrooms on their floor. First, they created hand-drawn maps of the location of the classrooms on their floor. Then, they transposed the classrooms into a computerized data file. Next, they collected information on the ethnicity and gender of teachers and students in each classroom and entered these data into an additional database. Using ARCVIEW, a desktop software program for mapping environmental, demographic, and social variables, they were able to link the databases to demonstrate variations across classrooms by gender and ethnicity of children and teachers. This visual display allowed them to make inferences about the degree to which teacher/student matching on these variables was occurring in their school, and to discuss whether or not mismatch made a difference in quality of education (Berg, personal communication, 1998).

Definition:
GIS refers to Geographic Information System, a computerized means of organizing quantitative data in space to illustrate social patterns

Cross Reference:
See Book 4, Chapter 2, on spatial data for a discussion on GIS use in ethnography

These activities can be more intrusive than they may seem at first glance, especially if they take place in more private places. Walking from one residential hamlet to another in rural hill country in Sri Lanka and counting house sites is a highly visible task, and it is likely to appear suspicious or even threatening to villagers who have not met the researcher and do not know what he or she is doing. The following example illustrates a circumstance in which mapping was not only not possible but dangerous.

EXAMPLE 5.6 ━◆━●━◆━●━◆━

AN EXAMPLE OF A SITUATION IN WHICH MAPPING
THROUGH OBSERVATION WAS DANGEROUS

One of the first tasks LeCompte wanted to carry out in "Pinnacle," the town where she did a 5-year study of the school district, was to create a map of major institutions in the community. Many public places were easily accessible. From driving through the town, LeCompte learned that most commercial enterprises, such as hotels, the grocery store, a trading post, and several restaurants, were located along the highways that intersected in a "T" in the middle of town, along with the post office, offices of the tribal police, the state highway department, the offices for subsidized housing, a large field where the weekly flea market was held, and the clinic. Located in a large fenced compound on the north-south highway were the compound of the Indian boarding school, all of the public school buildings, and the school's district headquarters, with the exception of the elementary school, which was down a main side road next to the Indian Health Services office and hospital compound. Other features, such as the water plant and the city dump, also were accessible.

However, housing in Pinnacle was exceedingly segregated, by ethnicity and by occupation. Only Navajo people from the Pinnacle area could own land in the town, so the major employers provided housing in compounds for their non-Navajo staff and for Indian staff not from the area. This housing was arranged in four large walled compounds: one next to the education buildings for teachers and educational staff, another across the highway from the public school complex for the Bureau of Indian Affairs boarding school staff, one attached to the hospital for their staff, and one adjacent to the public school complex for employees of the nearby coal mine. A fifth small complex was located within the compound of the elementary school.

Mapping where these areas were was fairly easy, but adding any details meant that LeCompte encountered hostility. Most local Navajo lived on "the hill," an area west of the main highway. This also was where most churches, some small stores, the community gardens, and an area where local Indian men gathered to drink illegally were located. Nonlocals were welcome only in the public areas and in housing compounds related to their employment. LeCompte could hang out around the schools and the teacher housing, and in any of the public areas, including the flea market. However, even going by car onto "the hill" was greeted with suspicion, although she had been working in the community as a consultant for several years. Rocks were thrown, and feedback from local people made it clear that nonlocals should not venture out of their designated areas. Doing house-to-house mapping was out of the question, even in the compounds where many non-Indians lived; a map including major roads and institutions such as churches was assembled only after many months of talking to local teachers and making forays through town by car in the company of a Navajo teacher aide. Fortunately, a detailed map of the community was not necessary data for LeCompte's study of district instructional practices.

The research team of Schensul, Schensul, and Velazquez encountered similar problems while they were conducting health surveys among contracted laborers living in migrant labor encampments in Homestead, Florida. Resident camps were privately owned, and researchers entering them to map and enumerate households without owners' permission exposed themselves and their respondents to the threat of violence from owners' security patrols.

On the other hand, counting the number of vendors' stands and the range of products available in a public market in rural Mexico is very unobtrusive because many people purchase items at the market, and the vendors come from all over the central part of the country and are accustomed to strangers.

Definition: Social differences are recognized patterns of differences in appearance, income, or lifestyle that set people apart from one another and often rank them in relation to one another

Socioeconomic or Other
Indicators of Social Differences

Social differences are an important component of any study. **Indicators** of the concept "social difference" can be readily observed in any community or other social setting. Socioeconomic differences—referring to differences among individuals, families, or groups by a combination of educational level, type of employment, and income—are easy to observe and are important in most ethnographic studies. Differences in socioeconomic status among individuals and groups can be inferred through observation by a respondent's characteristics and preferences:

Definition: An indicator is an element that researchers select from among the universe of possible behaviors, beliefs, or materials to represent a concept important in their research

- Choice of clothing
- Hair style
- Type and amount of jewelry
- Leisure time activities
- Speech and language patterns
- Television program preferences
- Choice of car
- Place of residence

Another way to observe socioeconomic differences at the community level is to look for differences in the physical structure of houses or homesteads or material items purchased with cash.

EXAMPLE 5.7   ➤•➤•➤

OBSERVING DIFFERENCES IN HOMESTEADS IN A
RURAL RICE-GROWING AREA OF SRI LANKA

A group of researchers that included the authors visited Division C of the Mahaveli Development Scheme, an internationally funded effort to move large numbers of people from their overpopulated highland villages to a newly irrigated dry zone in eastern Sri Lanka. Immigrants were given some resources to relocate and a plot for homesteading. Homesteads were arrayed along long irrigation channels, the use of which required cooperation among homesteaders to dig the canals and to ensure that people at both ends of a canal had access to water. The prosperity of households depended on cooperation over water and other factors, such as alternative sources of income in addition to rice agriculture, number of workers in the household, and the health of the household.

The research team visited and walked the length of several ditches, noting the size of the house, the composition of the walls (cinder block vs. mud and sticks), the materials used for roofing (palm fronds vs. tin sheets), the size of the clearing around the house, the presence of fruit-bearing trees, evidence of chickens and other cash animals, and visibility of store-bought cooking utensils. These and other items were used to create a scale included in a survey instrument that measured socioeconomic status of the household (Amarasiri de Silva, 1993).

➤•➤•➤

A similar procedure was used in new towns of Lima, Peru. A walk through several communities at various stages of development showed variations in household structures, indicating differences in household economic status and wealth, including the following:

- Straw versus cinderblock house walls
- Presence and type of roofing
- Presence and use of latrine on premises versus ground
- Presence of wooden front door
- Presence and number of windows
- Presence of a water storage tank, nearby street tap, or piped-in water
- Method of garbage disposal (dumping near the house, burning, or pickup)
- Legal or illegal (wire tapped or stolen) source of electical power

These indicators were not noticeable to the unexperienced eye, but they quickly became obvious to researchers when community physicians pointed them out.

A visit to even a small number of households often reveals the presence of a range of items purchased with disposable cash. These items will vary with the context—for example, in developing countries, items that signify important social differences are generally those that are manufactured and represent a modernized or urban lifestyle, such as electrical appliances, television sets, motorcycles, and indoor toilets. In more affluent countries, where it is common to own many such material items, some handmade goods (such as handwoven imported carpets, works of art, or finely handcrafted wooden furniture) have a similar symbolic value. It is necessary to discover beforehand which items are indicators of status differences.

Observers usually have many opportunities to ask about these items, including their cost, location of purchase, use, and importance in the life of the household. The items can

Cross Reference: See Book 5, Chapter 8, on the organization and management of quantitative data including index and scale development

Cross Reference: See Book 5, Chapter 8, on the construction of scales and indexes

be used to compose quantitative indexes or scales measuring wealth or level of development of the household. The qualitative data obtained through observation and interviewing help both to determine which items should be included in the scales and to interpret the meaning of the associations between scale or index scores and other variables later in the study.

There are many other domains that can be explored and clarified through observation. Formative theories will help to define what these are. However, observation in the field will always reveal new individual behaviors, social relations, material items, and other social things or facts whose meanings must be discovered through repeated observation and interviewing before they find their place in coding and conceptual taxonomies.

WRITING OBSERVATIONS: THE LANGUAGE OF FIELDNOTES

We have seen that observation is critical to the conduct of good ethnographic research. The challenge for the researcher lies in the transformation of observations into fieldnotes, which then constitute a scientific record of the experience for future reference. The more complete and accurate the fieldnotes, the easier it is for researchers to catalogue, code, and use them as data.

Writing good fieldnotes involves detailed and concrete observation and recording on a regular basis. When the researcher comes from the community in which the research is taking place, or after months in the field have produced familiarity with the field environment, detailed observations seem unnecessary because "everyone knows what is going on here." But ethnographers must remember that their fieldnotes may not be only for themselves, and if they take detailed notes, they may notice patterns over time that are not obvious in episodic observations.

Some important points to remember about keeping fieldnotes are the following:

- Behaviors should be defined behaviorally, rather than in terms of what they mean to the observer. For example, fidgeting with a pencil and keeping eyes downcast in a meeting may mean several things: boredom, disagreement, lack of understanding, anger, frustration, or preoccupation with another matter. Researchers should describe the behavior and avoid attributing meaning to it in the fieldnotes until they discover what the behavior communicates to others in the setting.

- Descriptions of an individual should include details of appearance, clothing, shoes, carriage, items carried by the person, and indicators of the status of the material items. For example, rather than describing a person in the train station as "poor and disheveled," it would be more accurate to describe the person as "dressed in blue jeans with shredded edges, an army jacket with dirt spots on the back and a torn collar, no belt, a white T-shirt with red smudges around the collar, and shoes with ripped edges, carrying a bulging backpack and a paper bag full of newspapers." People at the farewell party for the local newspaper editor might be elegantly dressed, but unless the ethnographer described what they were wearing, we would have no idea of the meaning of elegance in that environment.

- The physical state of the environment also should be described as if through the lens of a camera. A classroom might be described as bright and warm with a lot of visual stimulation, but the readers would understand the description better if it noted that "the walls are painted in warm shades of yellow and orange. Three of the four walls have collections of between 10 and 20 photographs, posters, children's drawings, and writing samples. Some of the writing samples are on colored construction paper. Others are accompanied by colorful outlines, frames, or drawings."

Pelto and Pelto (1978) offer the following good advice: "In every case the fieldworker should describe the observations themselves rather than the low level inferences derived from the observations" (p. 71). *Inferences and personal observations, reflections, hunches, and emotional reactions*

Cross Reference:
See Book 5, Chapter 5, on low inference descriptors

Key point

of the field researcher can be recorded separately from the stream of fieldnotes that describes the event or situation.

 Cross Reference: See Book 5, Chapter 2, for a discussion of inscription, description, and transcription as ways of organizing and recording observational data

Small notebooks about the size of a secretarial pad (5 × 7 inches) or smaller and pencils or pens are useful for helping ethnographers to recall and record their observations. Observers can note their observations using whatever shorthand memory-jogging devices they prefer. Once at home or with access to a typewriter or computer, they should transform their shorthand notes into detailed and lengthy descriptions as quickly as possible. Ethnographers can also record their observations in the field using small tape recorders. It is important to find a private location for recording purposes, because recording in public is likely to appear intrusive and to engender suspicion on the part of some observers. Although memory and recall improve with practice, no ethnographer should depend on memory alone for reconstructing fieldnotes, especially because memory is selective and easily biased, and recall diminishes notably, even on important topics, after 24 hours.

  Cross Reference: See Book 5, Chapter 2, on data recording and memory loss

Generally, we do not advise using computers in the field for recording observations because the sound of the keyboard is intrusive, and in some settings, new technology may be distracting. We also caution against carrying portable computers in vehicles used for transportation to and from field sites, despite their convenience for typing fieldnotes in between site visits. Portable computers and the fieldnotes stored in them are easily lost or removed with consequent loss of data and threats to confidentiality.

Cross Reference: See Book 6, Chapter 2, for a discussion of issues surrounding team-based data collection

For studies of short duration, with only 50 to 100 pages of fieldnotes, researchers may want to sort through their fieldnotes by hand, coding them as they go in large blocks of text. Larger studies produce many more pages of fieldnotes, especially when conducted by ethnographic field teams. In these cases, it is advisable to enter data into a computerized text management program. Most text management programs are designed to read text from standard word processing programs (such as MSWord or WordPerfect), and fieldnotes are formatted following instructions provided by the text management program. In general, regardless of the scope of a study, we always recommend keeping personal observations and first-level analyses separate from the observations themselves.

Cross Reference: See Book 5, Chapters 6 and 8, on the use of codebooks and computerized text management programs

A typical fieldnote form for personal use might look like the form in Figure 5.3.

Observer _____ Date _____	Event _____
Notes	Field Researchers' Comments

Figure 5.3. A fieldnote recording form.

The following material illustrates what part of a typical set of fieldnotes might look like. The notes are taken from an observation conducted by D. Scott Wilson, an ethnographer in a study led by anthropologist Margaret Weeks at the

Cross Reference: Other examples of fieldnotes can be found in Book 5 and in Nastasi's chapter on audiovisual techniques in Book 3

Institute for Community Research on the potential for introducing HIV prevention interventions into locations or sites where adults with drug addictions use drugs. Ethnographers in all AIDS studies carry and distribute materials that enable drug users to protect themselves against infection. The observation protocol involves sometimes actually observing people using drugs and learning from them whether they protect themselves, and what could help them do so better. In the following observation, the ethnographer reports on activities as they happened, describing how one informant obtains drugs and how the players in the scene use injected cocaine while protecting themselves with clean needles. The location is an informant's apartment.

EXAMPLE 5.8   ━●━●━●━

FIELDNOTES RECORDED AFTER OBSERVATIONS AND INFORMAL
INTERVIEWS WITH DRUG USERS IN A DRUG USE SITE

Fieldnotes: 5-1-98, 1:20 p.m.
Location: An apartment
D. Scott Wilson (ethnographer)
HRS (acronym for project entitled "High Risk Sites")

"So we went in and sat down. She was busy bouncing around and counting her money. It looked like $200 and some odd bucks she had. She said 'I just sent a boy to get a bag for me. He won't burn me for the nine dollars. I told him about that other kid who burned me for the nine dollars.' . . .

She was changing clothes and then APR20 [code for another informant based on date of first meeting] came back and they were just sort of bouncing around with the excitement of money day and getting drugs. I brought JAN24 a pack of cigarettes. JAN24 and APR20 left to go to the pawn shop leaving me alone in the apartment to wait for 'the boy' who had gone to cop the dope.

There were two bags of syringes on the table, one opened and one unopened. There were three empty dope bags on the table, 2 Roadrunners and a Titanic. Various other things scattered.

The guy who showed up was a guy who came to ICR two times already. He first showed up two weeks ago and I told him to come back next week. . . . He's a Black guy who's probably at least part Puerto Rican. He has a completely shaved head and a big bushy mustache, muscular arms with a tattoo on the left arm. He's fairly short of stature and he had two round things on his knees that look like the lids to tobacco cans under his pants, and he walks with a cane.

He showed up while JAN24 was out and I let him in. Apparently he had been there earlier in the day. He was somewhat suspicious of my presence but eventually he relaxed a little though he didn't really want to have any conversation with me. . . .

JAN24 got back and the guy pulled out what turned out to be powdered cocaine rather than dope . . . it was a pretty big tin of powdered cocaine. They dumped it in a spoon. JAN24 said 'And yes this is brand new syringe.' She drew up a forty into the syringe and put it in the spoon. She took half for herself and he took half and they both shot up right there. It didn't seem to have a huge effect on them."

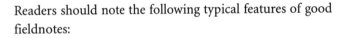

Readers should note the following typical features of good fieldnotes:

- Exact quotes are included with selected words to convey to the readers a sense of being there and meeting the actors in the scene.
- Pseudonyms or unique identities (numbers/letters) are used throughout to ensure anonymity and confidentiality.
- The observation notes describe the activities in the sequence in which they happened.
- The researcher described the appearance of the newcomer who brought the drugs to the observation site without making any low-level inferences about the meaning of the appearance.
- The notes included relevant history related to incidents or individuals to situate the event.
- The researcher has differentiated his own summary of the events and conversation from the direct quotes of the speakers.
- The date, place, time, and name of the researcher are recorded at the top of the set of notes.

Cross Reference:
See Chapter 2 of this book, and Book 5, Chapters 7, 10, and 11, on units, variables, factors, and domains

These notes are compiled along with others into a database of observations and informal interviews with respondents in inside and outside locations where adults use drugs in different parts of the city. The notes have been content coded by domains, factors, and variables. They will be analyzed by seeking associations among units, patterns, and structures.

SUMMARY

In this chapter, we have reviewed techniques and approaches to open-ended observations in field settings. To summarize, participant observation is useful

- To document the first stages of entry into a new field situation
- To gather information on unoperationalized or as-yet undefined concepts or cultural domains identified as important in the formative theoretical model or set of research questions and hypotheses guiding the study
- To identify new cultural domains that can be added to enrich the formative theoretical model
- To provide descriptive information that can enhance and complement the interpretation of any quantitative data gathered by the study

In-depth interviewing fulfills some of the same purposes. However, the interviewing and recording techniques used for in-depth or exploratory interviewing and the circumstances under which these interviews take place are often different. In the next chapter, we turn to the techniques and uses of in-depth exploratory interviewing.

6

IN-DEPTH, OPEN-ENDED INTERVIEWING

In-depth, open-ended interviewing is the most technically challenging and, at the same time, the most innovative and exciting form of ethnographic interviewing. By **in-depth,** we mean exploring a topic in detail to deepen the interviewer's knowledge of the topic. **Open-ended** refers to the fact that the interviewer is open to any and all relevant responses. There are no correct answers, and the interviewee is not asked to select from a series of alternative choices. *Exploratory* refers to the purpose of the interview—to explore domains believed to be important to the study and about which little is known. This open-ended, exploratory interview format allows researchers maximum flexibility in exploring any topic in depth and in covering new topics as they arise. The main purposes of in-depth, open-ended interviewing are to

- Explore undefined domains in the formative conceptual model
- Identify new domains
- Break down domains into component factors and subfactors
- Obtain orienting information about the context and history of the study and the study site

Definition:
In-depth interviewing refers to exploration of any and all facets of a topic in detail

Definition:
An open-ended question leaves the response open to the discretion of the interviewee and is not bounded by alternatives provided by the interviewer or constraints on length of the response

121

- Build understanding and positive relationships between the interviewer and the person being interviewed

A good exploratory interview calls for an alert mind, logical thinking, and excellent communication skills. At every point, the interviewer must

- Keep in mind how the topic relates to and illuminates the larger questions asked by the study
- Determine whether the person being interviewed is staying on topic, and if not, how to reintroduce the topic
- Understand what logical connections the interviewee is making in the discussion when those connections are likely to be quite different from those of the interviewer
- Decide whether or not to pursue new ideas and directions
- Probe for the meaning of terms
- Recognize when the interviewee's ideas are clearly expressed, and when they need to be elaborated to make sure that they can be understood by everyone who reads the notes or transcripts

These, taken together, constitute an exciting challenge and require considerable practice.

 Key point

 Cross Reference: See this book, Chapters 2 and 3, for information on theoretical frameworks

Cross Reference: See this book, Chapter 4, for a discussion of key informants and cultural experts

WHO AND WHEN TO INTERVIEW

Exploratory interviewing is intended to expand the researcher's knowledge of areas about which little is known. In-depth interviews follow the format of the formative theoretical framework and explore the main domains in the study, initial hypotheses, and contextual factors related to the study. People identified by researchers or community members as knowledgeable about the topics targeted for exploration are selected as key informants or cultural experts to be interviewed. It is not necessary to interview many key informants to obtain a large amount of information about a subject; however, at this stage of the research, it *is* necessary to find key informants who are well informed. It is precisely because they are so much more well informed about the subject than the ethnographer that Werner and Schoepfle (1987) refer to these cultural experts as consultants.

In the following example, exploratory interviews were used to disconfirm a prevailing belief in the drug abuse literature that youth follow a single route to hard drug use from gateway drugs to hallucinogens to cocaine and heroin. These same interviews were used to identify the presence of alternative pathways that could be measured and confirmed through quantitative data collection later.

➤•➤•➤   **EXAMPLE 6.1**

EXPLORING PATHWAYS TO HARD DRUG USE IN YOUTH AND YOUNG ADULTS

A study of the progression from marijuana and alcohol use to cocaine, heroin, and other drugs among youth and young adults in Hartford took the position, contrary to research literature, that youth followed different pathways as they became involved in the use of different types of drugs. In-depth interviews with young adults already injecting heroin asked about the timing and circumstances of their initiation into the use of any drug. These interviews revealed that, as we expected, young adults followed a variety of different pathways to injecting heroin or using crack rather than a single trajectory. Exploration of the social context of initiation of each drug pointed to the importance of gender, ethnicity, relationships among friends and partners, and availability of drugs in influencing which path a young adult might choose.

➤•➤•➤

The next example demonstrates how in-depth interviewing can provide information about major domains identified as influencing changes in male-female relationships among young adults on the island of Mauritius in the Indian Ocean.

EXAMPLE 6.2   ➤•➤•➤

EXPLORING THE CONTEXT OF MALE-FEMALE RELATIONSHIPS
AMONG YOUTH AND YOUNG ADULTS IN MAURITIUS

The formative theoretical model developed in this study of sexual risk among young, unmarried women in the Mauritius industrial workforce suggested that the cultural domains of "family," "peers," and "work" were important in shaping attitudes and behaviors with respect to male-female relationships. Even Mauritian research partners and health educators, however, were uncertain about how these domains were structured and what changes actually were taking place in them that might create opportunities for interaction and intimacy between young women and men. To explore these domains, and to identify factors within each domain related to the research topic, the research team decided to interview people knowledgeable about family life, work situations, and relationships among peers.

In the family domain, they recognized differences in family attitudes and relationships among the three major ethnic-religious groups in Mauritius—Christian-Creoles of African-French descent, and Indo-Mauritians, Hindus, and Muslims. They decided to interview family service providers from agencies serving each of these groups, as well as a small sample of parents, to find out which behaviors were appropriate for young men and women.

To explore the domain of peers, researchers decided to interview a small sample of approximately 20 males and females proportionate to each of the three ethnic-religious groups to find out in what kinds of activities they were involved with same-sex and opposite-sex peers, where they went separately and together, when males and females met and in what circumstances, and the range of relationships considered appropriate for this age group of unmarried young adults.

To understand opportunities for social interaction between young women and men in the workplace, they decided to interview shop supervisors in several of the larger industrial complexes in the general vicinity of the capital city of Port Louis. Floor supervisors were responsible for the whereabouts of workers and could tell researchers where men and women congregated both during and after the workday, whether they had observed any friendship or intimate relationships among workers or workers and supervisors, and if there were social activities during the workweek where men and women could socialize together.

These interviews produced information about changing aspects of social life for young Mauritians and supplied important subdomains for further investigation. For example, under the domain "family," in-depth interviews identified the factors "family relationships," "family activities," "family economic status and work situation," and "family health status." All of these factors seemed to be associated with whether or not a young woman had economic resources, free time, and opportunities to relate to men outside the household.

Under the domain "peers," interviews identified the factors: "social activities" (compartmentalized into same-sex/opposite-sex activities), "types of relationships," "locations where intimate encounters take place," and "types of intimate behaviors." Interviews about the work setting revealed other areas for consideration as important factors, including "social settings where male-female interaction occurs," "work relationships," and "requirements for upward mobility" (Schensul, Oodit, et al., 1994).

Exploratory interviews can occur throughout the course of an ethnographic study any time a domain or a concept at any other level of abstraction calls for additional investigation or clarification. Their intention is to discover new information and expand existing understanding. The general rule of thumb is to identify the domains in which new information is needed and to interview local experts on topics associated with these domains. Despite the fact that representation is not the purpose of in-depth exploratory interviews, when selecting key informants, ethnographers should take into consideration any major factors, such as ethnicity, class, or age, that might have significant bearing on the perspective of the respondent. This ensures breadth of perspective. In the Mauritius case, the formative theoretical model determined which three domains would guide the in-depth interviewing strategy. To understand the parental domain, we chose to interview a family service provider and one parent of a young, unmarried woman between 16 and 24 years of age working in the industrial sector from each of the three major ethnic groups. Family ethnicity was important in the Mauritian case because rules of protection and propriety with respect to female sexuality were known to be different across groups.

PREPARING FOR THE INTERVIEW

 Cross Reference: See also Book 3, Chapters 1 and 2, for guidelines for setting up effective interviews

To prepare for an exploratory interview, ethnographers must

- Revisit the study questions and the formative theoretical model
- Develop some general questions for use in the interview
- Make an appointment to conduct the interview and identify a proper location for it
- Have recording supplies and devices ready

Revisiting the Study Questions and Preparing Questions and Probes

Definition: A probe is a neutral question that encourages the interviewee to think more deeply, clearly, or broadly about an issue

An exploratory interview may be unstructured, but it is not unplanned. It includes a set of open-ended questions, drawn from the study questions and formative theoretical model, each of which has associated with it a set of **probes.** Some typical probes to encourage additional information include the following:

- Neutral agreement or acknowledgment of the statement ("Oh yes, I see"; "um-hm")
- Repeating what the person has said in a questioning way ("You sent your brother to seek money for hospital payment before you took your 2-year-old son to the emergency room?")
- Asking for more information ("Could you tell me a little more about why Henry called for a curriculum revision?")

- Asking for clarification on internal differences in what the person has said ("You said earlier that you were under 21, but now you told me that you went to a club that cards [i.e., asks for identification from clients under the legal age]—how old are you really?")

- Asking for an opinion ("Just now you have said that the girls in that town all work in the textile industry. What do *you* think about that?")

- Asking for clarification of the meaning of a term ("You used the word 'play'. What did you mean by that? Can you give me some examples of what you mean by 'play' "?)

A set of questions for an exploratory interview with a curriculum director about the introduction of a new curriculum might look like the following example:

TABLE 6.1 Questions Used in an Exploratory Interview

Interviewer: So you've just begun to implement a new social development curriculum in Hillside School. How is it going? (*Probes:* who is using it, who is not, how is it different from the old one, what kinds of advantages does it have over the old one, and what problems)

Interviewer: How are you introducing it to the teachers? (*Probes:* how about the training process, any technical assistance, monitoring in the classroom, special help teachers need)

Interviewer: Does it address some of the main social and health problems children face in this school system? (*Probes:* What are the main problems children face? How are they incorporated into the curriculum? How will this new curriculum improve the chances for changing chil-dren's behavior or circumstances over the standard curriculum currently in use?)

Interviewer: Has introduction of the curriculum resulted in any changes in your department? (*Probes:* in staffing, organization, time to do other things, tension level, activities, etc.)

Interviewer: Has introduction of the curriculum resulted in any changes in any of the schools? (*Probes:* in school activities, teacher cooperation, spillover into other aspects of the curriculum, new programs, etc.)

Returning to Mauritius, we present the set of exploratory interview questions used to interview peers in Mauritius about their social activities with peers in Table 6.2.

TABLE 6.2 Exploratory Interview Guide: Interviewing Youth
About Activities With Peers

- Do you have any free time at work, after work, or at any other time to do things with your friends? (*Probes:* when; what does free time mean; do they have family obligations that reduce their free time; do they have different groups of friends, and if so, what are they?)

- What kinds of activities do you do with your friends? (*Probes:* get a list of activities and ask in detail what each of them involves, where it takes place, and how long and how often they do it; ask with which friends—same-sex or opposite-sex friends— they do the activities)

- Do any of these activities involve couples—boyfriend and girlfriend? (*Probes:* which ones, and why these and not others?)

- Are there any activities your parents do not permit you to do? (*Probe:* which ones; why; do they do them anyway, and if so, how?)

Many things can interfere with the timing and conduct of an interview, including other priorities in the lives of the respondents. Most respondents are asked to volunteer their time for in-depth interviews (although increasingly, in larger projects, key informants may be paid for their time). Other priorities may come up, or they may forget and plan something else at the time of the interview. It is always wise to reconfirm the interview appointment if possible, either

Key point by telephone or by stopping by the interview site. *Researchers should never take personally the inability of a key informant to meet a scheduled interview appointment.* Assume that the lapse is unintended unless it happens several times without explanation.

Using Maps and Other Elicitation Tools to Obtain Interview Data

Maps, organizational charts, and material items are usually thought of as useful in obtaining standardized responses from a sample of participants. But they can also be very helpful in generating responses in open-ended interviewing. Mapping as a data-gathering technique has gained somewhat increased attention in recent years. A number of social scientists have popularized the concept of "social mapping" as a means to gain the direct involvement of community people in data gathering, leading to community development, agricultural innovation, and other programs that depend on community participation (Chambers, 1992).

For social mapping, community people (usually rural villagers) are asked to create a map of their village or neighborhood, usually by using locally available materials such as colored powders (*rangoli* powder in India) for making the village map on a flat (dirt) surface. Usually, the social mapping is carried out as a group process, sometimes with considerable numbers of participants. *As we already have indicated in Example 5.6, it is important to remember that ethnographers should not engage in mapping activities until they have determined whether and how the mapping they plan could be sensitive or offensive to members of the community.*

Key point

Involving individuals in creating and responding to maps is also a useful technique for interviewing individual informants. Anthropologist Lakshmi Ramchandar has made effective use of a mapping technique in which she draws a rough-and-ready map, based on instructions from her informants. This technique is effective in motivating and focusing the informant on key data and, at the same time, avoids the painful preliminaries that informants go through if they are expected to draw the maps themselves. The mapping was especially productive in Lakshmi's interviews with village health nurses (VHNs) concerning abortions in the local population. The following excerpts from Lakshmi's fieldnotes give the flavor of this data-gathering technique used to map the VHN's area. The names of village health nurses, doctors, and villages have been changed to pseudonyms. Her own comments are in parentheses.

EXAMPLE 6.3 ━━●━━●━━

USING MAPPING TO OBTAIN INFORMATION ABOUT ACCESSIBILITY
TO REPRODUCTIVE HEALTH CARE

Lakshmi: "Tell me all about your villages and how they are distributed. (I took out my big sheet of paper and started drawing a circle.) This is for my own understanding and to help me visualize the community. We will draw the map together. I will draw the map, of course, roughly, but you help me in putting the information in the right place, OK?"

Prabha: "I have 6 villages (Note: I drew six circles), so you draw 6 circles, and then I will give you the names of the villages and you fill in those circles. The villages are the following: Tirukampatti (3,200 population); the subcenter is located in this village. The government has given me the building."

(I filled in this information in one of the circles I had drawn in the center. After recording this information I asked Prabha what I should write next.)

Prabha: "Write Kendaipalyam." (She then pointed to one circle and asked me to write Devannapuram. She next pointed with her finger and asked me to write Nanja, Koundan, Pudur, Dhorkatha, and finally Palayur. I completed filling the circles, recording the information, that is, writing in the names of the villages.)

(Then, Prabha started telling me the distances from the subcenter to each of the 6 villages. She told me that the distance between Kendaipalyam and the subcenter was 2 kms; between Palayur and subcenter 4 kms. The other 3 villages were between one and a half to 2 kilometers from the center.)

Lakshmi: "Could you please show me the places or locations where there are private practitioners or nursing homes doing MTP (abortions)?"

Prabha: (Pointing to the half-drawn map—She began to give me information about all the private doctors and nursing homes in her area. She pointed towards Palayur.) "It is 10 kms from Pattaupalyam Taluka hospital; then, in the same direction, there are a cluster of private nursing homes." She said: "Write Dr. Girija, Dr. Subha, Dr. Purushothaman, Dr. Hariharan" (all private physicians).

(After this string was completed, she then shifted the pointer to the East of Palayur. Another big cluster of private (pvt) doctors surrounded this area. She gave me the names of those doctors.) "Tenmozi (pvt/gynecologist), 15 kms from Palayur Taramadai PHC, and Dr. Jayaram (pvt); Dr. Rangaraj (pvt), Dr. Malarkodi (pvt), and Linnama (pvt unqualified practitioner). CMC [Coimbatore Medical College] is 50 kms away from her area."

Lakshmi: "Do you know anything about Sandira?"

Prabha: "Yes, I know her; she is an unqualified provider. She does illegal abortions and many women go to her. Knowing she is unqualified, I do not refer any of my clients to her. I have not met her either. But many people in the surrounding area have reported to me about her."

Prabha had heard about Sandira, whose business is only handling such illegal terminations. Sandira has her private practice away from the main city of Coimbatore. She is quite well-known in the surrounding area. Many poor women who cannot afford the cost of going to big nursing homes or private clinics go to Sandira. (The story ends with the woman going to Sandira for abortion, without consulting Prabha.)

(Note: At this point in the interview, Lakshmi was writing in her notebook. The map remained in front of them as an orienting system. At any time, Lakshmi could return to the map; but at this point, she was writing everything into the small notepad.)

Lakshmi: "Have you come across any post-abortion complication cases in the last two years?" (This question is an oblique way of referring to Linnama and her lack of qualifications.)

Prabha: "No, I have not come across any such cases."

Lakshmi summarizes with this description of her work area, based on the mapping interview.

"The map of the village health nurse has a population of 3,200 spread out unevenly in 6 villages. There are two government facilities located in opposite directions; one is an intermediate referral facility (Taluka) 10 kms away, and the other—the Community Ministry Center—is a tertiary facility 55 kms from the subcenter. The Primary Health Care Center is 15 kms from the SC. According to the village health nurse, there are no qualified private doctors or clinics in the subcenter area/

villages. There is one unqualified provider (Linnama) who is accessible to all the villages. The village health nurse said people from her villages go to Linnama on their own. But she does not refer any of her clients to her, even though she has come across no post-abortion complication cases (from this provider) in the last 2 years." [End of the excerpt from fieldnotes]

Lakshmi initially began the mapping technique to get a clear picture of the microlevel data about abortion services seen from the village and village health nurse perspective. However, she found that the nurses' conceptual maps reached beyond their microlevel concerns at the individual and village levels and linked to broader referral systems at the intermediate and macrolevels—the region and general health care facilities. Furthermore, these conceptual mappings showed complex intermingling of the private and government sectors. Thus, the technique of mapping plus interviewing provided Lakshmi with a powerful analytic device for understanding the linkages and networking between the microlevel and macrolevel of the abortion services.

━●━●━●━

The techniques used by researcher Ramchandar to stimulate discussion about the location and provision of clinical, abortion, and sterilization services to women in southern India can be used with other sorts of elicitation materials for open-ended interviews with adults and children. Chambers (1992, p. 301) notes that the staff of a development agency in India involved villagers in placing small models of houses and other constructions in their proper positions in relation to one another in a replica of the village. Using this as a base, villagers participated in marking the roofs of houses in the model with names of household heads, presence of adult illiterates, educational and immunization status of children, pregnant women, and cattle ownership. New information could be added to the model as it emerged. The end product was a permanent, mapped record of the data that was easy to interpret and available to every resident of the village.

Nitza Diaz, a researcher studying perceptions of body image among Puerto Rican adult women and young girls in Hartford, found that women were not comfortable when asked directly about their own bodies. She was able to initiate interviews by asking women to talk about their views of female body types as represented by line drawings depicting a range of women's bodies in different shapes, heights, and sizes (Diaz, 1998). Similarly, researchers Romero and Berg at the Institute for Community Research discovered that it was easier to do in-depth interviews with preadolescent girls about their attitudes toward alcohol use if they were allowed to draw a picture about the topic while they were talking about it. The children's reservations at talking about this sensitive topic were allayed when they used the picture as a point of discussion (Romero & Berg, 1997).

All of these tools offer ways to help people feel comfortable in interviews and to encourage them to talk about things of interest both to them and to the interviewers.

BEGINNING AN UNSTRUCTURED INTERVIEW

Steps in Beginning an Exploratory Interview

- Introduce yourself and the project, including the organizations sponsoring it.
- Ensure confidentiality, and explain how you will protect privacy.
- Tell interviewees that their views are very important to you and to the project, and explain why.
- Ask permission to record interviews by tape-recording and in writing.
- Make interviewees comfortable by asking how they are, how their day went, how their family is, or some other culturally appropriate small talk.

In addition to following the above guidelines, researchers should assess the interview surroundings. If noise levels are too high to record, it may be necessary to take notes instead or change the location of the interview. If the interview is in someone's home, other family members or visitors may be present. It may be socially inappropriate for the ethnographer to ask them to leave; in this case, their views will become incorporated into and will alter the interview.

EXAMPLE 6.4   ◗•◗•◗

CONDUCTING INTERVIEWS WITH MINA'S GRANDMOTHER

Angela Johnson, a graduate student in education, planned to do a life history of Mrs. Chavez, the grandmother of Angela's friend, Mina. Mrs. Chavez was in her late 80s; both she and her husband had been teachers in the mountains of New Mexico long before Anglo settlers set up white schools. Upon arriving at Mrs. Chavez's house with Mina, Angela found that another of Mrs. Chavez's daughters and her preteen son and daughter were visiting as well and were working with Mrs. Chavez in the kitchen to prepare a meal. Both women were chatting and cooking. Mina joined in, while the two children ran in and out of the house constantly, necessitating a running disciplinary commentary from all the women. Angela did not have another opportunity to interview Mrs. Chavez, so she set up her tape recorder near the kitchen stove and began asking questions. She soon discovered that Mrs. Chavez often forgot critical words in English that she needed to answer the questions. Her daughter and granddaughter joined in, translating, adding words, amplifying Mrs. Chavez's descriptions of life in the old days, and even contesting some of her recollections. Meanwhile, the tape recorder picked up the sounds of food cooking, children running in and out, doors banging, the dog barking, and all of the overlapping conversations among the three women and the interviewer. To make sense of the interview, Angela had to transcribe all of the conversations, but doing so left her wondering how much of the story she recorded was that of Mrs. Chavez and how much had been contributed by her daughter and granddaughter.

◗•◗•◗

Although Angela Johnson could not do so for her inter-   **Key point**
view with Mrs. Chavez, researchers should generally follow
the guidelines for organizing interview locations detailed in
Book 3, Chapter 3 on focused group interviews.

And regardless of the difficulties under which interviews
are conducted, *remember to be sensitive to the time con-*   **Key point**
straints and life situations of interviewees. They may be
taking time away from work or another personal commitment to be interviewed, they may have family problems that   **Cross**
are affecting their emotional status that they do not wish to   **Reference:**
reveal, or family members may be waiting for them to fulfill   See Book 3,
an obligation. They may need advice or support with a   Chapter 2, on
personal problem, which the ethnographer might or might   focused group
not be able to help them solve. These factors influence the   interviews for
quality and tone of the interview. If ethnographers feel that   information on how
circumstances are impeding their ability to conduct a qual-   to choose the best
ity interview, it may be wise to reschedule it.   sites for interviews

STRUCTURING OPEN-ENDED INTERVIEWS

Open-ended, exploratory interviews can be long and seem
unfocused. This is because when interviewers give respondents an opportunity to speak about something important
to them, respondents tend to reflect on many additional
topics, which may be of great interest to them but of lesser
interest to the researcher. *The apparent looseness of the*   **Key point**
open-ended interview is deceptive; a good ethnographer
does extensive preparation for such data collection and has
developed a set of general questions to guide the interview
prior to beginning.

An in-depth interview is a special kind of conversation.
It requires a reciprocal relationship between the interviewer
and interviewee, one that honors the rules that people
normally follow for good conversation in the given cultural
setting, as well as rules for good interviewing (Levy &

Holland, 1994). To conduct a good in-depth interview, the interviewer must know enough about the local culture to avoid violating principles of polite conversation. In some settings, for example, interruptions are not only acceptable but expected; in others, they signify disrespect for the speaker. Some cultures require good listeners to acknowledge a speaker's points in midsentence with a nod, "m-hm," or "yes" (or equivalent in other languages); doing so ensures a smooth flow of thought. Ignorance of such conventions may result in an ethnographic interview that goes widely astray or nowhere at all.

Keeping an interviewee on track requires ethnographers to memorize the question sequence in which they are interested and to return to it after a respectful wait for the interviewee to finish his or her digression. English phrases that help to return the speaker to the topic include "As you were saying about X . . . ," or "Remember what we were talking about a few minutes ago?" or "A little while ago, you told me that (something occurred). Can you tell me more about it?" These reminders help to distract the speaker and refocus on the topic at hand.

Below are three hints to guide open-ended interviews that help to keep informants on topic while not interrupting the natural flow of the interview.

Hints for Guiding Open-Ended Interviews

- Identify and return to topics to clarify unclear or incomplete information.
- Define domains of culture by asking for lists of things.
- Ask for narratives of experience.

Identify and Return to Unclear or Incomplete Information.

Researchers should keep track of terms, points, and ideas that they do not understand by taking notes during the interview. These areas of confusion can be noted in the margins of the interview instrument or through some other recall device so that they can be revisited later on during the interview. Phrases useful for this purpose are the following:

- What did you *mean by* the word "comadre"?
- Would you *explain* chenna agriculture for me?
- What *kind* of rice is that?
- What is the *difference between* line skating and ice skating?
- Is the municipio *the same as* the village?
- Would you mind *repeating that sequence* again? I missed your explanation about how you make milk rice and for what occasions.

Define Domains of Culture by Asking for Lists of Things

Interviewers can elicit lists as one excellent way to obtain detailed information on important domains of culture. Listing should always be accompanied by the respondents' definitions and explanations for each of the items on the list because these ethnographic data are central to understanding the domain. Some examples of listing questions are the following:

Cross Reference: See Book 3, Chapter 3, listing techniques and their uses

- What games do teens play in this neighborhood?
- Where do adults get together around here?
- What kinds of youth groups are there in this community?
- What issues are people concerned with in this town?

- Who are the people with power in Cleveland?
- What are the main sources of employment in Peradeniya?
- What are the names of the most common children's illnesses in this town?

Questions such as these produce lists that can be the basis for probing questions about meaning, locations, participation patterns, duration, and other characteristics of each of the items on the list.

Ask for Narratives of Experience

Narratives and storytelling permit interviewees to speak from experience about situations that illustrate points important for the researcher's study. Researchers use narratives to obtain information from the informant's perspective about episodes from beginning to end. Narratives begin with questions such as: "Tell me about your last experience with a health problem. What happened first?" The narrative is continued or sustained as the researcher probes with questions such as, "What happened then? And after that?" Additional probes encourage the speaker to remember, for example, what the problem was, who was there, what the speaker and others did to address the problem, whether they used medication, from whom they sought advice, and so on. Targeted life history narratives such as that illustrated below use the same technique to obtain information about the history and sequencing of specific behaviors of research interest.

A NARRATIVE ACCOUNT OF ENTRY INTO ALCOHOL AND DRUG USE

Project:	Pathway
Interview:	"Joey" (pseudonym, transcribed)
Date:	9/22/98
Interviewer:	Lorie Broomhall

L: What drugs are you doing now? (screening question)

J: I sniff dope and I smoke reddies.

L: OK, you sniff dope and you smoke reddies. OK, so what I want to talk about, I want to go way back.

L: And so, take me back to the day when you didn't do anything. And tell me how it all began.

J: OK, I can go back to 11. Um, drugs wasn't in my life at all. But it all happened on a birfday, on a birfday. And, uh, a friend of mine, he used to smoke weed, and, uh, and he's like, you know, it's your birfday. My twelf birfday, as a matter a fact. And he was like, you know, I am gonna get you high, you know. So we went to this little park, matter a fact right down on the street, on Southern Street, is a little park like right near the parole office over there, it's like a little park. And we sat in there and he rolled it up and we smoked. It was my first time ever smokin', and I was wired. I mean, it had me like, you know, dizzy, like I couldn't even hardly walk or anything. It's like my first time, and I went in the house, I laid down, but the main thing to me is alcohol, and that was an early age, 13 I started drinking, and I love alcohol because it just changed my whole frame of mind. You know what I'm sayin'? I mean, when I drink, I am big man, nobody tougher than me, I speak my mind, I don't care what you think. You know it's all about me, alcohol when I drink. You probably smell some on my breath right now. I just drank some Bacardi. And, um, to me, alcohol, it's like an energy. You know, when I drink it's like I'm the hawk, you know, and then I start, I start drinking with, I still continue with the marijuana at the same time.

L: Was there any alcohol or weed in your house, in your family?

J: Um, my mother doesn't do anything. She'll drink occasionally, but I had an aunt that lived next door where she, she shoots up. She recently died, well, not recently, about 4 years ago she died of (mumble). She shot up, she did it all. She used to do those hallucinogens. Stuff like that. But, um, far as me, though, it was weed and alcohol. Early age, 13.

L: And you were always doing it with your friends?

J: Yeah, yep. I mean, if I go to the store, I have to get somebody to give me the drink first because I was young, you know. And then, um, I usually, yeah, drink with someone, smoke with someone. That's the type of thing you don't want to do by yourself. You know, you gotta, when you get high like that you gotta have communication. You know, whachu gonna do? You gonna get high by yourself and just sit in the dark in a daze? You know there is nothin' outa that, you know? And, um, I was doin' that up until about 16.

L: And how often were you drinking and smoking?

J: Oh, wow. Four or five forty ounces a day, probably six or seven. Like and then uh—

L: Six or seven forty ounces a day?

J: Yeah. Six or seven forty ounces a day. And the weed, the weed, at the age of 13 was probably like, like a bag or two a day, 'cause the alcohol really cut the weed down when I started drinking, and I liked the alcohol. But when I reached that age, 16, that's when I started dealin'.

L: Dealin'?

J: Dealin'.

L: To whom?

J: To whoever wanted to buy.

L: What were you dealin'?

J: I was dealin' cocaine. Powder. Not ready rock. Back when I, back then when I was 16, it was powder goin' around. There was no reddies here in Hartford. It was strictly powder caine. You would have to cook the 'caine up yourself.

━●━●━●━

This excerpt shows how an experienced ethnographic interviewer obtains information in a first interview with a young drug user about his early exposure to alcohol and drugs. Anthropologist Broomhall asks sequenced questions about initiation and use of alcohol and drugs, and uses probes to explore new topics related to use, such as drug selling.

SELF-MANAGEMENT DURING INTERVIEWING

Researchers can maintain the high quality of interview data if they follow three simple principles:

> ### Hints for Interview Self Management
>
> - Maintain the flow of the interviewee's story
> - Maintain a positive researcher-respondent relationship
> - Avoid interviewer bias

Maintaining the Flow of the Interviewee's Narrative

Interviewers can inadvertently alter the flow of an informant's story in ways that change or restrict what the informant is trying to say. Seven of the most common ways this occurs are the following:

- Phrasing a question as a statement (e.g., when the interviewer repeats as a fact something an informant has stated only tentatively):

  Informant: So we live sort of on the edge of town.

  Interviewer: So you live in a rural area, correct?

  Informant: Well, um, that's correct.

In this case, it is not possible to tell whether the informant really lives in a rural area or is simply agreeing with the interviewer to avoid a conflict.

- Failing to notice that the informant has provided an alternative meaning to the one asked for by the interviewer. For example, interviewers may not really hear that an alternative has been offered, or they may ignore or reformulate the alternative:

    Informant: We were trying to figure out how to assess the arts students, so . . .

    Interviewer: You were using some tests, right?

    Informant: No, we were looking at portfolios.

    Interviewer: What kinds of tests did you use?

- Finishing sentences for the interviewee, even when the interviewer is fairly certain that he or she knows what the interviewee will say:

    Informant: I was about to begin graduate school . . .

    Interviewer: When your mother died.

    Informant: Yes, and the problem then was . . .

    Interviewer: That you had to take care of your siblings.

- Failing to clarify the referents for terms such as *stuff* or *things* or *junk,* which have meaning only in context:

    Interviewer: What materials do you need to create a collage?

    Respondent: Well, glue, colored paper, all sorts of stuff, you know, other things, you know what I mean . . .

- Incorrectly assuming that the meanings of slang words are self-evident:

    Respondent: That's *phat!* (pronounced "fat" in English but meaning attractive).

    Interviewer: (to self) It's not very nice to refer to someone that way (assuming that the speaker means "heavy").

- Prematurely determining the beginnings and endings of episodes in the narrative in ways that cut short what the informant is saying
- Asking questions that the informant does not understand or in such a way that the informant stops talking

It is important for the researcher to try to figure out how informants themselves pace their stories and string together episodes in them so that they can create a coherent whole, in their own words, for the study.

Maintaining a Positive Researcher-Respondent Relationship

Equally important to the kinds of conversational etiquette outlined previously is general cultural etiquette. We have already alluded to some behaviors that are necessary to keep the conversation flowing, such as proper responses, appropriate questioning behavior, and paying attention to respondents' needs and personal situations. Ethnographers also should consider the following cautions in ensuring an open flow of communication:

- Avoid offering opinions or making judgments about what the interviewee says, despite having strong feelings on the topic. Researcher judgments (regardless of whether they are positive or negative) will influence respondents' ideas and answers.
- Avoid showing surprise, disgust, or other strong emotions, regardless of personal opinion.
- Accept hospitality when offered. Most people in most cultures offer food or drink when they are interviewed, and refusing may insult your host. Unless the safety factor is critical or researchers have dietary or alcohol restrictions, they should accept and consume at least some of whatever food or drink is offered.
- Be aware of the general condition of the informant. If he or she is ill, intoxicated, or emotionally upset, the information provided may not be of the highest quality.

Avoiding Interviewer Bias

The rules listed above help to ensure conversation. Avoiding interviewer bias requires attention to other considerations. Because in-depth interviews are designed to obtain the perspective of the interviewee, anything that interferes with this purpose is detrimental to the process. Perhaps the most serious source of bias comes from interviewers themselves; fortunately, interviewer bias is the most manageable. Among the principal sources of interviewer bias are the following:

- Asking leading questions
- Failing to follow up on or omitting topics that the interviewee introduces
- Redirecting the story or interrupting it
- Failing to recognize reactions of the interviewee to the interviewer's personal characteristics, including dress, age, race, gender, body size, or apparent social status
- Asking questions that include or suggest the desired responses (e.g., questions that begin with "Don't you think that . . .")
- Using nonverbal cues (such as head, face, and body movements) to indicate the "right answer" to a question, or the response with which the researcher agrees
- Stating opinions on an issue. Researchers should avoid volunteering opinions at all; if forced to do so, they should wait until after the interview is over

RECORDING YOUR INTERVIEWS

Cross Reference: See Book 5, Chapter 2, on inscription, description, and transcription

Interviews can be recorded in three ways: written, taped, and videotaped. Writing brief notes that include reminders of both the questions the researcher has already asked and the answers given is the most typical way of recording an interview. It is inexpensive; it does not depend on electronic equipment which might fail; and the researcher controls the transcription process. The primary disadvantage of notetaking is that it distracts the interviewer from the openness of direct communication with the interviewee; it is also difficult to write quickly—and legibly—enough to record everything an informant says.

Interviews are often audiotaped. The obvious advantage of taping interviews is accuracy of recording. There are, however, several disadvantages associated with audiotaping. Audiotaping interviews can be expensive, requiring high-quality tape recorders, blank tapes, working batteries or an available electrical outlet, and time and money for transcription. Tape-recorded interviews are often lengthy, and they will require as much as 3 or 4 hours of transcription time for every hour of taped interview. If the interview takes place in a noisy environment, the quality of the recording may be poor. Finally, the equipment may fail. Some researchers audiotape their own notes with less risk of encountering technical problems. However, the challenges of transcribing any recorded fieldnotes remain formidable.

Videotaping usually is not used for in-depth interviewing because of its cost and the inconvenience of transcribing videotaped interviews. Confidentiality is more difficult to ensure with videotaped data because the faces and other physical characteristics of the interviewees are easy to distinguish. We do not recommend the use of videotaping for in-depth interviews unless the interviews are to be used in a video production on the research topic.

Cross Reference:
See Book 3, Chapter 1, on audiovisual recording

SUMMARY

In Chapters 5 and 6, we have discussed two fundamental approaches to ethnographic data collection: exploratory observation and exploratory unstructured or in-depth interviewing. We refer to them as exploratory because they

- Are relatively unstructured in advance
- Are designed to permit an open exchange between the researcher and participants in the study

- ■ Allow the researcher to explore areas, cultural domains, or topics of interest in great depth without presupposing any specific responses or conclusions
- ■ Are likely to reveal new points, directions, and ideas for further exploration

Although we define them as unstructured, neither type of activity is unplanned. Effective exploratory interviewing and observation are guided by the design of the research and the primary research questions, the formative research model, and some general questions that the researcher has about the specific topic to be explored. The process of interviewing and observation is guided further by the formulation of preliminary hypotheses or hunches about cultural patterns, social relationships, and why certain things happen as they do. Thus, although engaged in both types of data collection activities, the researcher is also involved in low-level theoretical formulations that will be tested again and again against the formative theoretical model and new data emerging from the field.

The goal of ethnography is to be able to describe one or more cultural domains in terms that are understandable both to other social scientists and to the people who are represented by the description—that is, to create a local theory of culture that corresponds to that held by most actors in the situation and that also can be interpreted in cosmopolitan or disciplinary terms. Observation and interviewing are two critical activities that allow researchers to enrich formative ethnographic theory by asking interpretive questions and observing behaviors that are habitual or unconscious and thus are unlikely to be described voluntarily by their actors in words.

We have mentioned two purposes here: (a) constructing meanings, interpretations, and associations (theories) that correspond to, are recognizable by, and have significance for actors in the setting; and (b) constructing meanings, interpretations, and associations (theories) that relate to discipline-based or interdisciplinary conceptual frameworks. To do both of these things, we must be as detailed as possible in our descriptions of events, relationships, linguistic terms, and activities and their meaning to participants in the setting. At the same time, we must be able to organize these building blocks into larger units, patterns, and structures that make sense of what we are seeing in relation to similar research conducted elsewhere. This dual purpose has different implications for observation and interviewing.

In observation, we try to capture important aspects of what we see in concrete detail. At first, we may not be sure of what we are seeing because we cannot attribute local meaning to it. Thus, we try to describe as much as possible in rich and concrete detail without knowing exactly what these details mean, or which details are important. Later, we will know enough to be able to select observational settings more systematically, and to focus our observations on units of behavior or events, or relationships that we know from prior experience and discussions with participants have meaning directly related to the topic of study.

In interviewing, we use a similar sequence but with the added advantage of being able to capture in participants' own words what they see, believe, and report doing with respect to a specific topic. Of course, their descriptions or reports are influenced to some degree by our questions and the way we pursue sequences of questions in our quest for knowledge. At the same time, participants or informants make active or passive decisions about how to frame their stories and why. For this reason, we have pointed to the variety of techniques that researchers can use to produce more valid and reliable information when interviewing. In Book 5, we review both qualitative and quantitative data reduction techniques.

The ultimate ethnographic objective is to reduce social and cultural reality to produce a coherent description of a

Cross Reference:
See Chapter 11 in this book and Book 3, Chapter 2, for a discussion of reliability and validity in interviewing

social situation. By helping us to learn more about the range of factors that bear on an issue, exploratory or in-depth interviews and unstructured observations are the first step in the process of data selection and reduction.

This chapter has provided readers with the tools needed to conduct in-depth, open-ended interviews for exploratory purposes in field settings. As we mentioned earlier, in-depth interviews challenge the researcher because they are unpredictable. But it is exactly their unpredictability that makes them an exciting tool for exploration in the early stages of a study, and also at the end of a study, when the first results appear and call for verification in the community. In the next chapter, we turn our attention to semistructured interviews, which focus on open-ended exploration of a much more narrow range of topics with a larger and more representative sample of respondents.

Cross Reference: See Book 5 for more detailed instructions for carrying out recursive analysis of qualitative data

7

SEMISTRUCTURED INTERVIEWING

REASONS FOR CONDUCTING SEMISTRUCTURED INTERVIEWS

Semistructured interviews combine the flexibility of the unstructured, open-ended interview with the directionality and agenda of the survey instrument to produce focused, qualitative, textual data at the factor level. The questions on a semistructured interview guide are preformulated, but the answers to those questions are open-ended, they can be fully expanded at the discretion of the interviewer and the interviewee, and can be enhanced by probes.

Some researchers differentiate only between unstructured and semistructured interviews (cf. Fontana & Frey, 1994). Others recognize that semistructured interviews play an important role in the development of exploratory models and the preparation for more systematic forms of investigation (Weller, 1998). Johnson (1998) makes a useful distinction between exploratory and explanatory research, suggesting that "exploratory approaches are used to develop hypotheses and more generally to make probes for circumscription, description and interpretation of less well understood topics" (p. 139). In his way of approaching ethnographic research, "exploratory research can be the

Definition: Semistructured interviews consist of predetermined questions related to domains of interest, administered to a representative sample of respondents to confirm study domains, and identify factors, variables, and items or attributes of variables for analysis or use in a survey

primary focus of a given design or just one of many components" (p. 139).

Exploratory research, which includes semistructured interviewing, provides the basis for survey and other forms of explanatory research that can test theoretical hunches or propositions (Boster & Johnson, 1989; Goldin, 1996; Koester, 1996; Koester, Booth, & Zhang, 1996).

Cross Reference: Refer to Table 2.1 in Chapter 2 in this book for a summary and examples of these terms

In the schema we propose here, semistructured interviews are best suited for exploring and delineating **factors** and **subfactors**, whereas ethnographic surveys—which we address in Chapter 8 of this book—are designed to test theory by eliciting and associating quantitative information at the **variable** level.

Semistructured interviews are used to accomplish the following objectives:

- Further clarify the central domains and factors in the study
- Operationalize factors into variables
- Develop preliminary hypotheses
- Develop a qualitative base for the construction of an ethnographic survey

Clarifying the Central Domains and Factors in the Study

Formative ethnographic theory building and modeling are based on the identification of and hypothesized relationships among major independent and dependent domains. The initial identification of these domains comes from prior research related to the topic, informant knowledge, and researcher experience. Exploratory interviewing and observation provide new insights, as well as confirmation of domains and factors. Semistructured interviewing further confirms or disconfirms the validity of domains for the study and adds new domains as they arise.

➤●➤●➤　　　　　　　　　　　　　　**EXAMPLE 7.1**

CONFIRMING DOMAINS AND IDENTIFYING FACTORS

The primary domains in studies of AIDS risk in Mauritius and Sri Lanka are family, work, and peers (independent domains), and sex, knowledge, attitudes, and behavior (dependent domains). Semistructured interviews based on questions related to each of these domains provided important information regarding whether the list of domains needed expansion or reduction (it did not) and which factors identified within these domains were likely to be related to one another.

➤●➤●➤

Operationalize Factors Into Variables

One of the primary objectives of semistructured interviewing is to identify the variables that are the constituent elements of the factors and subfactors within the domains in the formative model. To achieve this objective, questions in a semistructured interview are framed at the factor level. For example, in our study of exposure to AIDS risk in Mauritius, we were interested in the ways in which the domain "family" was associated with the domain "sexual risk." In in-depth interviews with a small number of female respondents, we asked about the domain of family. One important factor that emerged through these interviews was "discipline in the family." In a semistructured interview schedule administered to 90 young women, this factor was phrased as a question designed to elicit more information about family discipline: "Tell me about the ways in which discipline occurs in your family." The responses included discussion and negotiation, physical forms of discipline, restricting activity to the household, and several other categories. "Physical discipline" became a variable (see Tables 2.1, this book, and 8.1, Book 5) and the semistructured interviews produced the elements or attributes of the variable—an array of different "types of physical discipline."

Develop Preliminary Hypotheses

By the time researchers decide to use semistructured interviewing, they have already generated a series of hypotheses linking domains. Semistructured interview data can produce information that links factors and variables within and across domains. For example, some of the women who responded to the semistructured interviews administered in Mauritius reported that parental discipline became stricter once they entered the industrial workforce.

> *Hypothesis 1:* Relationship between stricter parental discipline, an independent factor under the domain "family," and employment in the industrial sector

Respondents also said that the more they worked—for example, increasing hours of overtime—the greater the level of family discipline they encountered.

> *Hypothesis 2:* Relationship between stricter discipline, a variable within the factor "family discipline," and more hours of work, a variable within the factor "employment in the industrial sector"

Develop a Qualitative Base for the Construction of the Ethnographic Survey

Semistructured interviewing establishes a firm qualitative foundation for the construction of an ethnographically informed survey (see Chapter 8) by creating the conceptual taxonomy of domains, factors, variables, and variable attributes that can be transformed into the items on a survey instrument. Doing so also establishes the coding system for both the text and survey data.

The first step in developing a semistructured interview guide involves working from the domain code categories identified in unstructured interviews and the observation phase of ethnographic research. These domains and categories form the basis for questions in the semistructured interview. The qualitative data resulting from responses to these questions are, then, the primary source for the variables that form the basis of the ethnographic survey.

In the Mauritius research, analysis of the "work" domain identified the following factors:

- Work *impact on lifestyle*
- Work *impact on social and familial relationships*
- *Reasons for* working *in the EPZ*
- *Attitudes* about work
- *Nature of the* work *unit*
- *Relationships with men* at work
- *Relationships with women* at work
- Travel to work
- Participation in industry or union *social (after-work) activities*
- Relationships with *supervisors*
- *Health and family planning services* at the work site

The researchers then formulated between one and five questions (more questions if it is believed that subfactors must be taken into account between factor and variable levels) for each of the work domain factors listed above.

CONSTRUCTING A SEMISTRUCTURED INTERVIEW SCHEDULE

Steps in Building the Questions for the Interview

The semistructured interview is built in the following way: The transcribed in-depth interviews and observational data obtained from the unstructured data collection observations are analyzed by domain. The domains yield factors that are identified because they appear repeatedly in the text data. The data do not provide enough information to know in advance exactly how important these factors are,

Cross Reference: See Book 5, Chapter 5, for a discussion of identifying factors from the "ground up"

how widespread they are in the population, or what they mean. Semistructured interviews, however, will help to answer these questions. That is why such interviews are constructed around these factors or subfactors. Social science researchers have devoted considerable time and energy to describing ways of formulating good questions for different types of interviews (Babbie, 1995; Fink, 1995; Sudman & Bradburn, 1982). Semistructured interview questions are created following guidelines outlined in the following box.

> ### Guidelines for the Construction of Good Semistructured Interview Questions
>
> ■ Make sure that questions use terms and phrases that are understandable to respondents.
>
> ■ Keep the length of the questions at a minimum; remember that probes play a key role and that subfactors and variables are further operationalized through probes.
>
> ■ Use terminology appropriate to the respondents' command of language, cultural background, age, gender, level of knowledge, and any other relevant characteristics.
>
> ■ Avoid questions that lead the respondent to answers or are biased.
>
> ■ Avoid questions that make use of either a positive or a negative association; for example, "How similar are your views on birth control to those of Mother Teresa?" "What do you think of the Nazi-like practices of ethnic cleansing in the Kosovo Province of the former Yugoslavia?"
>
> ■ Avoid double-barrelled questions that really are two questions in one; for example, "How often do you drink Coca-Cola and coffee?" or "When did you last attend a concert or a ballet performance?"
>
> ■ Try to avoid negatively worded questions: for example, "Do you agree or disagree with the following statement: 'Teachers should not use language proficiency tests to group students for ability'?"
>
> ■ Avoid asking people to rank order information in a semistructured interview unless it is absolutely necessary. Rank

orderings require complex instructions that informants frequently misunderstand.

- Avoid asking questions that require performing several tasks; for example, "From this list of 10 reading programs, first circle the names of the three reading programs you use most often, and then put an 'X' next to the name of the one you prefer."

- Do not ask questions that can be answered with a "yes" or "no" when what you really want is as lengthy a description as possible.

- Be sensitive to the cultural context or social meanings involved in the questions asked in the interview.

Ordering Questions in an Interview

Researchers need to consider how to order and sequence questions in both semistructured and structured interviews. In general, questions should be ordered as follows:

- Temporally: From earlier events to more recent events
- According to complexity: From simpler topics to more complex ones
- According to topics or domains: Group all questions on the same or similar topics together
- By level of abstraction within domains: From the most concrete to the most abstract issues
- In accordance with the threat level: From the least sensitive or threatening to the most sensitive or threatening; place the most sensitive topics last.

Some methodologists argue that researchers should warm up respondents by beginning with interesting but nonthreatening questions, and then follow with more challenging material. To that end, there is considerable disagreement as to what constitutes a threatening or sensitive question. In the United States, demographic questions typically are defined as nonthreatening; interviewers often begin by asking for this information. However, some kinds of demographic information, including age and income, can be very sensitive to many respondents. Furthermore, what is *not* sensitive in one culture may be extremely sensitive in another. In repressive societies, it can be dangerous to reveal information about ethnic or religious affiliation; where population controls are enforced, telling an interviewer how many children a family has can result in reprisals. In yet other societies, revealing one's own name or the names of one's kinfolk is taboo.

Other researchers argue that the most important information should be asked for first, so that if informants weary of the interview, the researcher has at least covered the most important issues before the informant stops talking.

EXAMPLE 7.2 ━▶•◀━•▶

ADMINISTRATION OF A SEMISTRUCTURED INTERVIEW

In the Mauritius study, a total of 120 workers (90 women and 30 men) were selected to participate in semistructured interviews. Both men and women were divided evenly among the three ethno-religious groups: Indo-Hindu, Creole-Catholic, and Indo-Muslim. Researchers conducted interviews in the cafeterias of the five largest industries on the island. Personnel managers arranged for time off; the average length of time for the interview was 45 minutes.

Seven interviewers were trained in conducting interviews and recording fieldnotes, and they were given a set of instructions typical of most training materials:

■ Explain the nature of the research and receive oral consent from participants.
■ Ask the demographic questions first.
■ Ask questions about work after the demographic questions.
■ Avoid repetition by recording answers that interviewees give to questions you have not yet asked *when they give them,* even if the answer was included as a part of an earlier question.
■ As much as possible, sequence the topics or domains of the semistructured interview guide so that they flow naturally with the conversation.
■ Avoid getting too far away from the main study topics or domains.
■ With the time allotment set at one hour, do not feel that all questions need to be asked; rather, emphasize those factors about which the respondent most wants to talk.

━▶•◀━•▶

TABLE 7.1 Work Sections of Semistructured Interview Schedule Used in Mauritius Study

PART II: RESPONDENT'S OPINIONS ABOUT WORKING WOMEN
2.1 What is your opinion about working women in Mauritius?
2.2 According to you, what type of work is better suited to women?
2.3 What major changes do you perceive in the lifestyle of working women of Mauritius?
2.4 What, in your view, is the basic difference in the lifestyle of a working woman and a nonworking woman today?
2.5 How would you describe a working woman's relationship with (a) her family, (b) her boyfriend/husband, (c) a female friend?
2.6 How does your family feel about your work?

PART III: QUESTIONS ON RESPONDENT'S WORK
3.1 For what reasons did you take up employment? (probe reasons for working—for money or other reasons)
3.2 Did you have any previous work experience or training for your present job?
3.3 What were you doing prior to taking up your present job? (probe reasons for quiting previous job)
3.4 What are your feelings about your work?
3.5 Please, could you describe to me one of your typical working days?
3.6 Do you work overtime? How often? What are your views concerning overtime?
3.7 Do you have "night shifts" in your present work? What are your views on night work?
3.8 How many people work in your section (of the factory), male and female?
3.9 How much do you earn in a month? (Ask about mode of payment—i.e., paid on piece rate, monthly, or weekly basis?)
3.10 Could you tell me what positive/negative impacts your work has had on your life?

Table 7.1 illustrates a section of the semistructured interview schedule used in the Mauritius study. The questions come from the "work" domain and relate to the dimensions of work (factors, subfactors) that arose in the in-depth or exploratory research phase.

ANALYSIS OF SEMISTRUCTURED INTERVIEW DATA

The text data generated by the semistructured interviews in Mauritius were entered into **ETHNOGRAPH**. We created code names for the domains, factors, subfactors, and associated codes. These codes were then applied to the data (some of which are illustrated in the italicized blocks below) and coded by domain ("work") and factor (WEFFECT, e.g.,

Definition:
ETHNOGRAPH is a computerized data management and analysis program specifically designed for use by ethnographers

the impact of work on lifestyle). Selected segments of text illustrate the variables that emerged for WEFFECT:

"Working has also helped her in being independent financially and helping her family out. From her working experience, she has met all kinds of people and she has encountered different problems or conflicts with them. Now she feels more comfortable in dealing with them"

Factor	Variable
Work Effect	⎡ Comfort and experience in dealing with a wide diversity of people ⎣ Financial independence

"Now that she works, she finds it easier to make friends with boys . . ."

Factor	Variable
Work Effect	Male friends

"She gets money and she now has a boyfriend in the factory itself. She says now she finds it more interesting to work. Especially that her boyfriend works in the same factory. Ooma says that now [that] she works, she feels free and is not stupid. She can talk with people and she feels she is happy."

Factor	Variable
Work Effect	Gaining Knowledge
Work Effect	Having Money
Work Effect	Boyfriend in factory
Work Effect	Feels socially confident

"According to Faeza, women who work neglect their family. On the other side, the working women are financially independent. They can buy things and add to the needs of the house. She can dress well and buy clothes for herself. She is of the opinion that lifestyle of women has changed radically, and she thought that first noticeable change is independence. Long ago, non-working women stayed at home, they were housewives and knew only the four walls of their homes and their neighbors. Today, they are more free, self-sufficient, they have friends and are open-minded. The relationship of a working woman with her family is more open."

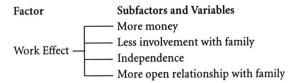

Factor	Subfactors and Variables
Work Effect	More money
	Less involvement with family
	Independence
	More open relationship with family

"She considers it a positive impact that work has had on her life, the fact that she can have all the [material] things she wants."

Domain	Factor
Work	Material possessions

A similar procedure was developed in the Sri Lanka study. Unstructured interviewing and observation had identified the following factors as part of the "family" domain:

- Mother
- Father
- Siblings
- Household composition
- Economics
- Material possessions
- Family relationships
- Shared family activities
- Parental discipline
- *Family problems*
- Extended family
- Middle East employment

Questions were formulated for each of these factors (as well as factors included in other domains in the formative theoretical model) and utilized to interview a total of 156 young adult males and females at the University of Peradeniya and in a low-income, urban community in Kandy.

Analysis of the segments coded as "family problems," a factor, revealed the following subfactors or variables:

*"He studied up to year 9 at Punga Sanipadhara Vidyalaya [a public high school] in Kandy and he had to put a stop to his studies due to four **deaths in the family** within that year and as **money problems** in the family started increasing."*

Family Problems ──────── Death in the family
└────────── Financial

*"Her main reason for her sorrow is **that another family is living with them.** When I asked whether there are problems at home, she said that she **doesn't like to live at home.**"*

Family Problems ──────── Crowding at home

*"Due to **terrorism**, they have **abandoned their lands** and home and have come to live at a rented house. Her mother suffers from **joint pains.** Most of the members of the family are living in their house and the **space is limited.**"*

Family Problems ──────── Health Problems
└────────── Residential Crowding

*"Every Friday they fast (Viratham). Her parents are very strict on religious activities. **They are very strict in selecting partners for their children.** They do not allow her go to night parties. Sometimes, they refuse to allow visiting friends in the house. She obeys her parents very much. Restriction is important, and she feels her parents are doing their duty for the children. But sometimes, children have **to break their rules in selecting a partner** and like (meaning 'similar') things."*

Family Problems ──────── Breaking family rules around
                          male-female partnerships

*"My parents quarrel quite often, and they don't eat when they get any problem. I think **understanding between father and mother is poor,** and the **financial situation** brings these problems."*

Family Problems ──────── Financial problems
└────────── Parental conflict

*"They (her parents) had a lot of **financial problems** at home which led her **mother to go to the Middle East** to work as a housemaid."*

Family Problems ──────── Absent parent

"Her father is an alcoholic and comes home with his friends and drinks. He fights with the family when he's not given money he needs to drink."

Family Problems ———— Father's alcoholism ———┐
└——————————————— Family conflicts with father

"Talking about her family problems, she said her father won't take alcohol or eat pork. But most of the time, he is away from home. He is so busy that he gets little time to spend with the family. And also, her father's two younger sisters are widows. So according to their religion [Islam], it's the duty of an elder brother to look after them after their parents' death. So she tells that her father had to earn for all of them, and they have financial problems.

Family Problems ———┬—— Father's limited time with family
├—— Financial problems
└—— Extended family's need for care

This analysis leads to a list of family problems, each of which could be treated as a variable, or an item or attribute of a variable.

- Financial problems
- Health problems
- Poor housing conditions (residential overcrowding)
- Problems related to care of extended family members
- Missing parents
- Alcohol and drug use
- Family conflicts
- Parent-daughter conflicts
- Male-female relations

These procedures for identifying variables and items or attributes should be followed with respect to all of the questions in each of the domains included in the semistructured interview schedule.

SEMISTRUCTURED OBSERVATIONS

Semistructured observation schedules are important in investigating behaviors that are observable by researchers but difficult to discuss, because people are not aware of them. Conducting observational research follows the same pattern as the collection of ethnographic data through interviewing—that is, it involves a continuum from

- Open ended and exploratory data collection (as described in Chapter 5 of this book), to
- More carefully defined and systematic but open ended data collection, to
- Structured observational schedules designed to quantify observations and test hypotheses using statistical analytical techniques

Observation schedules focus on observed behaviors. Semistructured observational schedules focus on observable behaviors that occur regularly. The objectives of semistructured observation are similar to those for interviewing: (a) to identify factors associated with domains, (b) to identify variables associated with factors, and (c) to identify items or attributes of variables that can be recorded systematically by presence/absence or degree.

Physicians, epidemiologists, and medical social scientists have conducted semistructured observations to help them learn how mothers care for children with diarrhea or upper respiratory illnesses, or when they wish to understand dietary inputs by watching how people purchase, prepare, distribute, and eat food. Semistructured observation requires an observational protocol similar to that used in semistructured interviewing, in which the major domains and factors believed important in the study are listed and partially defined, but the observer is required to identify and record in detail the behaviors believed to be important. Semistructured observations also can be conducted in schools and classrooms, where patterns of behavior tend to be somewhat regularized, and researchers can observe both pattern repetition and deviation. Deviation is important because one objective of research is to capture the range of variation in behavioral responses to the designated situation.

Several important points are important to keep in mind when conducting semistructured observations:

Cross Reference: See Book 3, Chapter 2, on the use of audiovisual recording techniques for recording human behavior in situ

- Observations can be intrusive, especially in households or classrooms; semistructured (as well as structured) observations require regular presence and, often, the use of a visual recording device. It is necessary to establish good rapport with participants in the study before beginning semistructured observations in field settings.

- Observations of complex social interactions are difficult to do alone because a single observer may not be able to capture all of the activities going on among all of the participants in a large event or a classroom. For example, it may be impossible for observers to observe a classroom teacher using cooperative learning methods and, at the same time, observe small working groups of students involved in shared learning activities. To collect enough desired data, it may be necessary to conduct observations of this type with a colleague.

- Semistructured observations require as much thought, prior knowledge, and disaggregation of already gathered text data as other forms of data collection; researchers must prepare in advance.

- It goes without saying that behaviors to be observed must be observable; researchers in Mauritius and Sri Lanka could observe locations where young people met and could even observe certain expressions of affection in public settings such as parks and lovers lanes, but they could not observe intimate behaviors placing young women at risk for sexually transmitted infections. On the other hand, Allison Bingham, in a time-location study of exposure to malaria in a malaria-endemic area, found that it was entirely possible (although potentially risky!) to time observations of farmers' exposure to malaria-carrying mosquitoes each evening as they walked home from their farmlands (Bingham, 1998).

SUMMARY

Semistructured interviews and observations can be an end-point for qualitative data gathering. We begin our investigation with open-ended interviewing and observation, which has the lowest power of representation and the broadest range of exploratory potential. As we learn what to look for, we increase the power of representation and decrease the range of topics and subtopics that we can explore. Semistructured interviewing and observation offer us the most systematic opportunity for the collection of qualitative data. An ethnographic research project may end here with a report of exploratory or descriptive data, or it may continue on to transform qualitatively defined factors and variables into quantitative measures amenable to investigation using the techniques of survey research—systematic, structured, and standardized data collection; random sampling with a large sample size; and hypothesis testing through statistical analyses. In the next chapter, we use the same structures—formative theory and research model, domains, factors, and variables—to guide the construction of an ethnographic survey or self-administered questionnnaire.

8 ━━●━━●━━●━━

STRUCTURED ETHNOGRAPHIC DATA COLLECTION: ETHNOGRAPHIC SURVEYS

THE ROLE OF STRUCTURED DATA COLLECTION

Ethnography attempts to understand social and cultural phenomena from the perspective of participants in the social setting under study. To do so, the approach builds conceptual models using qualitative techniques and then validates or tests them both qualitatively and quantitatively. Structured ethnographic data collection offers a way to transform exploratory and semistructured data into instruments that measure relationships among cultural domains and variables quantitatively and test their relationships with a representative sample of the population (see Babbie, 1995, pp. 51 and 55, for a diagram of this process).

In Chapters 5 and 6, we discussed the role of exploratory or unstructured data collection methods in uncovering critical ethnographic domains and factors. Chapter 7 reviews the important contribution of semistructured data collection methods, especially semistructured, open-ended interviewing, in enriching description and defining the range of variation in knowledge, attitudes, beliefs, behaviors, social organization, and patterned event sequences at the variable (unit) and item (fact) levels in a cultural group or organization.

In this chapter, we discuss the role of structured data collection methods in ethnography. We concentrate on constructing survey instruments, the most typical way of collecting data from a representative sample of respondents in a population. In addition to self-report on surveys, there are other types of structured data collection. These include unobtrusive measures of behavior (cf. Bernard, 1995) at specific points in time (e.g., timed observations of patterns of use of emergency rooms, or time-activity accounts of individuals in relation to exposure to disease-carrying mosquitos). Like ethnographic surveying, direct systematic observation of behavior can help to avoid the bias that inevitably occurs when ethnographers engage in opportunistic participant observation in the field (Johnson & Sackett, 1998). Bonnie Nastasi's chapter in Book 3 on audiovisual methods of data collection in ethnographic research provides a thorough discussion of techniques for the systematic collection of quantifiable observational data.

Cross Reference: See Book 3, Chapter 1, on audiovisual methods in ethnographic research

Structured ethnographic data collection moves ethnographers beyond the collection of information about cultural consensus and structural descriptions to an examination of relationships among independent and dependent cultural domains. The purpose of using structured data collection methods is to

- Select variables within domains and factors for measurement
- Predict and test the relationships among variables nested within factors and domains against the formative ethnographic model
- Discover hypothesized and new, unexpected associations among variables for which explanations can be sought in the existing qualitative database or in additional ethnographic research

Even the most homogeneous communities, institutions, and work settings display wide variation in their members' knowledge, attitudes, beliefs, and behaviors (Pelto & Pelto, 1978). Domains such as educational performance, teenage pregnancy, and activities of daily living also are variably distributed in any population. Structured ethnographic data collection gives us the opportunity to test quantitatively hypotheses that we have generated from formative theory, which was built and refined through the course of collecting unstructured and semistructured data.

The difference between structured ethnographic data collection and standard surveys centers on the fact that ethnographers base their quantitative research measures on locally based formative ethnographic research. By contrast, non-ethnographic quantitative research often is generated *a priori* on the basis of the researcher's experience alone or on another researcher's theoretical perspective using instruments established for other purposes and other populations. (See Aday, 1989, for an approach to traditional survey construction, and Gay, 1985, for uses of standardized survey instruments.)

DEFINING ETHNOGRAPHIC SURVEYS

We use the term *ethnographic survey* to refer to closed-ended instruments and observation schedules designed to collect quantitative ethnographic data that:

- Follow from and are built on unstructured and semistructured observation and interviewing
- Are based on items derived from transformations of cultural domains to factors and then to variables in the local setting as we have described in Chapter 2 of this book
- Gain validity and reliability from prior investigation in the local setting

Cross Reference:
See Book 5, Chapters 8 and 9, on the organization, management, and analysis of ethnographically informed quantitative data

- Enable researchers to triangulate the results of quantitative analysis using bivariate and multivariate statistics with qualitative data generated through the use of comparable coding categories

- Do not stand alone; but used in conjunction with other data sources, they provide a comprehensive picture of the phenomena in question in the local setting

- Generate results calling for further qualitative data collection and analysis, either to resolve contradictions between qualitative and quantitative data or for further explanation of why observable quantitative relationships have occurred

Ethnographic surveys are *not*

- The first data collection operation in a research project; preferably, they are the last step in a study

- The product of a process in which research staff generate survey items based only on their own personal experience; rather, the items emerge from the systematic analysis of qualitative data

Cross Reference:
See Chapter 10 of this book for a discussion of validity in ethnographic research

- Opportunities for replication of standardized indexes used in other studies and/or validated on national samples (e.g., "locus of control" or "depression" scales); instead, their strength lies in the fact that the survey variables and items emerge from the local context. The local foundations of the survey enhance its validity.

- Part of the discovery process; instead, they are designed to determine the degree to which the ideas, information, and results that emerged during the discovery process from in-depth investigation with a limited and selective sample can be generalized to the whole population. Thus, variables should not include opportunities for open-ended responses or a category of "Other." If these alternatives are necessary, then qualitative data collection was insufficient in that area of the survey.

Ethnographic surveys share many of the characteristics of other types of surveys:

- They can be administered face to face (structured interview) or self-administered (questionnaire).

■ They use common formats for questionnaire construction (e.g., rankings, ratings, true/false questions).

■ They require pilot-testing to ensure that the population will understand the questions and to establish the adequacy and range of the distribution of responses for each variable.

■ They usually use probabilistic, preferably random, selection and sampling procedures.

They differ from other types of quantitative surveys in a number of ways. First, construction of ethnographic surveys is based on prior experience in the field situation. They may incorporate instruments or questions drawn from other studies, including nationally validated instruments, but their strength is their ability to describe, in an ethnographic context, the meaning and variation of elements of local culture. Thus, they are employed toward the endpoint in the testing of midrange or local theory. Ethnographic surveys measure constructs that the study population understands and has identified as relevant, and that are included in the theoretical model. Ethnographic survey questions and the results they generate are meaningful only when they are connected with the qualitative data obtained from the same field site and integrated into the theoretical model.

STEPS IN THE CONSTRUCTION OF THE ETHNOGRAPHIC SURVEY

Ethnographic surveys flow from the systematic collection and analysis of ethnographic data. The data are organized into domains, which are then operationalized as factors, subfactors, and variables. Researchers using these data to construct their survey will be faced with the need to select from among a large number of factors and variables those to include in the survey instrument.

As we have described earlier, data collection starts with unstructured interviewing and observation at the domain level, guided by formative theory. Ethnographic researchers use these data, the literature, and insights from study participants to delineate new domains, identify factors, and eliminate domains that have proved to be less significant than first thought.

Moving down the ladder of abstraction, factors become the basis for developing questions for a semistructured instrument. Semistructured interviews create the first opportunity in the data collection process for researchers to ask specific and focused questions that initiate an exchange between researcher and a number of respondents. The answers to these questions, and the subsequent probes that seek further clarification of answers to them, generate variables and items or attributes that constitute the components of variables that are the basic building blocks for a quantitative survey. Example 8.1 shows how the process diagrammed in Figure 8.1 looks in practice.

Cross Reference:
See Chapter 2, this book, Figure 2.1 for a synopsis of the concept of levels of abstraction and operationalization

Cross Reference:
See Book 5, Chapter 8 for a definition of variables and their attributes or the items of which they are composed

Continuum of Abstraction	Method	Results
	Unstructured Observation and Interviews →	Description of domains, macrostructural features, cultural continuities
	Semistructured Observation and Interviews →	Description of factors and sub-factors, identification of cultural variation
	Ethnographic Survey →	Identification of variables and testing of associations predictive models

Figure 8.1. Methods of data collection associated with the continuum of abstraction.

EXTRACTING FACTORS AND VARIABLES FROM UNSTRUCTURED AND SEMISTRUCTURED INTERVIEW DATA

In the Mauritius research, the "work" domain was identified as one of the major components of the formative theoretical model. One important factor that emerged in unstructured interviewing was "reasons young women enter the workforce." In the semistructured interview schedule, researchers investigated this factor by asking the following question in Creole, the language spoken by every Mauritian, "For what reasons did you take up employment in the Export Processing Zone?" The resulting text was situated in the "work" domain and coded using the ETHNOGRAPH text search program with the assigned factor code name "WHYWRK" (why work?). Content analysis of the text coded under the factor "WHYWRK" resulted in the identification of five categories or groupings of reasons why women chose to enter the workforce:

1. To be financially independent
2. To support the family
3. To be away from home
4. To join friends who are also working
5. Because of family problems

Because many of the women mentioned multiple reasons for entering the workforce, the variable "why women entered the EPZ" was then transformed into a ranking question in the ethnographic survey with the following format:

"Here are five reasons why women take up employment. I would like you to rank each reason from 1-5 in terms of their order of importance (1 = highest and 5 = lowest)."

For data analysis purposes, each response was treated as a separate ordinal variable in the form of a Likert scale. When the scores for each question were summed and averaged,[1] the results showed that the most frequently chosen reason was "to support family" (mean = 2.03), with "financial independence" (mean = 2.61) in second place.

There were many significant differences in their relationships with men and sexual behavior between young women who were motivated to join the EPZ workforce for their own development or personal interests (Reasons 1, 3, and 4) and those who entered the workforce as a result of family motivation (Reasons 2 and 5).

━•━•━

This example illustrates the points made in Figure 8.1 that each level of methodology contributes

- A unique set of results specific to that level
- A basis for further operationalization and increasingly focused research methods
- An opportunity for cross-checking (triangulation) one set of results with another on the same issue
- A follow-up procedure to build on and further elucidate results

As Example 8.1 demonstrates, the first step in the process of ethnographic survey construction is analysis of data obtained from semistructured interviews and observations. These data are in the form of text, generated by recording the respondents' answers to questions and typing up field-notes. For purposes of constructing the ethnographic survey, these text data are analyzed by searching for and identifying variables that operationalize factors, as well as finding the attributes or items that make up these variables as they are expressed in the population. Thus, a search of the code WSAT (work satisfaction, a factor) in the responses to the semistructured interview question "How do you feel about your work in the EPZ?" identified two groups of respondents: those who were satisfied with their work life in the EPZ and those who were not. A further analysis of the responses to the question abstracted under the code WSAT identified a number of subfactors and variables, including perceptions of

Cross Reference:
See Book 1 and Chapters 4 and 5 of this book for further guidance in identifying items, variables, factors, and domains; also see Book 5 for analysis of text data

- Quality of relationships with co-workers
- Relations with supervisor
- Amount of job training
- Level of tiredness
- Physical effects of work tasks

- Adequacy of salary
- Amount of time off during work hours
- Amount of free time after work

In terms of the process of operationalization, we have moved in the following fashion (see Figure 8.2):

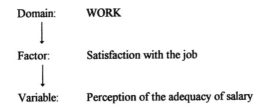

Domain:	**WORK**
Factor:	Satisfaction with the job
Variable:	Perception of the adequacy of salary

Figure 8.2. Moving conceptually from the domain to the variable level.

One approach that our research team has taken to make this process of transformation easier has been to work with enlarged models mounted on several sheets of posterboard or newsprint and taped to a large wall. A standard rule of thumb is to select two to five independent domains and one (or no more than two) related dependent domains for inclusion in the survey. The ethnographic surveys constructed for use in Mauritius and Sri Lanka included the three independent domains "family," "peer," and "work/community," and the dependent domain "sexuality." The study of pathways to high-risk drug use being conducted in Hartford includes the independent domains "family," "school," "peer," "violence," and "social networks," and the dependent domain "high-risk drug use." Figure 8.3 illustrates the way in which the relationships among domains can be diagrammed. The same process was used in a study of arts programming, described in Book 5.

The next rule of thumb for survey construction is to review the analyzed secondary and primary (in-depth and

Cross Reference:
See Book 5 for a discussion of a similar process used in a study of arts programming

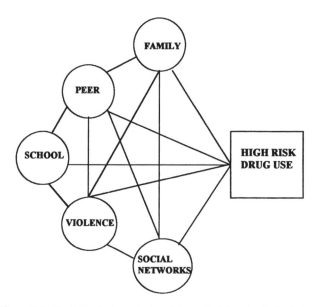

Figure 8.3. Displaying independent and dependent domains for inclusion in the survey instrument.

semistructured) data for the purpose of identifying four or five factors in each domain, and up to six variables in each factor. These can be listed on the wall on a separate sheet of paper in the form of a taxonomy, as shown in Figure 8.4a.

The next step is to superimpose factors that are candidates for inclusion in the ethnographic survey instrument onto the conceptual model, as illustrated in Figure 8.4b.

Finally, we demonstrate in Figure 8.5 how variables are included in the model by using the factor "socioeconomic status" as an example. Below it, we list the variables that are indicators of socioeconomic status in this study:

- Household income
- Material style of life
- Occupation of household head
- Number in household working

FAMILY DOMAIN
Factors
  Socioeconomic status
  Education level of primary caregiver
  Birthplace of parents
  Migration history
  Drug use of family members

PEER DOMAIN
Factors
  Number of peers
  Number of activities with peers
  Drug use with peers
  History of court exposure of peers
  Drug use of peers
  Peer pressure to use drugs or alcohol

SCHOOL DOMAIN
Factors
  History of school performance
  Exposure to drugs in school
  Exposure to alcohol in school
  School norms related to drug use

VIOLENCE DOMAIN
Factors
  Exposure to violence
  Perpetration of violence
  Drugs and violence
  History of arrests or court involvement

SOCIAL NETWORKS DOMAIN
Factors
  Size of social network
  Composition of social network
  Density of social network
  Density of risk network
  Centrality of ego

DRUG USE DOMAIN
Factors
  Number of drugs used
  Frequency

Figure 8.4a. A taxonomy of domains and factors.

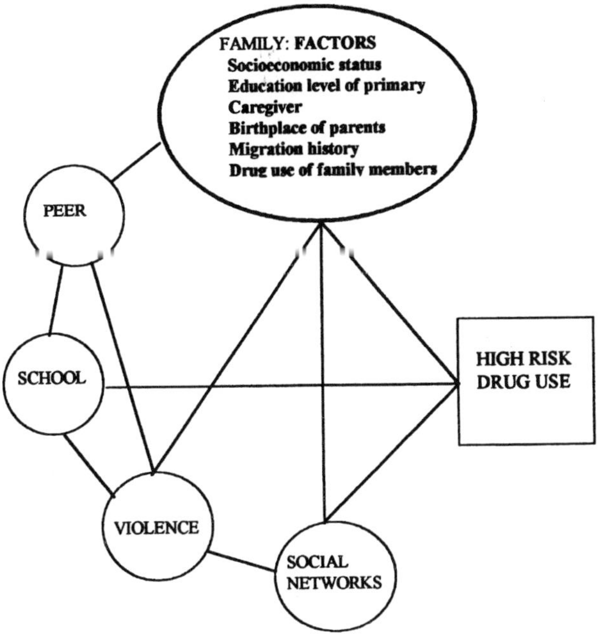

Figure 8.4b. A taxonomy of factors for survey construction.

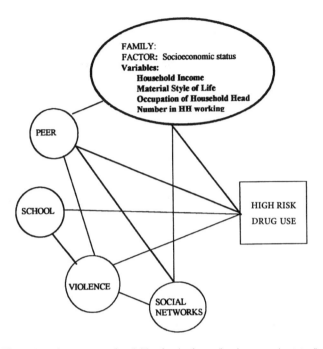

Figure 8.5. A taxonomy of variables for the factor "socioeconomic status" in the domain "family."

  The process of breaking down six domains into approximaely six factors each, with up to seven variables in each factor, gives us more than 200 variables on the bottom tier of the conceptual taxonomy or tree diagram. This number of variables may seem daunting at first, and the appearance of the new "office wallpaper," brightened with colored construction paper with different colors representing different levels (domain, factor, and variable), may surprise visitors who are not familiar with its meaning. It will, however, provide a sense of the distribution of identified variables by factor and domain, illustrating where the distribution of variables is uneven, and where there are gaps in knowledge that need to be addressed to ensure that the survey covers every relevant topic in an adequate manner.

Formulating an ethnographic survey instrument calls for careful selection at both the factor and the variable levels because researchers cannot cram into a single instrument questions about every single factor or variable of interest. Looking at a complete list of factors and variables arrayed on the theoretical model makes the selection/deselection process at these levels more systematic and explicit.

We use our wall hanging to generate the following criteria for selection and deselection:

- Are there *factors* within any domain *that have not been well operationalized*—that is, any factors lacking a sufficient number of variables? If other factors within the domain are well-operationalized, a less well operationalized one could be a candidate for deselection.

- Are there *factors* that *include too many variables?* If so, redundant or less relevant variables could be identified and eliminated.

- Is there an adequate *balance of factors to domains?* A significant imbalance may guide the deselection process by pointing to domains that are less well represented by factors in the existing data and are thus less important for the study.

- Is there a limitation on time and resources for conducting the interview, taking into consideration sample size, incentives for respondents, and the duration of the study? These limitations help to determine how many domains, factors, and variables can be included in a survey instrument (although they do not necessarily determine which ones are actually selected).

It is more difficult to provide concrete guidelines for how to choose one variable over another. A variable that is difficult to format may need to be eliminated. Redundancy is also a good reason for rejecting a variable, except in cases where having more questions about the same factor increases reliability. When in doubt, researchers must rely on the decision of the lead researcher or principal investigator, who will determine the final selection based on revisiting the conceptual model. The tree diagram allows other members of the research team who may be more familiar with the ethnographic data to have input into the formation of the ethnographic survey.

The process we have described here calls for editing down variables identified in the ethnographic text and other complementary sources of data, rather than inventing variables. The more conscious and intentional the process is, the less mysterious the construction of a survey instrument will seem. Having selected the final variable list, researchers are now ready for the conversion of these variables into questions on the survey instrument.

The Construction of Variables

Cross Reference: See Book 5, Chapter 8, on the organization and management of quantitative data

Variables consist of attributes (or items) that vary. Ethnographic data collection in Stages 1 and 2 assists us in defining attributes, organizing them into variables, and, eventually, determining how the variables are to be constructed.

The construction of variables involves several important qualities:

Critical Considerations in the Construction of Variables

- Attributes should be exhaustive
- Attributes should be mutually exclusive
- Attributes and questions should avoid using two or more nouns or verbs

---

Exhaustiveness. The attributes or units of which a variable is composed should be *exhaustive*. That is, every observation with regard to that variable should be able to be classified into one of the attributes; there should never be a response that fits an attribute other than one already included in the variable. Attributes can be made exhaustive by adding the categories "other," "none of the above," and "don't know." Researchers should remember, however, that responses to "other" will have to be coded for use later on, and the category should be avoided whenever possible.

➤•➤•➤ **EXAMPLE 8.2**

EXAMPLES OF EXHAUSTIVENESS IN ITEM SELECTION IN THE CONSTRUCTION OF CLOSED-ENDED RESPONSES ON AN ETHNOGRAPHIC SURVEY

1. Main reason for thinking of dropping out of school:
   ___ Harassment by teachers
   ___ Harassment by students
   ___ Poor grades
   ___ Need to help family financially by working full-time
   ___ Had a baby
   ___ Other

2. Future education/career paths. What educational option is most likely for you in the future? You may select only one of the following choices.
   ___ Join the army
   ___ Go to college
   ___ Go to a technical school
   ___ Get on-the-job technical training
   ___ Don't know

3. Where were you the *first* time you tried a drug (not alcohol)?
   ___ Have never used drugs
   ___ With friends at a party
   ___ With friends in a car
   ___ At a public event (concert, game, dance, etc.)
   ___ At school during regular school day
   ___ At home with friends or family members
   ___ Alone (at home or elsewhere)

➤•➤•➤

Mutual exclusiveness. Attributes must be mutually exclusive. When there are optional responses, it should not be possible to respond to two attributes simultaneously with respect to the *same variable*. For example, "Where do you live most of the time?" should include all of the possible places where a person could live and should request the respondent to select *only one location* where he or she lives most of the time.[2]

The following example illustrates flaws in the construction of a question measuring a variable called "employment."

EXAMPLE 8.3   ━━●━◆━●━━

FLAWS IN THE CONSTRUCTION OF A QUESTION ON AN ETHNOGRAPHIC SURVEY

What is your current employment status?

___ Full-time employment
___ Part-time employment
___ Unemployed

━━●━◆━●━━

The question is problematic because the responses are not mutually exclusive. A respondent could check both of the first two statements because he or she has both a full-time *and* a part-time job. To correct the problem, the researcher could do one of several things:

- Include part-time employment under the general category "employed" and provide only two optional responses: employed or unemployed. This option would result in lost data.
- Offer the respondent only one choice, which would result in the respondent's choosing the most salient or important option. This strategy could result in inaccurate data as someone could check "part-time" because it is more lucrative, but hold full-time employment as well.

- Indicate that full-time employment takes precedence over part-time employment. In this case, only those *not working full-time* would check the part-time employment box. This would also result in incomplete data because full-time employees might also work part-time but would not have the opportunity to indicate this in the survey.
- Leave the question as it is, after obtaining enough information to know that the options are indeed mutually exclusive in that setting.
- Ask two or several questions designed to elicit the full range of full- and part-time work combinations.

Researchers are advised to consider seriously the following point: <u>*Avoid double-barrelled questions with two or more subjects or verbs.*</u> **Key point** Inexperienced researchers sometimes include questions in surveys that contain two or more subjects or verbs, such as "Has the use of alcohol or drugs ever influenced you to engage in an illegal or violent act?" This is a poor strategy for question construction because neither the respondent nor the researcher knows to which of the subjects—alcohol or drugs—or adjectives—illegal or violent—the response refers. The question should be disaggregated into two questions, each of which contains two variables:

Has the use of alcohol ever influenced you to engage in

- an illegal act?
- a violent act?

Has the use of drugs ever influenced you to engage in

- an illegal act?
- a violent act?

These are basic characteristics of question construction eliciting clearcut information about variables. Up to this point, we have applied them only to those variables for which respondents are asked to select one response alternative from among several choices. Respondents also may be asked to compare one attribute to another, that is, to determine relationships among attributes. For example, they can rank attributes from high to low or in relation to one another (first, second, third, etc.). Attributes also can be scored. It is important to know what choices researchers have when constructing variables and why they should choose one type of variable over another, because data analytic procedures differ depending on the type of variable used.

Types of Variables or Measures

- Nominal measures
- Ordinal measures
- Interval measures
- Ratio measures

Definition: Nominal measures are variables with exhaustive and mutually exclusive attributes that are qualitatively but not quantitatively different

Nominal measures. Nominal measures are variables whose attributes are exhaustive and mutually exclusive. They vary in terms of quality but not in amount. Nominal variables are *categorically* different, that is, they can be differentiated by name or label but not by quantity. For example, in an international training program that brings together people from different countries, people could be grouped by country. The variable would be "country of origin." All of the people from Zimbabwe, Ireland, Peru, and Indonesia would differ by one characteristic: "country of origin." All of those from Zimbabwe would share the same characteristic "Zimbabwe as country of origin." People can be arranged in the same way by gender (male vs. female), food preference (vegetarian vs. nonvegetarian), home tenancy (home ownership vs. rental) or meeting attendance (present vs. absent). But the differences between these attributes *cannot be ranked.* They are merely categorically or qualitatively *different.*

Ordinal measures. Variables with attributes that can be ordered by ranking are referred to as ordinal measures. Ranking means that different attributes have relatively more or less of the variable, but the differences *are not measured in absolute terms.* For example, we can establish a ranking by educational level. Respondents would be instructed to choose only one from among the following items.

> ___ Completed elementary school
> ___ Middle school
> ___ High school
> ___ Less than college degree but some college
> ___ Completed college degree
> ___ Postcollege education

Definition: Ordinal measures are variables that can be ranked, where the differences between ranked levels are only relative and not measured in standardized units

These are mutually exclusive and are ranked in terms of "amount of education." Yet the specific amount of education, as measured by classes, or years, is not indicated. The so-called distances between levels do not have any meaning other than "more or less than." Likert scales, which ask respondents to rank a preference or opinion from 1 (highest) to 5 (lowest), are ordinal measures.

Guttman scales are ordinal scales that demonstrate logical orderly accrual of attributes or items, that is, they demonstrate the presence of a ranking in a set of related items that might rank differently in different cultures or with different populations.

Cross Reference: See Book 5, Chapter 8, for an example of a Guttman scale

Interval measures. When the distance between ranked attributes has meaning as measured with a standard unit of measurement, the variables are referred to as interval measures. It is difficult to find variables in social science research

Definition: Interval measures are variables for which the ranked distance between attributes is determined by a standard unit of measurement that does not begin at a zero point (e.g., units on the thermostat, or IQ)

that are true interval measures that are not based on a zero startpoint. Some authors give the example of IQ or other intelligence scores, in which the distance between a score of 100 and 120 is considered to be the same as the distance between 90 and 110. However, for a living person, the startpoint could not be zero—that is, no living person could be considered to have no intelligence functions at all.

Ratio measures. Ratio measures are based on a zero point. Actual age, absolute income in monetary units, numbers of people in personal networks, or spatial units such as miles or kilometers are ratio measures.

Transforming Variables by Selecting or Creating Items That Vary

Our next task is to disaggregate a variable into its constituent items or attributes and to reconstitute those attributes into a question that will appear in the ethnographic survey instrument and will measure the variable. Example 8.4 illustrates the relationship between a variable and a variable-level question, and the reframing of the question to obtain responses to items or attributes.

EXAMPLE 8.4   ━●━●━●━

RELATIONSHIP BETWEEN VARIABLES AND ITEMS

Variable: Reasons for working in the EPZ, Mauritius

Semistructured Survey Question: Why do women work in the Export Processing Zone in Mauritius?

Responses or Attributes (Items): Five reasons why women take up employment

- To be financially independent
- To support the family
- To be away from home
- Friends are also working
- Family problems

Ethnographic Survey Question: Here are five reasons why women take up employment. I would like you to rank each reason (item) from 1 to 5 in terms of their importance when you took up employment, where 1 means most important and 5 means least important.

___ To be financially independent
___ To support the family
___ To be away from home
___ Friends also are working
___ Family problems

⬥•⬥•⬥

Suggestions and Guidelines for the Construction of Survey Questions

In the following box, we list some suggestions for the formulation and construction of survey questions. The primary messages we want to convey to researchers are to make sure that questions are clearly phrased and to avoid biasing respondents toward favoring one answer over another, and to design questions that research participants can understand easily.

Suggestions for Constructing Survey Questions

- Select either a question or a statement format.
- Avoid open-ended questions.
- Make sure that all items are stated clearly.
- Make sure that items are mutually exclusive.
- Avoid statements that include combinations (and/or) in either noun or verb.
- Make sure respondents can answer the question.
- Make sure the questions are relevant to the topic.
- Keep questions and item responses as short as possible.
- Avoid alternating negatively phrased items with positively phrased items in the same scale.
- Avoid questions and terms that have hidden meanings that could obfuscate the question.

Formatting Survey Questions in Relation to Types of Variables

Researchers can choose from a broad range of question format options when transforming variables into items. Typical survey question formats are the following:

- Fill in—Respondent completes the response with the correct answer
- Multiple-choice—Respondent chooses one from among as many as 15 choices
- Likert—Respondent rates an item from high to low on a 3-, 4-, or 5-point scale
- Semantic differential—Respondent locates a cultural domain in relation to a series of items consisting of adjectival opposites
- Ranking—Respondent is asked to order each item in relation to the others in a finite and given list of no more than 10 items
- Rating—Respondent is asked to rate an individual item in importance, usually from 1 to 10
- Category—Respondent is asked to choose one of two or more categorically distinct options

These question format options are summarized in Table 8.1, along with examples of questions and type of measure.

In Table 8.2, we show how researchers can create and format questions representing variables within the same factor and domain. Here, we have chosen the factor "family income." In our study of AIDS risk in Mauritius, family income is situated in the "family" domain. All of the questions in the table relate to the factor "family income." They represent seven different variables, each an indicator of a slightly different cultural construct and each measured differently. Selection of the appropriate format is based on the nature of the variable, the education and experience of respondents (both of which influence their ability to respond accurately), and the results of pretesting.

TABLE 8.1   Question Format Table, With Examples

Question Format	Example	Measure (nominal, ordinal, interval, ratio)
Fill-in	How old are you now? Exact age _____	Ratio
	Are you a _____ male _____ female	Categorical

Multiple-choice	Please choose one answer only.
	I believe that women in this community:
	— should remain at home to raise children and
	  should not earn money
	— should earn money doing traditional women's
	  work (sewing, selling food in the marketplace, etc.)
	— should be able to do any work men can do
		Nominal

Likert	What would you say is your risk of exposure to AIDS in the next 5 years? (1 is highest, 5 is lowest) _____1 _____2 _____3 _____4 _____5	Nominal
Semantic differential	Where would you locate the term "applied research" on the following scales: useful _ _ _ _ _ useless wealth _ _ _ _ _ poverty weak _ _ _ _ _ powerful	Nominal
Rating	Rate **each** of the following from 1 (highest) to 4 (lowest) in terms of how important they are to you: _____ car _____ computer _____ TV _____ stereo/CD player	Nominal
Ranking	Rank the following from 1 (highest) to 4 (lowest) in terms of how important they are to you: car computer _____ TV _____ stereo/CD player	Nominal
Positive/negative (yes/no)	Do you expect to be living in this area 5 years from now? _____ yes _____no	Categorical

Piloting and Pretesting the Survey

Testing an ethnographic survey should take place in two steps, piloting the instrument with a small sample to assess

TABLE 8.2 Different Ways of Formatting Variables for the Factor "Family Income"

Format	Question	Variable	Cultural Construct	Scale or Measure
Positive/negative—yes/no	Please indicate whether your monthly income is ___ less than $600 ___ more than $600	Estimated monthly income	Demographic	Nominal—categorical
Fill-in	What is your monthly household income?	Exact monthly income	Demographic variable	Ratio—continuous
Multiple-choice	What is your average monthly income? Check the response that applied most directly to you. ___ $100-$499 ___ $1,000-$1,999 ___ $500-$999 ___ $2,000 and above	Estimated average monthly income	Demographic variable	Nominal—categorical
Likert	How satisfied are you with your monthly income on a scale from 1 (highest) to 5 (lowest)? 1 ___ ___ ___ 5	Satisfaction with income	Perception	Ordinal—continuous
Semantic differential	How do you consider your monthly income? Please check the place that applies. High ___ Low Adequate ___ Inadequate	Characteristics of monthly income	Attitude	Ordinal—continuous
Rating	Please rate from 1 to 10 (highest to lowest) how lowest) how likely it is that your monthly income will enable you to purchase each of the following items in the next year: ___ television ___ microwave oven ___ automobile ___ living room couch ___ motorcycle ___ radio ___ stereo ___ indoor toilet	Probability of purchase of MSL items	Expectancy	Ordinal—continuous
Ranking	Please rank from 1 to 6 the following items in terms of sequence of purchase: ___ television ___ microwave oven ___ automobile ___ living room couch ___ motorcycle ___ radio	Importance of MSL items	Attitude	Ordinal—continuous

the clarity of the questions and the timing of administration, and pretesting the instrument on a larger sample to
assess validity and adequacy of variable and scale construction.

Piloting the Instrument. The instrument should be reviewed with a small group of respondents from the study
population for sequencing, flow and **skip patterns**, language use, comprehension, and length. The review can take
place in a focus group setting, through individual interviews, or both. Any issues regarding the construction, conception, and flow of the instrument can be taken up with
respondents during administration on a question-by-ques-
tion basis or afterward. The instrument then should be
redrafted for pretesting.

Definition: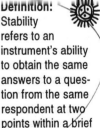
Skip patterns
are instructions to
the interviewer to
move from one set
of questions to
another consistent
with the logic of the
instrument

Pretesting the Instrument. The instrument should be pretested with a representative sample of between 60 and 80
respondents from the target population or a similar population in a nearby area. Between 20% and 50% of those
interviewed should be interviewed again with the same
instrument during a 2-week time frame to check for consistency of responses from the first to the second administration. A high correlation between selected responses from
Time 1 and Time 2 suggests that the instrument is stable,
that is, that the questions are structured so that they will be
highly likely to obtain the same answer from the same
respondent more than once. The data collected from the
larger pilot study are useful for the same purposes as the
first pilot phase. However, these data also serve other important purposes:

Definition:
Stability
refers to an
instrument's ability
to obtain the same
answers to a ques-
tion from the same
respondent at two
points within a brief
time period

- They permit checking for internal reliability and consistency
  by cross-tabulating similar questions to see if they correlate.
- They permit checking for stability.
- They enable the creation of scales with good reliability scores.

- They permit researchers to evaluate variables for variation adequate to test hypotheses.
- They enable researchers to eliminate variables that do not show enough variation (i.e., where all the responses are the same).
- They permit researchers to eliminate potential scale items that do not scale.

Any instrument, regardless of the source of the questions, should be pretested on the local population involved in the study. Pretesting prevents problems associated with validity and stability, and it allows researchers to test the degree to which scales assessed for reliability and validity with national samples measure variables in the same way locally.

Pretesting an instrument is especially important in the construction of ethnographic surveys where most variables, including those measured by scales, are derived from field research rather than from nationally validated instruments. The pretest permits researchers to validate the instrument and determine its reliability in the field setting prior to using it on a larger sample.

The issue of sampling is critically important in ethnographic surveying. For this reason, we have devoted much of an entire chapter to a consideration of systematic and probability sampling in ethnographic research.

Cross Reference: See Chapter 10 of this book for more information on sampling in ethnographic research

ADMINISTRATION OF ETHNOGRAPHIC INTERVIEWS

Cross Reference: See Book 1 on the interpersonal nature of ethnography and researcher as instrument of data collection, and Book 6, Chapter 1, on the researcher's role

Researchers should administer ethnographic interviews to respondents directly in a face-to-face interview. Face-to-face interviews are preferable because respondents often make additional comments during the interview process. These additional comments constitute ethnographic data that add to understanding the respondent's life and may also add to overall data in the study. Direct administration of interviews can create more rapport between the interviewer and respondent, leading to more valid responses. Furthermore, as we have said elsewhere, we also believe that face-to-face administration and direct knowledge acquisition give researchers a better intuitive understanding of the responses.

The conditions for face-to-face administration of ethnographic surveys are similar to those outlined as necessary in supporting the acquisition of good information from focused group interviews. The interview should take place in a quiet, private place, with few or no interruptions. Ideally, it should be conducted away from other family or community members who could influence the opinion of the respondent directly (e.g., see Angela Johnson's predicament, described in Chapter 6). This is not always possible, especially in communities where trust of strangers is low, or where it is the custom that people—especially women—be accompanied at all times. Under these circumstances, interviewers must do their best to minimize the input of others by telling them that they will be able to respond later in their own interview, or that the opinion of the respondent right now is the most important.

Interviewee fatigue or restlessness can be a problem in a long interview; other problems occur when the respondent has small children or other family obligations, or is sick, disabled, or addicted. Interviewers can always terminate an interview before it is completed and make appointments to return to complete it. Researchers may also decide that the interview itself is too long to be administered in a single session, and schedule two sessions to complete it. Two-session survey interviews are costly and time-consuming, and we caution researchers to avoid them if possible.

Face-to-face administration of ethnographic surveys helps researchers to avoid problems stemming from illiteracy, poor reading comprehension, and mixed language ability. However, it can take a great deal of time and effort to

Cross Reference: See Book 3, Chapter 2, on focused group interviews

locate respondents; find safe places for administration of the interview; and complete the interview without the intrusion of other family members, friends, and personal obligations.

One solution is to use a self-administered instrument. The creation of a self-administered instrument may take longer because researchers must be sure that the questions asked are transparent—that is, completely comprehensible to anyone likely to become involved in the study. Furthermore, self-administered instruments are useful only with literate populations. It is easiest to administer them in places where respondents normally gather for other purposes—for example, classrooms and adult learning centers, clinic waiting rooms, check-cashing lines, and after-school programs for youth. However, prior arrangements for administration must be made with staff at these settings.

EXAMPLE 8.5 ━●━●━●

SELF-ADMINISTERED QUESTIONNAIRES WITH UNIVERSITY STUDENTS IN SRI LANKA

In a project on youth and sexual risk in Sri Lanka, members of the research team organized respondents—urban youth and university students—into small groups of 6 to 10 members that were proctored by members of the research team. With each group, the proctors reviewed the questionnaire in blocks. Respondents completed one self-administered block of questions as a group and then received instructions before they moved on to the next block of questions. Proctors were also available to answer any questions or to clarify issues if youth did not understand. Most of the youth in the study had an 11th-grade educational level or more and were literate. As the questionnnaires were handed in, proctors checked them and asked respondents to fill in any incomplete answers.

This approach made it possible to collect more than 600 completed instruments in less than 3 weeks, despite electricity blackouts and other kinds of logistical problems.

━●━●━●

It is also possible to invite large numbers of respondents to a central location to complete questionnaires. Even with monetary incentives, food, a party, or a raffle, these events often require transportation, baby-sitting, or child care. Researchers must devote considerable time and attention to the social relationships that build the trust necessary to bring people to the session.

➤•➤•➤   **EXAMPLE 8.6**

SELF-ADMINISTERED QUESTIONNAIRES WITH
MOTHERS AND DAUGHTERS IN HARTFORD

Urban Women Against Substance Abuse (UWASA) is an intervention study testing whether improving mother-daughter communication in girls 9 to 12 years of age can prevent early initiation of drug and sex risk behaviors. The study design calls for the recruitment and testing of three 1-year cycles of 40 girls and their mothers and then comparing the results of a 9-month intervention with both to a matched control group of mother-daughter pairs. Testing using self-administered instruments for both girls and their mothers (or mother-equivalents) is conducted at baseline (prior to the beginning of the intervention cycle) and at three time points thereafter: immediately following the intervention, and at 6-month, 15-month, and 24-month points. During the second and third cycles, up to 120 mother and daughter pairs needed to be assessed at approximately the same time, because data collection time points for several cycles overlapped. To overcome this challenge, the small evaluation staff of three decided to hold "testing parties." Treatment and control mothers and daughters from each cycle were invited to their own special events at the Institute for Community Research. They were separated into two groups, one for mothers and the other for girls. Program staff proctored each setting, handing out questionnaires in English or Spanish, making sure that mothers and girls understood all the questions, reviewing questionnaires as they were completed, and sending respondents back to complete questions that had not been filled in. At least one member of the evaluation staff was available for mothers who did not read either English or Spanish well. In these cases, staff members read the questions and responses to the respondent, who then checked the appropriate answer.

Both mothers and daughters received an incentive. In addition, they could participate in a raffle. Following the completion of the testing, mothers and daughters joined a reception. Baby-sitters cared for small children, and mothers and daughters were transported to and from each testing session by program staff and hired drivers. In this way, program staff could test between 50% and 75% of each cohort at the same time, leaving only a small number of responses to be obtained through door-to-door collection of the data. This method reduced evaluation staff time in the field by more than 60%.

━•━•━

Despite hidden costs, self-administered questionnaires offer researchers many advantages. They are less costly to administer, they take less time, they are effective with most study populations whose reading and comprehension levels are good, and they offer ready opportunities to increase sample size. At the same time, they may not capture the entire sample desired for the study, because some respondents might never arrive at a central location despite incentives. Furthermore, it is possible to identify patterned misunderstanding of specific questions only after the data have been collected and analyzed, not during the administration of the survey. For these reasons, self-administered instruments require more initial effort to ensure the accumulation of valid data.

ANALYSIS OF QUANTITATIVE DATA

Cross Reference: See Book 5, Chapters 8 and 9, on organization, management, and analysis of quantitative survey data

Analyzing ethnographic survey data can be more systematic and structured than is true for other kinds of survey data because the analysis follows the guidelines set by the formative theoretical model and the conceptual taxonomy of domains, factors, and variables. In this section, we outline the steps in quantitative data analysis only briefly. We refer readers to Chapters 8 and 9 in Book 5, where these steps are treated in greater detail.

The first step in quantitative survey data analysis requires the production of **frequencies** for each of the variables in the study. Computer analysis programs such as SPSS, SAS, or EPI-Info provide summary information on each variable (e.g., frequency, means, and range) that helps researchers to describe the variable and interpret the meaning of the results. Surveys usually include large numbers of variables that should be reduced for further analysis. Data "crunching" (reduction) occurs through combining variables in a variety of ways. Once the data are prepared for analysis, they are ready for use in hypothesis testing. To test hypotheses, researchers revisit the original research model and use the data to examine the relationships among domains, factors, and variables. Hypothesis testing involves comparing the means of variables for two groups of people within the sample, or examining the associations among variables, two or more at a time. Using statistical techniques to associate two variables is referred to as bivariate analysis. Using statistical techniques to associate groups of variables or more than two variables is referred to as multivariate analysis.

Researchers generate many new hypotheses during the course of data analysis that are based on the original model and on new ideas that emerge by interacting with the data. Qualitative data already collected in the study can help to interpret the meaning of these new hypotheses. The final step in analysis is reporting on and interpreting the results and deciding which unanswered questions will guide the next study.

INTEGRATING QUALITATIVE AND QUANTITATIVE DATA

Triangulation of data for verification of results and the integration of qualitative and quantitative data are critical components of ethnographic research. The problem for

Definition:
Frequencies are the number and percentage of times that each item or attribute appears in the response to the question addressing the variable

Cross Reference:
See Book 5, Chapter 9, for a discussion of descriptive statistics

Cross Reference:
See Book 5, Chapter 8, for a discussion of quantitative data crunching strategies

Cross Reference:
See Book 5, Chapter 9, for a detailed discussion of the ways in which hypotheses can be tested; also see Table 9.3 for a summary of the statistical techniques that are used to determine whether the associations are significant or not, and that can be used for bivariate or multivariate analysis

Cross Reference: See Book 5, Chapters 10 and 11, for instructions on how to report and interpret ethnographic data

ethnographers lies in how to integrate the results of each kind of data analysis so that they complement and reinforce one another. Integration involves returning to modeling and operationalization, which form a common basis for both the qualitative and quantitative data collection and analysis procedures in an ethnographic study.

The qualitative data generated from the unstructured and semistructured interviews are coded into domains, factors, and variables and stored in computerized form with a text-based data management program. The quantitative data are organized and stored in the form of scales and indexes representing the *identical* variables, factors, and subfactors. The meeting of these two comparable data sets at the factor and subfactor level provides an opportunity for both triangulation and integration.

The approach to coding qualitative data that we have found most effective is exemplified by the conceptual taxonomy or the "tree diagram." Text data are coded by domains, factors, and subfactors,[3] based on these levels in the taxonomy. When a text-based computer management program (e.g., ETHNOGRAPH) searches for a domain such as "work," it will retrieve all of the codes for the factors and subfactors in the "work" domain, as well as any other coded domains and factors in the same block of text. Researchers can then examine associations among domains, factors, and subfactors in that block of text in line with the conceptual model. Furthermore, text management programs allow researchers to request blocks of text that include any two or more specified codes. This is a second way in which researchers can seek associations among domains and factors in textual data.

Cross Reference: See Book 1, Chapter 7, and Book 5, Chapters 4, 5, and 7, for instructions on analysis of qualitative data

Quantitative data analysis explores the associations between two or more variables either within or across domains and factors in much the same way that researchers do when they look for associated blocks of text. Using the theoretical model as a guide, ethnographers can explore the same associations in their qualitative and quantitative data, and they can use one type of data to help validate, interpret, and raise questions about the other.

➤•➤•➤ **EXAMPLE 8.7**

INTEGRATING QUALITATIVE AND QUANTITATIVE DATA IN A STUDY OF WOMEN, WORK, AND AIDS IN MAURITIUS

Statistical analysis of quantitative data obtained from the ethnographically informed survey conducted among young women in the workforce in Mauritius showed that contrary to researchers' beliefs, peers contributed little to AIDS knowledge. To our surprise, family and work settings both played a significant role in providing young women with information about the potential for sexual transmission of AIDS.

It was difficult for us to understand how Mauritian families, who rarely, according to our ethnographic data, addressed issues of sexuality, could or would contribute to their daughters' AIDS knowledge. A review of the qualitative data showed that parents considered work in the EPZ as a risk factor for unsupervised relationships with men. Text data showed that fathers in particular were using the threat of HIV/AIDS to dissuade their daughters from any sexual involvement in the hopes of reducing their contact with their male co-workers.

➤•➤•➤

SUMMARY

In this chapter, we have covered most of the primary considerations in the construction, administration, and analysis of ethnographically informed surveys or questionnaires. The approach we have evolved is designed to systematize the formulation of surveys from conceptual model to the construction of questionnaires. It also provides a structure for the analysis of data, proceeding from intradomain analysis to interdomain analysis. Finally, the approach we are suggesting simplifies the integration of qualitative and quantitative data by structuring both forms of data collection along parallel conceptual tracks.

The following box summarizes the steps in formulating an ethnographic survey:

- Analyze the qualitative text data resulting from the unstructured and semistructured data collection methods
- Use the analysis to modify the formative theoretical model by subtracting or adding domains, factors, and variables
- Construct a complete tree diagram or conceptual taxonomy that includes all of the identified domains and their associated factors and variables. The tree diagram provides a guide to the careful selection and elimination of variables.

The next steps in survey development and implementation are to

- Develop questions using a variety of question formats
- Pilot test the instrument with a small group
- Pretest the instrument with a larger sample to develop scales and eliminate variables that do not show variation
- Finalize the instrument for use in the field
- Administer the instrument to a systematic or probability sample of respondents
- Provide a structured approach to the analysis of quantitative survey data
- Integrate qualitative and quantitative data

Sampling is a critical issue in ethnographic research and poses different challenges for unstructured, semistructured, and systematic or structured data collection. We discuss these issues along with ways of ensuring validity and reliability in ethnographic research in Chapters 10 and 11 of this book. In the next chapter, we discuss how to complement the collection of interview, observational, and survey data with secondary and archival data as the final step in completing data collection for the story the ethnographer eventually will tell.

NOTES

1. As noted in Book 5, Chapter 9, strictly speaking, the responses for ordinal variables (rankings without fixed values between levels) should not be summed, but treating ordinal variables as if they were interval or ratio scales is, nevertheless, a common practice and was done in this study.

2. The question could read, "Where do you live at the present time?" In this case, those who live in several different locations could check each one. However, the question would be structured in the form of not one but multiple variables. Each variable would be a location (i.e., New York, Houston, Colorado, Hartford, Essex-on-the-Shore, and San Miguel Allende) with a "yes/no" response.

3. It is not advisable to code text data at the variable level because coding is very time-consuming, and coders generally cannot remember efficiently anything below the subfactor level in any conceptual/coding taxonomy.

9

USING ARCHIVAL AND SECONDARY DATA

 The collection of primary data is a major effort requiring a significant outlay of person power, time, money, equipment, and resources. Any approach to data collection and analysis that can shortcut the process, add important information, and save valuable resources is an advantage for ethnographic researchers. Using data and information collected by others can serve these purposes. At the same time, the use of archival and secondary data can further enhance the comprehensiveness of data collection, understanding of results, and its cross-cultural and cross-national comparability and generalizability. The purposes of this chapter are to define and describe archival and secondary data sources that are both available and potentially useful in ethnographic research, identify how to access and analyze these data sources, and demonstrate how they can be integrated with other forms of data collection in the ethnographic endeavor.

ARCHIVAL AND SECONDARY DATA: DEFINITIONS AND SOURCES

Archival and secondary data can be defined as qualitative or quantitative data collected for governmental, research,

Definition:
Archival and
secondary data
are qualitative and
quantitative data
collected and stored
for research, service,
and other official and
unofficial purposes by
researchers, service
organizations, and
others. They are stored
in the format in which
they were collected
or transformed into
computer-readable
data

Definition:
Archival data
are materials
originally collected
for bureaucratic or
administrative
purposes that are
transformed into
data for research
purposes

Definition:
Secondary
data are raw data
that other
researchers collect
for their own
purposes and that
ethnographers can
access for other uses

Definition:
Local
secondary data are
data gathered by
other researchers on
the population
under study

Definition:
Nonlocal
secondary data
are data obtained
from related
research conducted
elsewhere on related
topics/populations

education, or service purposes and available to researchers in usable raw data forms and formats. The term *raw* refers to the fact that these data sets or sources are available in their unanalyzed and uninterpreted formats (case records, questionnaires, applications, forms, or numerical or text data coded and formatted into computer-readable data sets). They are organized and stored in their original sampling frames and units (e.g., cases of individuals, households, classrooms, communities, and countries).

Some texts use the terms *archival* and *secondary* data interchangeably. We find it useful to distinguish these terms as follows: **archival data** are materials collected for bureaucratic, service, or administrative purposes and transformed into research data. **Secondary data** are data collected by other researchers for their own research purposes that ethnographers can obtain either through public access or personal negotiation.

We also distinguish between local secondary data and nonlocal secondary data. **Local secondary data** are derived from the work of other researchers on the population under study; they are used to add to researcher understanding of the local situation and help to shape study design and formative theory, as well as interpret study results. **Nonlocal secondary data** are data obtained from research conducted elsewhere with comparable populations on similar topics.

These data offer researchers the opportunity to develop research models and test preliminary hypotheses prior to going into the field, and to situate their locally available data in the context of comparable populations or larger data sets. They also offer the opportunity for testing new hypotheses emerging from the study and clarifying the idiosyncratic features of single community studies.

A special class of nonlocal secondary data that has implications for local description consists of national or state data sets that permit data to be extracted on local geographic units or communities in which ethnographic research will be conducted. The United States' and other national census data, as well as many other such data sets, provide demographic, health, housing, and other important information about the population of study prior to entering the field and can be a useful supplement to primary data collection.

Researchers can find many sources of information about local communities in the form of reports, fact books, and maps. For a city such as Hartford, Connecticut, for example, researchers can obtain a demographic fact book for new residents, a Chamber of Commerce Summary of Business Activity, a report of the status of education in the Hartford public school system, and a Children's Health Report Card. These reports, labeled by librarians as "fugitive literature," are not available through the usual sources—universities, libraries, informational clearinghouses, and research centers. Researchers usually have to locate them through the agency that produced them. Key informants, other researchers working in the area—especially policy researchers—and legislative aides can sometimes provide information about the availability of such reports. These reports are the products of others' analyses of archival or secondary data and thus do not fit our definitions of either. Despite the challenges of locating these materials, they are important sources of descriptive information, and ethnographic researchers should make every effort to secure them during the early stages of their research.

LOCAL ARCHIVAL DATA

Local archival data are available on general demographic and socioeconomic characteristics of the research community or area as well as on specific aspects of the population of interest to researchers, such as health status or educational achievement levels. In the following pages, we discuss how to locate and use both forms of local archival data.

Local Archival Data on General Features of Communities

Local archival data that can be used to inventory the population and obtain information about social and geographic features of the community under study include the following:

- Areal and topographic maps that can identify physical features, roads, and residential and other building structures in rural communities and urban neighborhoods
- Municipal records of births; marriages; deaths; real estate transactions; and ownership of telephones, cars, and property
- Census, tax, and voting lists available in villages and neighborhoods of urban areas (e.g., the *gramasevana* [the lowest public official/office in Sri Lanka] has the list of all individuals in the unit over 18 years of age who are eligible to vote)
- Specialized surveys of water, soil, weather, agricultural production, and other features
- Service system records from health, social welfare, and education organizations
- Court proceedings and cases

Pelto and Pelto (1978) state: "Governments and their agents maintain a variety of records concerning population sizes, births and deaths, crimes, marriages and other social statistics. . . . Fieldworkers should make every attempt to obtain official archival data wherever possible" (p. 116). These archival data can serve as a means of describing the physical environment, establishing the composition of the study population, selecting samples, establishing observational settings, delineating community and population change

through time, and many other population development and
dynamics issues.

•—•—•—•

EXAMPLE 9.1

USING ARCHIVAL DATA IN THE STUDY OF URBAN COMMUNITIES

(*PUEBLOS JOVENES*) IN LIMA, PERU

Researchers Schensul, Schensul, and Zegarra initiated a study to explore the association between patterns of pediatric health problems and the evolution of communities
in the northwest quadrant of Lima. This study used the community as the unit of
analysis.

The city of Lima, Peru has expanded dramatically during the past two decades, as
rural residents from the highlands, jungle, and coastal areas have migrated to the city
in search of a better life. Limited availability of housing in the central city, as well as
the high cost of land and new housing, has resulted in the organization of *invasiones*
(invasions) of open public or private land on the outskirts of the city.

Professional organizers work with from 50 to more than 1,000 families to capture
a piece of land during the night and occupy it permanently. These organized "new
communities" establish temporary housing and seek official recognition so that they
can gain the geographic stability required to invest in the construction of permanent
housing. Residents also organize themselves at the block, block cluster, and community levels to take care of their health, social, and educational needs during the process
of advocating for recognition.

The study team conducted their research in the northwest quadrant of Lima, in a
relatively narrow canyon bordered by the foothills of the Andes. New towns, or
pueblos jovenes, were arrayed along the canyon from those closest to central Lima to
those further away. Some communities were located on the more desirable flatlands
in the center of the canyon, and others were located along the steep canyon walls.
Communities located closer to Lima were officially recognized as municipalities, were
older and more developed, and in which residents owned title to their own plots.
Communities situated at greater distances from central Lima tended to be newer and
unrecognized, with temporary housing and no infrastructural amenities. Communities located on the steep sides of the canyon experienced more economic and
physical disadvantages than did those on the canyon floor.

As a first step, the researchers found two maps in the City Planning Department: a topographical map of the canyon (Canto Grande) and a map that located the boundaries of each of the communities in the area of the canyon in which the research was to be conducted. Key informants added the boundaries of newer communities not included in the official map of Canto Grande, as well as official extensions to existing communities that had not yet been added to the official map.

Cross Reference: See Book 4, Chaper 2, on mapping spatial data for a more complete discussion of computerized maps

These maps proved crucial in the field in helping the research team to locate communities and define geographical and other visible variations among the communities that might relate to children's health. The maps also helped the team to understand spatial dimensions of community variation and development. The maps were digitized by Ellen Cromley, a medical geographer in the Department of Geography at the University of Connecticut, producing a three-dimensional view of the canyon showing the elevation of communities in the canyon in relation to one another, as well as a base map of Canto Grande upon which social, economic, political, and other community-level data could be overlaid for comparative purposes (Schensul, Schensul, & Zegarra, 1985).

━●━●━●━

Local Archival Data on Specific Domains of Interest

Local archival data can also be used to learn about particular domains or areas of interest to researchers. The following three sources illustrate the types of information usually available to researchers involved in health, education, and correctional issues.

Schooling and education. The local school system is an enormous repository of qualitative and quantitative information on individual students, their families, individual schools in the system, and the school system as a whole. These data include student demographic characteristics, student academic and test performance, student behavior, family economics and demographic characteristics, and teacher performance and behavior.

━●━●━   **EXAMPLE 9.2**

USING LOCAL SCHOOL-BASED ARCHIVAL DATA TO COLLECT INFORMATION ON CHILDREN'S ACTIVITIES

Researchers Jean Schensul, Diaz, and Woolley were interested in gathering information from children 7 to 10 years of age attending two schools in the Hartford public school system. Children were excluded from the study if they reported taking any form of medication for behavioral or learning problems, or if they had asthma. To obtain information about the number, gender, and ethnicity of children with diagnosed behavioral or learning problems that required medication, researchers met with representatives of the Central Board of Education in charge of school records. Although the records for individual children were confidential, these representatives were able to provide aggregate information about the classrooms that included children in the required age level. In this way, the researchers were able to select classrooms that had an adequate number of male and female children, broad ethnic representation, and small numbers of children on medication for hyperactivity (Schensul, Diaz, & Woolley, 1996).

━●━●━

The following example illustrates the use of historical documents obtained from schools and newspapers to document parents' attitudes toward education.

EXAMPLE 9.3   ══•══•══

USING HISTORICAL DOCUMENTS FROM SCHOOLS AND NEWSPAPERS TO
DEMONSTRATE A HISTORY OF LATINO PARENTS' INVOLVEMENT IN EDUCATION

Ruben Donato is studying the access of Latinos to education in the Colorado/New Mexico area during the period from 1910 to 1940, using the minutes of school board meetings, attendance records, curriculum documents, school board election statistics, and records of expenditures in white and Latino schools. This work follows from research he conducted in Los Angeles to challenge the idea that Latinos were not involved in the education of their children. He used newspaper archives to show that there was a consistent historical pattern of Latino concern and activism over educational issues.

══•══•══

Health services. Health care facilities such as hospitals, public ambulatory health centers, and private medical practices, as well as nontraditional health service providers (e.g., Ayurveda, acupuncture, and homeopathic medicine), maintain patient records. These records are likely to vary greatly in completeness and accuracy. In addition, they include only patients who use the service and thus are not a representative sample of the larger community. Nevertheless, they are an invaluable source of information about the characteristics of those using the service, the frequency of reported illnesses, and the treatments prescribed for these illnesses.

EXAMPLE 9.4   ══•══•══

COLLECTING CLINIC DATA FROM PUBLIC CLINICS IN THE
SAN JUAN DE LURIGANCHO AREA OF LIMA, PERU

To explore their hypothesis regarding a relationship between the level of community development of new communities in the northern quadrant of Lima and patterns of children's health problems, researchers S. Schensul, J. Schensul, and Zegarra obtained data on pediatric illness by community. They initiated a comprehensive review of records in the *Centros de Salud* serving the 30 communities. A program titled "Niño

Sano" (well child) kept comprehensive data on the health status of mothers and children, including heights and weights, family information, health problems of mother and child, and sociodemographic information on the family. The research team, with the assistance of clinic staff, collected a sample of at least 30 children's records for each *pueblo joven* in the area—a total of approximately 1,000 records. In a situation where it would have been impossible to collect primary health data, the clinic records were a vital source of information on the health status of children in the sample communities (Schensul, S., et al., 1985).

Legal, penal, and court system. Almost all formal civil and criminal courts in the world keep a qualitative record of their cases. These banks of case data can serve as an important record of community disputes, crimes, sentences, policies, and precedents. Sarah Blaffer Hrdy, for example, used wills and probate records to assess the social value differentially accorded to sons and daughters as reflected in inheritance patterns in the San Francisco Bay area. Police records can also be an important source of data on family disputes, gang violence, drug abuse, commercial sex workers, and other populations and issues (Needle, Coyle, Genser, & Trotter, 1995). Example 9.5 illustrates the use of local archival data for targeted sampling of people at risk for HIV/AIDS.

EXAMPLE 9.5

OBTAINING INFORMATION FROM POLICE RECORDS FOR USE IN RECRUITING
INJECTION DRUG USERS FOR DRUG AND AIDS PREVENTION PROGRAMMING

Researchers Weeks, Singer, and Schensul have been involved in AIDS and drug-related research for the past 12 years. This research has been based primarily in the city of Hartford. Much of the research has involved recruiting injection or other high-risk drug users and enrolling them in various types of intervention programs, or in studies to determine how best to conduct interventions designed to reduce both drug- and AIDS-related risks for themselves and their partners and families.

Recruiting people from streets, abandoned buildings, and other locations where they spend much of their time is a challenging task. One way to increase the likelihood of recruiting a larger and more representative sample is to identify the geographic areas where they are most likely to concentrate their activities.

Although drug use is not recorded in any archives, other information is recorded in different administrative reporting systems and can be combined to create a geographic map of what they termed "high-risk areas." Locational data sources available for this purpose included records of crimes, shootings, homicides, assaults, robberies, arrests for prostitution, arrests for drug sales, and locations of abandoned buildings. Institute for Community Research data managers coded these separate sources of information from police administrative databases and reproduced them in a neighborhood Geographic Information System (GIS) using a desktop computer mapping system (MapINFO). The neighborhoods that showed the highest concentrations of the above activities were those targeted for recruitment.

USING LOCAL ARCHIVAL DATA

A great deal of archival information is available in most communities. Researchers can locate these local archival sources by making the proper contacts with institutions and organizations, and by conducting interviews with key informants. However, they are not always fortunate enough to find these data already organized into clean and immediately usable quantitative or qualitative databases. Data are often stored—sometimes in disorganized ways—in filing cabinets and folders and must be collected, coded, and even computerized to be useful. The accumulation of such data requires considerable time and effort. It is important for ethnographic researchers to inventory the data and to select the data most likely to be central to the study in order to structure retrieval and sampling operations efficiently. The following examples illustrate two cases in which local archival data were collected. In the first example, a great deal of time was devoted to the collection of local archival data that did not relate to the research topic. In the second example, the archival data collected were directly useful to the study.

➤•➤•➤   **EXAMPLE 9.6**

COPYING ARCHIVAL DATA ON LEGAL DISPUTES
IN RURAL SOUTHWESTERN UGANDA

Researcher Stephen Schensul undertook a study in rural Uganda to examine the social and economic impact of the migration of rural village residents to the city of Kampala for wage labor. In the initial stages of the research, Schensul learned from one of the local chiefs that the local court kept transcripts of criminal cases and civil disputes. He hypothesized that those individuals who had migrated to Kampala for work might be more likely to be involved in criminal activity and, as a consequence of having more financial and property resources, would be involved in larger numbers of court-adjudicated civil disputes. Because he had no copy machine available in the isolated community in which he was working, he had to copy court records of disputes laboriously by hand. After much time and effort, he discovered little evidence that migrants had any greater court involvement than nonmigrants. Although the material was interesting, it turned out to be irrelevant to the central focus of the study (Schensul, 1969).

➤•➤•➤   **EXAMPLE 9.7**

USING LOCAL ARCHIVAL DATA TO OBTAIN INFORMATION
ON NAVAJO FOOD PROCUREMENT PATTERNS

On the other hand, Donna Deyhle (personal communication, 1995) found it useful and efficient in her study of dietary consumption practices on the Navajo Reservation to record data on food and nonfood purchases as derived from cash register receipts stored by local grocery stores and trading posts. This method was supplemented with interview data about what families bought on overnight shopping trips to larger towns off the reservation.

➤•➤•➤

Researchers wishing to access, record, and use local archival data should consider the following issues:

- Identification of the data
- Identification of the shortcomings of the archival data
- Decision-making regarding allocation of resources to archival data collection
- Procedures for storing and analyzing the archival data

Identification of the Data

The location and content of the data must be identified. Identification often occurs with the assistance of key informants both within and outside of the population under study. Steps in identification involve the following:

- Establishing who controls access to the data
- Identifying and carrying out formal and informal procedures necessary for gaining access to the data
- Obtaining or ensuring informed consent if the data describe individual cases (adults, minors, families)
- Developing a means for recording/copying the data, including machine copying, speaking the information into a tape recorder or voice-activated computer program, developing a coded format for the data, or scanning data directly into a computer.

Identification of the Shortcomings of the Archival Data

Archival data may have many shortcomings for purposes of the study, because they were or are being collected for entirely different purposes. To avoid wasting valuable resources, it is important to identify problems with the data in advance, before going to great lengths to record them. Incomplete items and missing documents are significant shortcomings in archival data. No archival data fully represent the study population. Clinic data, for example, record only those attending the clinic, not all cases of a disease. These same data sources may also record information inaccurately for research purposes (although the same recording may be appropriate for administrative purposes). Case records and billing forms for patients may record one diagnosis for purposes of billing rather than the two or three for which the patient is being treated, or they may subsume a specific illness under a broader domain (e.g., sometimes categorizing pneumonia as an upper respiratory infection).

Recording systems also can change. Thus, for example, when the definition of AIDS changed in the mid-1990s, far more cases of AIDS were recorded than previously, making it seem as if prevalence and incidence were increasing precipitously.

Decision Making Regarding Allocation of Resources to Archival Data Collection

Having decided that the archival data of interest are valuable to the study, researchers must make decisions about whether or not the resources required to capture or record the data are available, and how these resources should be allocated. Decisions about the allocation of time and resources to data retrieval may include the following:

- Determining how long it will take to obtain access to the physical location where the archival information is kept
- Determining how long it will take to record the data
- Determining how much archival or other staff cooperation is required to access the data
- Deciding whether to obtain all or only a sample of records

Procedures for Storing and Analyzing the Archival Data

Before investing time in recording local archival data, researchers should consider storage and analysis. Often, archival data must be copied by hand because of the environmental challenges of the field situation or the limited resources of the researcher. Researchers can save valuable time, however, if they can find ways of recording data directly into a qualitative or quantitative computer data management and analysis program. Decisions about storage, management, and analysis include the following:

- Selection of text search, text management, or quantitative data management and analysis programs
- Decisions about analytical procedures
- Decisions about when to use the data and in what form (for model development, contextual description, triangulation, or post-primary data collection hypothesis testing)
- How to triangulate the data with other archival, secondary, and primary qualitative and quantitative ethnographic data

LOCAL SOURCES OF SECONDARY DATA

As we said earlier, secondary data are original data sets that other researchers have created for their own purposes. Ethnographers can access these data sets with the permission of the original researchers. These sources of data may come from previous studies in the research community, including national studies that have selected the research community as a local site.

Previous Studies in the Same Communities

Fortunate researchers may be able to use the qualitative and quantitative data collected from studies previously conducted in the research community. The research initiated by Stephen Schensul and Mary Bymel in Chicago's West Side Mexican American community from 1968-1976 was carried on by Gwen Stern and other anthropologists over the course of two decades.

EXAMPLE 9.8

THE *CUARANTENA* AS A POSTPARTUM PRACTICE IN THE MEXICAN AMERICAN COMMUNITY ON THE WESTSIDE OF CHICAGO

Between 1969 and 1974, the Community Research Unit (CRU) of the Community Mental Health Program at the West Side Medical Complex (University of Illinois, Chicago) documented the role of Mexican traditions in the adaptation of newly arriving Mexicans to Chicago. One such tradition is the *cuarantena*: a 40-day post-partum period in which the new mother is excused from household chores; rarely leaves the house; and devotes herself to taking care of the new baby while relatives, friends, and neighbors take care of the family.

In 1974, the National Institute of Mental Health provided funding that enabled researchers Stephen Schensul and Gwen Stern to study the effects of the *cuarentena* on the health and mental health of Latino mothers during the postpartum period. The CRU's previous ethnographic research on traditional health practices suggested that the practice of the *cuarentena* would be as important as perinatal health care in producing positive maternal and infant health outcomes.

Research results showed that first-generation Mexican women who had migrated from Mexico were significantly more likely to participate in the *cuarantena* than were second- or third-generation Chicago Mexican-American residents. The study also found that those women who *expected* to practice the *cuarantena* had a less problem-atic pregnancy and fewer physical and emotional problems during the postpartum period than those who had no such expectations. Finally, the study showed that actual observation of the *cuarentena* predicted better maternal and child health outcomes. Stern and colleagues used these results to support the formation of a new organiza-tion, *Mujeres Latinas en Accion* (Latina Women in Action). The data also provided the basis for developing a program to assist pregnant women (particularly second- and third-generation young women) to construct a social support system and perinatal health practices comparable to the traditional *cuarentena* and appropriate to their lifestyles in urban Chicago. The new program provided the foundation for additional data collection on maternal and child health, adding to a growing corpus of qualitative and quantitative data on the health and social welfare of the westside Mexican community (Gaviria, Stern, & Schensul, 1982).

The work of anthropologists Jean and Stephen Schensul, Merrill Singer, and Margaret Weeks has contributed to a similar corpus of health, social, and cultural data on multi-ethnic communities and neighborhoods. For the past two decades, these anthropologists and their colleagues have been conducting collaborative ethnographic and epidemiologic research in Hartford, Connecticut through the Hispanic Health Council (1978 to present) and the Institute for Community Research (1987 to present). All of the original data sets from more than 35 studies on maternal and child health, substance abuse, HIV/AIDS, adolescent health, the health of older adults, and various types of health service utilization are maintained in both organizations and regularly are used to provide the foundation for new studies. Health social scientists associated with the University of Peradeniya and the Center for Intersectoral Community Health Studies in Kandy, Sri Lanka have been generating data on the health and development of urban and rural communities in central and eastern Sri Lanka from 1981 to the present. University and community partnerships such as these yield long-term relationships between social science research institutes, university departments, and local communities. The encouragement of funders such as the National Institutes of Health, the Centers for Disease Control, the World Health Organization, and the Centers for Disease Control to generate these partnerships suggests that the number of local secondary databases will grow dramatically over the next decade, enabling ethnographic researchers to begin their local research with the reanalysis of a substantial amount of previously collected text and numerical data.

NONLOCAL SOURCES OF SECONDARY DATA

We live in a survey-oriented world in which almost every aspect of human behavior has been surveyed, particularly in the industrialized countries. As a result, the United States, and its individual states, have hundreds of publicly available data sets starting with the U.S. Census and continuing with surveys of work, education, health, sexuality, adolescence, and many other issues. Similarly, most of the developing countries have demographic and topical survey data that include censuses; surveys conducted by ministries of health, planning, education, agriculture, and others; and surveys facilitated by international (World Health Organization, UNICEF, United Nations Development Program) and bilateral (USAID, Canadian International Development Agency, German Technological Assistance Agency) organizations. One of the largest international survey efforts, supported by USAID and conducted by Macro International, is the "Demographic and Health Survey" (DHS). DHS data have been collected from 64 countries since 1987, using the same basic format and questions. The Centers for Disease Control and their counterparts in 24 countries have collected cross-national data on reproductive health and contraception for the past 30 years with the Contraceptive Prevalence Survey. In the United States and internationally, demographers have led the way in developing, collecting data for, and analyzing large national and cross-national data sets.

Ethnographic researchers frequently underutilize state, national, and even international data sets, not realizing that they are an important source of information on local populations. Most of these data sets include social, economic, employment, health, education, and other sociodemographic and epidemiologic data. National censuses are the most well known and well utilized of these data sets. There are many other specialized national surveys that address specific topics such as AIDS and other STDs, maternal health, drug use, infant and child health, and agricultural production, and that can be reanalyzed for local use.

Example 9.9 illustrates how a state epidemiological database on sexually transmitted diseases can assist in planning for a local level intervention.

EXAMPLE 9.9   ◆–•–◆–•–◆

USING STATE SECONDARY DATA SETS FOR INTERVENTION PLANNING

As part of a project conducted with the Connecticut Department of Health, Stephen Schensul and Merrill Eisenberg focused on the factors associated with the rapid rise of STDs in one of the cities in Connecticut. An early step in the process was to map the spatial distribution of STD cases in the target city that were reported to the Department of Public Health. All cases of gonorrhea and syphilis must be reported. In practice, only a fraction of the cases are reported. Nevertheless, the research team believed that knowing how the cases were distributed geographically in the city would point to areas of high STD concentration, suggesting locations for more intensive ethnographic research.

The results of STD mapping, using the state's data base, showed that 55% of the cases came from two of the city's census tracts. Focusing on these high-incidence areas permitted researchers to target qualitative and quantitative research to those census tracts, and to concentrate planning for intervention in those same geographic areas (Schensul, Eisenberg, Glasgow, & Huettner, 1994).

The next example illustrates how national studies on related topics can inform the development of a study's theoretical framework.

EXAMPLE 9.10   ◆–•–◆–•–◆

USING ANALYSES OF NATIONAL SECONDARY DATABASES
TO STRENGTHEN A STUDY'S FORMATIVE THEORY

The formative theory for this study was generated based on the direct knowledge and experience of the administration of the Mauritius Family Planning Association, which had been providing health and family planning services in the industrial zone; and researchers Schensul and Schensul, who were familiar with AIDS risk in industrializing zones elsewhere in the world.

One of the members of this joint research team, Satindur Ragobar, was a faculty member of the University of Mauritius. She recalled the existence of two surveys of workers in the industrial sector conducted by the university. Prior to the start of the field study, the research team sought and obtained access to the raw data. This permitted the research team to disaggregate from the databases all cases of young women aged 15 to 25 years. Hypotheses were explored examining the associations among work, peer, and family domains; ethnicity; health; and dimensions of the work experience.

In 1989, the University of Mauritius conducted a national survey on "Health, Nutrition and Productivity of Workers in the EPZ Industries." The sample size for this survey was 2,500 EPZ workers, of which 1,217 were women and 689 were never-married women between the ages of 15 and 25. Although the focus of the survey was on other health issues, the demographic data allowed us to explore hypotheses related to the interaction of ethnicity with family structure and work issues. These analyses allowed us to identify for the first time several key differentiating factors in the family organization of young women in the EPZ. It also gave us our first indication that many of the young women were forced to work in the EPZ because of the loss of the male head of household due to death, divorce, separation, infirmity, or alcoholism.

The second survey, the national AIDS Knowledge, Attitudes, Beliefs and Practices (KABP) survey, was conducted in 1990 by the University of Mauritius in collaboration with the Ministry of Health and the World Health Organization. The national sample included more than 2,000 individuals, which, when disaggregated by EPZ employment, marital status, age, and gender, included 79 never-married women, ages 15 to 25, employed in the industrial sector. We were able to compare this group with a comparable group of nonemployed women to explore the relationship between work status and AIDS KABP. The survey instrument also proved to be useful in generating items for AIDS and condom knowledge scales. It was then possible to compare the results of the survey used in this study with results of the national AIDS study.

USING LARGE SECONDARY DATA SETS
FOR HYPOTHESIS TESTING AND
CROSS-CULTURAL COMPARISONS

The opportunity to "collect locally and compare globally" is a strength of ethnography. However, the diversity of our methods, as well as the locations of our research and our commitment to local research and theory development, makes such comparisons difficult. One approach, funded by international and bilateral agencies, is to organize multisite research and intervention projects with comparable qualitative and quantitative data collection methodologies (Pelto & Gove, 1992). These projects are costly, require much cross-site coordination, and are generally infrequent. A second approach is to organize ethnographically informed basic and intervention studies on a focused topic such as nutritional status of adolescents, or women and AIDS, and to compare the results across studies. Examples of this approach include the Women and AIDS studies funded by the International Center for Research on Women and summarized in their Phase I (1995) and Phase II (1997) report series (ICRW, 1995/1997), and the results of a cross-site study of the interaction of newcomers with established residents that was funded by the Ford Foundation (Lamphere, 1992).

Another alternative that ethnographers underutilize takes advantage of the increasing number of existing data sets resulting from the administration of a survey instrument to a nationally sampled population. Local data extracted from a national data set can be analyzed to test hypotheses emerging from local qualitative data collection. National data sets can be used to generate questions, hypotheses, and ideas that can guide a local study (see Chapters 2 and 3 for more information on this topic). Finally, these data sets are useful in testing hypotheses generated from local research. Below, we describe the steps involved in the use of these national and international data sets for testing locally derived hypotheses.

> ### Steps in Using International Data Sets
>
> - Delineation of the key results of local ethnographic research
> - Identifying and disaggregating appropriate data sets
> - Testing ethnographically informed hypotheses
> - Exploring the data sets to seek other associations with the dependent domain
> - Developing a new and expanded model

Delineation of the Key Results of Local Ethnographic Research

The results of local ethnographic research produce information limited in time and place, and hypotheses that can be tested on populations elsewhere. Large national and international data sets can provide the foundation for testing these locally derived hypotheses.

━●━●━● **EXAMPLE 9.11**

TESTING HYPOTHESES RELATED TO SOCIAL INEQUALITIES AND SEXUAL INITIATION IN SRI LANKA

In 1997, the Mellon Foundation funded a cross-national study to explore the relationship between social inequality and sexual initiation. Researchers Schensul and M.W.A. de Silva proposed using the Youth and Sexual Risk data set (de Silva et al., 1997) to explore this topic and added to it a substantial number of new interviews on sexual initiation.

In January 1998, researchers Stephen Schensul, de Silva, and P. Wedisinghe were at the Center for Intersectoral Community Health Studies offices in Kandy, Sri Lanka reviewing preliminary analysis of the new sexual initiation data and reanalyzing the qualitative and quantitative data sets from the previous study. Results of both studies pointed to a considerable amount of data on unprotected sex during first sexual encounters, and they were considering how to organize the results to reflect and interpret the circumstances under which risks occurred during these encounters. A gender-based analysis was not possible because females reported very limited sexual activity. The research team concluded that "age discordance" (not gender or behavior) was important in accounting for variations in the occurrence of risky behavior.

They defined age discordance as "the relative age difference between the respondent and sex partner in a sexual dyad." Age discordance was a proxy for the power imbalance between older and younger partners in sexual experience, emotional and physical maturity, socioeconomic status, power, and effective risk prevention communication. Age discordance was defined as positive (respondent younger than the partner) or negative (respondent older than the partner).[1] Researchers found a large number of examples of both types of age discordance at sexual initiation. The primary hypothesis emerging from the analysis of these data sets was that age discordance at sexual initiation predicted greater exposure to sexual risk later on.

A review of the scientific literature revealed little information on this topic. For this reason, the research team decided to conduct a secondary analysis of data on youth and reproductive health behavior based on available national and international data sets. The purpose of the analysis was to test the hypothesis as stated and to identify critical predictors (domains, factors, and variables) for use in a broader study of age discordance and sexual risk in Sri Lanka.

━•━•━

Identifying and Disaggregating
Appropriate Data Sets

The next step in testing the generalizability of locally supported hypotheses with large national and international data sets is to identify those data sets that are likely to be useful. Once these are identified, data analysts must disaggregate or subset them in terms of the target population (defined by age, gender, ethnicity, income level, or geographic location) and the variables believed to be appropriate for the proposed study. Researchers should recognize that these operations are complex and should not be tackled by novice data analysts.

SELECTING AND DISAGGREGATING APPROPRIATE LARGE DATA SETS FOR A STUDY OF AGE DISCORDANCE IN SRI LANKA

In the CICHS study of age discordance, we used subsets and selected variables from the following data sets: *Demographic and Health Survey (DHS)* data collected in six sub-Saharan countries—Uganda, Zambia, Zimbabwe, Benin, Central African Republic, and Cote D'Ivoire—on a variety of health, fertility, mortality, and nutrition topics, as well as on sexual activity, knowledge, and behaviors regarding AIDS and other sexually transmitted infections. This data set included no information about premarital partners.

The *National Longitudinal Study of Adolescent Health Data UNC, Chapel Hill (Add Health)* study (Wave I, 1994) was designed to measure the impact of the social environment on adolescent health through the examination of behavioral and demographic factors affecting youth in their communities. The data set contains 6,503 cases—3,356 females and 3,147 males from Grades 7 to 12. Information is available on age, gender, and other characteristics for three partners so that it is possible to be precise about difference between the age of the respondent and the age of the partners.

The *Contraceptive Prevalence Survey (CPS)* has been administered in almost 30 countries but is not as publicly available as the other data sets described. Access to each country-data set has to be negotiated separately either with the specific Ministry of Health or with the individual project officer at the CDC. As a result of working with two participants from Jamaica, we had the Jamaican CPS, from which we extracted for unmarried young women and men 15 to 24 years old. There were 970 young women and 1,041 young men. The data set for males was more extensive, including sections on sex education, current sexual activity, and knowledge of AIDS, whereas the data for females were limited to demographic and contraceptive use variables.

➤•➤•➤

Testing Ethnographically Informed Hypotheses

A major challenge in using a data set created with purposes only partially related to the research topic at hand is to find the appropriate variables with which to test the main hypotheses. Once these variables are located or created, researchers can look for associations among independent and dependent variables. These processes are described in the following example.

➤•➤•➤

EXAMPLE 9.13

CONSIDERING THE RELATIONSHIP BETWEEN AGE
DISCORDANCE AND SEXUAL RISK

Continuing the example cited above, researchers first created the variables "positive age discordance" and "negative age discordance" in each of the data sets. Next, they identified variables in the available data sets related to the major hypothesis to be tested. These included "age at first sex" and several outcomes related to sexual risks, emotional well-being, conformance to cultural values, and life adjustment.

The data sets generally confirmed the primary hypothesis and related secondary hypotheses. The results are as follows.

Perceptions of future sexual risks. Positive age discordance and earlier age at first sex were related to expectations that one will contract STDs or HIV/AIDS.

Contraceptives. Lower level of knowledge about contraceptives (including condoms) was related to lower likelihood of using contraceptives/condoms at first sexual experience, early age of initiation into sex, and premarital pregnancy at an early age.

Risky sex. Both age discordance and earlier age at first sex were related to higher levels of sexual risk (more subsequent sexual partners, higher incidence of STDs, and greater likelihood of involvement in coercive sex).

Substance abuse. For both males and females, first sexual experience with older partners was related to use of several substances, including tobacco, alcohol, cocaine, and other illegal drugs.

Emotional problems. For females, first sexual experience with older males was related to poor self-esteem. For males, early age at first sex was related to poor self-esteem, suicide ideation and attempts, and greater involvement in physical fighting.

Premarital pregnancy/fatherhood. For females, both early age of sexual initiation and negative age discordance (with an older partner) were related to higher incidence of premarital pregnancy.

━●━●━

Exploring the Data Sets to Seek Other Associations With the Dependent Domain

Large data sets include variables other than those researchers may have considered in the original formulation of the hypotheses to be tested cross-nationally. Thus, an advantage of working with large data sets is the opportunity they provide to explore associations with variables from new domains.

━●━●━   **EXAMPLE 9.14**

TESTING NEW HYPOTHESES

In the same study, we also explored precursors to age-discordant relationships situated in the domains "family," "work," "school," "peers," and "demographic factors." The results are as follows:

Demographic. Lower age at first sex was related to residence in a rural (vs. urban) community, fewer years of education, lower economic status, unemployment, and (for females) working in a setting away from family.

Family. Positive age discordance (i.e., older partner) at first sex was related to unhappy family relationships, a desire to leave home, lack of attention from family members, and low levels of family activity. Living in a single-parent family was related to positive age discordance (for females) and lower age at first sex (for males).

Family problems. Family problems, characterized by alcohol use in the household, were related to age discordance in first sexual experience. Strict parental discipline and oversight were related to higher age at first sex.

Peers. For males, earlier age at first sex was related to engagement in negative activities with male peers. That is, male youth who were initiated into sex at an early age were more likely to engage, with peers, in high levels of smoking, alcohol use, and visiting commercial sex workers.

School. Both age discordance and early age at first sex were related to school difficulties (e.g., suspension, expulsion) and negative school experiences.

Developing a New and Expanded Model

Large data sets can be used to identify new domains, factors, and variables that can form the basis for a new formative theoretical model that can take the researcher "back to the field" to conduct additional ethnographic research.

SECONDARY/ARCHIVAL QUALITATIVE DATA

As yet, there are few instances where ethnographers have shared or developed a common set of fieldnotes. Most ethnographers, still, do not prepare their fieldnotes for other researchers to use. Ethnographers see their text data (observations and informal interviews) as a personal record of their field experience and usually do not write fieldnotes for a wider audience. Their notes may vary in quality and completeness, and ensuring confidentiality can be a problem because descriptions of people and places are usually quite detailed, enabling other readers to identify them if special precautions are not taken. Finally, personal fieldnotes may not be coded systematically.

 Cross Reference: See Book 5, Chapter 6, on coding and computer management of text data

This pattern is changing with the increasing use of computer-based text coding, management, and search programs. Schensul, Weeks, and Singer have described several examples of such exchanges among members of ethnographic research teams in Book 6. These examples reflect ethnography conducted on comparable topics by overlapping teams of researchers in the same general field site. They involve practices such as assigning code numbers or unique identifiers to key informants and locations, and developing a common coding system and codebook with unique codes assigned to subprojects. Researchers on any of the participating ethnographic study teams receive copies of all of the coded fieldnotes from any of the studies and can recode them for their own purposes without tampering with the common coded data set. Members of the research team who wish to use fieldnotes for a publication invite those ethnographers who collected the data to join them as co-authors. These data sets are formatted so that they can be stored and used eventually as secondary qualitative data sets.

Cross Reference: See Book 6, Chapter 2, on building research partnerships and data sharing

With properly defined coding categories (conceptual taxonomies) available to them, researchers new to these data sets could then choose to recode the fieldnotes from the perspective of their specific interests. Secondary data analysts could work directly with the author of the notes or independently as long as the author's contribution was fully acknowledged.

The technological advances necessary to prepare text data for broader public use are available. To date, there have been few discussions of the ethical aspects of sharing fieldnotes or the effect of making fieldnotes public on the quality and substance of the fieldnotes. These topics remain to be addressed. In the meantime, ethnographers depend on qualitative archival resources that consist of already processed data. These are in the form of ethnographies organized into databases.

Three current databases include a large number of descriptive ethnographies. The units of analysis in these databases are named cultural groups further identified as bands, tribes, kingdoms, and other bounded groups. Databases include the following:

- *Atlas of World Cultures*—1,264 ethnographies along with a reduced collection of 862 ethnographies assessed as "well described" (Murdock, 1967)
- *Standard Ethnographic Sample*—containing 285 societies or cultures (Naroll & Sipes, 1973)
- The Human Relations Area Files Sample—the HRAF collection of 360 cultures is the only one of these databases that provides ethnographic text; the others provide only coded text databases (Ember & Ember, 1998)

Cross Reference: See Book 5, Chapter 4, for an example of the HRAF coding system

George Peter Murdock, a leader in cross-cultural research, led a global effort to compile an organized collection of ethnographies at the Yale Institute for Human Relations that has allowed scholars to compare cultures of the world. His subject classification (coding) system has been applied not only to ethnographies but also to numerous other studies on cultural topics. Ember and Ember provide a full description of cross-cultural ethnographic databases, noting that the sources they cite have been available on CD-ROM and the Internet since 1994 (Ember & Ember, 1998). Like reports, these ethnographic materials are useful in the preparation of research models and designs, and in situating the results of local ethnographic research in a global context.

SUMMARY

Ethnographic researchers can make good use of secondary and archival data in developing local theory and situating their studies locally and globally. In this chapter, we have seen that these data can contribute to initial conceptualization and to the substantive data collection of an ethnographic study. They can provide the opportunity to test field-generated hypotheses at the national and international level.

Ethnographic methodology and perspectives have become an important component of international health and development programs because they deliver the localized, socioculturally specific knowledge essential to appropriate implementation. This in-the-field orientation is an aspect of ethnography that gives "voice" to groups that are marginalized, modifies top-down programs, and contributes to a greater balance between the professionals and the community. At the same time, ethnography has been criticized for being too localized, generating data with limited comparability to other settings, and lacking comprehensive theories validated by data collection in cross-national settings. The global and comparative ethnology of the past, some would argue, has given way to a utilitarian ethnography devoid of a search for cross-cultural principles and models.

The use of the newly available large national and international data sets may provide a partial answer to this global ethnographic-ethnological dilemma. Almost every country is now committed to a census, as well as to other surveys that include contraceptive prevalence, family planning, and many other issues. International and bilateral agencies are increasingly promoting the development and use of comparable survey instruments that include core questions and questions tailored to the interests and needs of each participating country.

This approach calls for ethnographers to use the scientific literature and locally conducted ethnographic research to generate hypotheses for testing by analyzing large secondary or archival data sources. It also requires explaining and interpreting the results of these statistical analyses through the collection of additional qualitative and quantitative data in local field situations. In the future, computer-based text search programs may give us the opportunity to explore and compare large qualitative data sets as well. The interplay between local and global primary, secondary, and archival data can produce the national and international comparisons that build on ethnographic traditions and strengths.

NOTE

1. Here "positive" and "negative" do not refer to concepts of good and bad. They refer to the age of the partner relative to the respondent.

10 ━●━●━●━

ETHNOGRAPHIC SAMPLING

Historically, ethnographers sought to study entire populations. Populations usually are made up of human beings, but they also can constitute communities, organizations, programs, animals, places, things, time periods, documents, words, phrases, sentences or paragraphs in interview texts and transcripts, specific activities or bits of behavior, or any form of unit whatsoever. The populations that ethnographers once studied were conceived of as intact, bounded, and rather small groups, often on islands, in remote villages, or otherwise located in exotic places. Under such conditions, it was not difficult to contact, and to study intensively, every member or unit in a population. However, current ethnographic practice often involves the study of large groups that may be embedded within other groups, organizations, activities, or settings; they may even be scattered over a number of sites. In such cases, studying every single member of a population is not possible, and researchers must engage in **sampling**.

Definition: Sampling is the process of identifying from a large population a smaller group which not ony shares the former's characteristics but is more manageable to study

231

Key point

Researchers study both populations and samples. They study samples when the populations in which they are interested are too large or unwieldy to study, usually because of limitations on resources, time, or personnel available to conduct a larger-scale investigation. Researchers choose samples from larger populations using a number of strategies. The objective of sampling always is to generate a small group that represents as accurately as possible the characteristics of the population. However, some forms of sampling—particularly those using probabilistic methods to choose units from a comprehensive list of the population—guarantee more accuracy in sampling than do others. The list from which a sample is drawn is called a **sampling frame.** Sometimes, researchers cannot create a comprehensive sampling frame because they are unable to identify and enumerate all members of a population; in these cases, other systematic strategies for choosing people or units to study must be employed.

 Definition: A sampling frame is a comprehensive list of all members or units within a population, from which samples are chosen

Definition: Selection is the process of establishing criteria for choice of a research population

While they are deciding upon the population to study, researchers also must consider issues of **selection** and whether or not sampling will be appropriate for the particular phenomenon under study. Selection is a conceptually or theoretically informed process by which researchers become interested in studying a particular issue, phenomenon, or group of people, and then go about establishing a set of criteria for identifying and bounding that issue, phenomenon, or group for an actual research project. As we shall indicate in this chapter, researchers interested in some kinds of topics *should not* use samples. Where populations are very small, sampling is not needed. Where the phenomenon is unknown, sampling is inappropriate. For example, early research into the causes and characteristics of the intellectual disability autism was based on clinical studies of every known case of autism; these were, in turn, analyzed as a body so as to compile some comprehensive description of the disorder. Sampling would have omitted important information about the undescribed ailment contained in unsampled cases. Even when a population's characteristics are known, certain kinds of sampling also are inappropriate. As we will point out, good sampling frames require that every member, or at least all categories of members in a population, be represented; if all categories are not clearly identified, sampling would cause researchers inadvertently to omit important segments of the population. For example, because AIDS was initially identified in the United States as a disease of adult homosexual males, researchers did not investigate whether or not heterosexual males and females could contract it. Furthermore, in the absence of reliable tests for AIDS, researchers missed many infected individuals because of the long period of time between initial infection with HIV and the onset of actual AIDS symptoms.

Many researchers use **convenience samples**, so called because they are selected from any group conveniently accessible to the researcher. Studies of adolescent behavior in general, for example, could be undertaken in the high school nearest to the researcher's office—with the usual cautions that such populations may not be representative of *all* adolescents in a given society. Convenience samples should be used only when the research is exploratory or when specific variations in the population have little effect on the phenomenon under study. For example, a study recently undertaken of how very young children who have not yet learned to read use books in their preschool classrooms (Cumbo, 1998) was conducted with a convenience sample of children in the preschool that the researcher's 4-year-old daughter attended.

Definition: A convenience sample consists of any group readily accessible to the researcher that reasonably might be assumed to possess characteristics relevant to the study

Regardless of whether samples or populations are used, researchers must define the populations and sampling units that they plan to study with precision and in operational terms. This precision is necessary because they must know specifically from which groups to sample, and then they must identify discrete individuals or units from the given population for observation, questioning, interviewing, or counting.

Sometimes, the first steps in selection and sampling involve defining the boundaries of the population or universe to be studied, if these boundaries are not known. For example, initial ethnographic study of commercial sex workers in Sri Lanka revealed three different groups of women working in different settings—those residing and serving in large tourist hotels, those living at home or with friends and working with smaller local inns and residences, and those living on the street and working in more public locations. Together, these three groups constituted the overall population to be sampled for a study of commercial sex work and AIDS risk in an urban area of Sri Lanka. Once the population had been so described, units for analysis and sampling had to be defined. Here are some simple rules for defining units:

Cross Reference: See Book 1, Chapter 5, for a detailed description of how to define, bound, and operationalize units of analysis and sampling units

- They must be countable.
- They must be measurable and observable.
- They must be locatable.
- They must be distinct and distinguishable; that is, the researcher must be able to identify their beginnings and endings and distinguish one unit clearly from others.

In this chapter, we first discuss the ways in which ethnographers locate and select members of a population based upon specific selection criteria, followed by a description of strategies for using probabilistic and random procedures in ethnographic research. We end the chapter with a discussion of requirements for and general cautions about the use of sampling procedures.

APPROACHES TO SELECTION
IN ETHNOGRAPHIC RESEARCH

Ethnographic research involves a search for cultural patterning within a community or group. Researchers know that they have identified ethnographic patterns and structures when they are able to identify similarities or systematic differences in themes, units, and structures over time and across different spaces or groups in a cultural scene. Confirming such variability—or its absence—requires that researchers select for study populations that maximize the chances that they will find the patterns for which they are searching; doing so involves engaging in **criterion-based selection** in the early stages of the research project (see LeCompte & Preissle, 1993, chap. 3, for a more detailed discussion of criterion-based selection and sampling procedures than is possible in this chapter). Researchers use criterion-based selection to choose the population or set of units they want to study. First, they identify their theoretical, conceptual, or topical interests; then, they try to decide what kind of population would best enable them to explore those interests. These decisions are based on criteria establishing how or why the particular population matches with the theoretical or descriptive interests of the researcher, or how the population facilitates answering the research question. For example, researchers interested in studying the degree to which students in a community fail to graduate from high school might decide to study dropouts. However, because dropouts are notoriously difficult to locate, they might need to define a different, but similar and more accessible, population as a substitute, such as potential dropouts.

Definition: Criterion-based selection involves choosing study participants or units because they possess characteristics related to the study's central questions

EXAMPLE 10.1 ➤•➤•➤

STUDYING POTENTIAL DROPOUTS IN PINNACLE

In the study of school failure that LeCompte and her associates conducted for the "Pinnacle" school district, the criteria for selection were all students in Grades 9 through 12 who had failed at least two major subjects (math, language arts, science, or social studies) in the previous semester. Of particular interest were those students who had failed three or more such classes. The researchers used this criterion for selection, reasoning that students who had already dropped out of school would be difficult to find for interviews without extensive, and expensive, fieldwork, and that students who had already failed major courses were at risk of falling so far behind that they would not be able to graduate with their peers, a factor that often leads to a decision to drop out of school.

LeCompte decided to study potential, rather than actual, dropouts. A sampling frame for potential dropouts was available because the school district had records of every student who matched the criterion that LeCompte established: failure in at least two major subjects. *It is important*

Key point *to remember that criterion-based selection strategies do not use probabilistic techniques to generate groups for study; therefore, criterion-based selection does not create random samples or permit researchers to generalize their results to larger populations without further research or careful comparisons (see discussion of "comparable case selection," below) among results from other studies.*

The most common approaches to criterion-based selection are the following:

- Extreme or dichotomous case selection
- Typical case selection
- Intensive case finding
- Unique case selection
- Reputational case selection and chain referral selection
- Bellwether or ideal case selection

- Comparable case selection (LeCompte & Preissle, 1993)
- Targeted selection

Regardless of the type of criterion-based selection used, researchers should, whenever possible, select more than one person, activity, item, or unit to study, and then explore the same issues with each. This is because the experiences or characteristics of one person or unit are not enough to establish a *pattern* of experiences or characteristics of a whole population of similar units or people. The purpose of ethnography is, after all, to confirm patterns, establish the existence of variability, and then map the range of variability within the group under study. Lack of variability confirms the existence of patterns; variability calls for further and more systematic ethnographic exploration of the range of variation.

Selection to Determine Population Differences

The first four criterion-based selection procedures—extreme or dichotomous, typical, intensive, and unique case selection—are used when researchers want to explore specific kinds of variation in a group, or to determine differences among members in a population of interest.

Extreme or dichotomous case selection. **Extreme or dichotomous case selection** requires that researchers first define a characteristic that interests them and then create a scale or continuum by which individual members of a population can be arrayed in accordance with how much of that characteristic they possess—from little or none to the highest level of that characteristic. For example, if measured by grades, a continuum of academic performance of high school students would range from all Fs to all As. If qualitative measures were used, researchers could ask teachers to array students along a continuum from those they believed

Definition: Extreme cases are those representing the ends of a defined population continuum

to be the worst students to those they thought to be the best. Extreme cases are those members or units in a population that are most highly saturated with, or have the highest proportion of, the characteristics the researcher wants to study. Examples of extreme cases include geniuses, musical child prodigies, Nobel prize winners, or psychopaths, each of which is saturated with intelligence, creativity, or mental illness, respectively. Whereas extreme case selection usually involves only those individuals at one end of the continuum, dichotomous case selection requires selecting individuals from both ends of a continuum. For example, a study of the social relationships of young women from households at the highest and lowest socioeconomic levels (i.e., both ends of a socioeconomic continuum) in Mauritius is a dichotomous case study.

Typical case selection. In contrast to extreme case selection, typical case selection is used when researchers want to study average people or units. Researchers first must determine what the average or mean characteristics of a population are and then locate individuals for study who have the same characteristics as that average. Typical case selection of teachers in the United States, for example, would involve selecting married women of European-American ancestry and middle-class origins betwen the ages of 32 and 50, because statistics indicate that these descriptors characterize the average North American teacher.

Definition: Typical case selection involves selection based on a known average for the population

Intensive case selection based on high-density locations. Intensive case selection using a geographic approach is based on the assumption that people who behave in similar ways tend to live, work, or relax together. Thus, they can be most easily found in the geographic areas where these activities take place. Intensive case selection can be used to explore any cultural domain in which behaviors and geographic location overlap. The sites themselves can be considered units of observation and analysis if behavior conducted in them is the topic of study. Ethnographers studying youth culture, for example, can find—and recruit among—African American high school youth (a population of interest) on basketball courts (a behavior identified with the population) in local parks (a geographic location where the behavior occurs). Identifying lower-income, urban women residents (a population of interest) is easier if recruitment occurs at banks (locations or sites where behaviors in which the population is known to engage occurs) where women cash their welfare checks (behaviors in which the population engages) or in public clinic waiting rooms where they wait to have their children seen by doctors (a behavior in which the population engages) or receive nutritional supplements (another behavior in which the population engages). This approach can be applied to any area of research in which individuals are involved in activities in geographically designated public or semipublic areas, including street corners, playgrounds, shopping malls, sports events, empty lots, lunchrooms, bus stops, taxi stands, dance clubs, or McDonald's restaurants, from which people can be recruited for interviewing purposes. *Although such procedures are used all the time, ethnographers should note, however, that operating on the basis of assumptions about the population that may be stereotypic ("All African-American male youth play basketball" or "All low-income women are on welfare or make use of public clinics") risks missing segments of the population that do not engage in such behaviors and therefore do not frequent the locations in which the ethnographer chooses to recruit.*

Key point

Unique case selection. In contrast to typical case selection, which identifies those activities, events, or individuals *most* common within a population, **unique case selection** seeks the *least* common: cases or events that are set apart from the normal flow of events or not amenable to repetition. Natu-

Definition:
Unique case selection means selecting for study a nonreplicable person, event, or situation

ral disasters, such as volcanic eruptions or hurricanes, are such unique events, as is the unexpected influx of immigrants to a community. For example, a unique case with significant impact on educational systems occurred when schools in a small community near Denver, Colorado, experienced sudden increases in their Cambodian immigrant enrollment. Cambodian families choose to live near one another, and when the large apartment complex in which the majority of Cambodians in Denver lived was closed, the entire community moved, as a group, to another apartment complex in the nearby community. This meant that the bilingual education classes for Cambodians in Denver suddenly had no students, whereas the smaller community had to accommodate a large number of students for which district officials were unprepared.

Selection That Is Used to Further Explore Research Questions

Other kinds of criterion-based selection can be used to explore either the degree to which cultural patterns or themes exist in a more generalized population, or the conditions under which a particular innovation or intervention can be successful. These forms include the following:

- Reputational case selection[1]
- Chain referral selection
- Bellwether case selection

Definition: Reputational selection involves asking experts from, or participants in, the community who are familiar with the criteria of interest to the researcher to recommend individuals for participation in the study

Reputational case selection. **Reputational case selection** requires that researchers get help from community experts to identify suitable people or units to study. Researchers first must decide what kind of individual or units they want to study. Then, they ask community experts to name others who—because of their reputations—are known to be the best examples of the kind of people the researchers want to study. For example, researchers might ask hospital administrators to identify the most competent administrators in the medical establishment of a community. Similarly, automobile dealers and mechanics can be asked to identify expert mechanics. Study populations of trustworthy drug dealers (identified by drug users and other dealers), talented music students (identified by music teachers), and uncooperative patients with mental illnesses (identified by doctors and staff in their care facility) can be identified in the same way.

Chain referral selection. Chain referral selection is similar to reputational case selection. In **chain referral selection** (Diaz, Barruti, & Doncel, 1992), each initial study participant suggests to the researcher the next person or set of people to be contacted, based on a set of criteria the researcher has established in advance. Starting points or **index respondents** for a chain of referrals are selected on the basis of their conformity with known criteria. They are interviewed and then asked to identify other people they know who also fit these criteria—for example, they are the same age, engage in similar behaviors (they play a musical instrument or are football fans), or share a characteristic (they are all high school dropouts). The people whom the index person names are then interviewed. This means that all of the people in the study population not only share at least one or several characteristics important to the study, but they also are linked to the index person in an association that can be characterized ethnographically, or in terms of other shared cultural characteristics.

Chain referral is particularly useful in studies of hidden populations. It has been used to study drug subcultures, such as cocaine users in the Netherlands (Bieleman, Diaz, Merlo, & Kaplan, 1993); users of multiple drugs in Mexico (Medina-Mora, Ortiz, Caudillo, & López, 1982); injection drug users in Hartford, Connecticut; youth networks in

Definition: Chain referral selection asks participants in an activity or people who possess specific characteristics to identify others known to them who share those activities or characteristics

Definition: Index respondents are individuals who fit the criteria for the study and whom the researcher first asks to generate other names for a study population

Cross Reference: See Book 4, Chapter 3, on conducting research with hidden populations

Atlanta and Puerto Rico; and gang members in a variety of locations (Moore, 1991).

EXAMPLE 10.2 ━●━●━

USING A CHAIN REFERRAL APPROACH TO SAMPLE
HARD-TO-FIND YOUTHFUL SUBSTANCE ABUSERS

Researchers in Hartford, Connecticut were unable to identify the universe or population of high-risk young drug users because they did not attend school or after-school programs, and they were irregularly employed. In addition, researchers had no way of knowing how many young adults in Hartford were between the ages of 16 and 24, and how many fit the criteria for the study: that they were regular users of either alcohol or marijuana and were experimenting with at least one other drug. The researchers developed a targeted sampling plan in which they identified a certain number of index individuals in each of six neighborhoods (see our discussion of targeted sampling later in this chapter). These individuals were then asked to list all of the people close to them to whom they turn for social, emotional, and financial support, and with whom they had ingested drugs or engaged in sexual activity over the past 6 months. All of the individuals mentioned by the index people who fit the criteria for the study were interviewed. The index person was asked to help bring the study individuals to the researcher and was offered a financial incentive to do so—a strategy that the researchers had used successfully in other Hartford-based drug and HIV/AIDS studies.

━●━●━

Procedures for chain referral selection involve interviewing the individuals named by index respondents with the same questions asked of the index respondents themselves. These individuals are asked to name others in their social network in the same manner to be interviewed with the same instrument. As with any nonrandom selection procedure, chain referral selection is likely to ensure that the group selected for study is saturated with the characteristics that the researcher wants to study, but the degree to which the individuals interviewed represent any particular population other than themselves is difficult to ascertain in the absence of other kinds of corroboratory data. One way to address this problem is to compare results obtained from chain referral procedures with other data obtained with the same or similar populations (see our discussion of comparable case selection, below).

Chain referral selection can be used in network research to identify clusters of people engaged in similar activities and to determine how information or specific behaviors are diffused through networks. As Robert Trotter's contribution to the **Ethnographer's Toolkit** demonstrates, this information is useful for both intervention and descriptive purposes.

Chain referral can be combined with randomized sampling techniques (see the discussion of probabilistic sampling techniques later in this chapter) to increase the generalizability of the study's results to other populations or groups. For example, if the index people name more contacts or "alters" who possess the appropriate characteristics for inclusion in the study than an ethnographer has resources to study, several of them may be chosen using randomized techniques for more intensive investigation. In such a case, the ethnographer could have reasonable confidence that information obtained from the randomly selected sample also would characterize all of the index person's named contacts—whether or not they were included in the study.

Bellwether or ideal case selection. **Ideal cases** are what Wolf (1999) calls "no wonder!!" cases. For example, Borko and Peressini (personal communication, 1998), who study innovative mathematics programs, have selected for their research schools where teachers have the best training and facilities, and administrators are the most supportive of the innovations. Under these conditions, success of the programs is "no wonder"; in fact, the only "wonder" would be if the programs actually failed, contrary to expectations.

Cross Reference: See Book 4, Chapter 1, for a discussion of network research

Definition: Bellwether or ideal cases are those in which the optimum conditions for observing what the researcher wants to study are found

Cross Reference: See Book 1 for a discussion of the conditions required for conducting experimental and quasi-experimental research

Bellwether or ideal case selection is especially good for examining the effects of an intervention—once initial field-work has determined an appropriate strategy for that inter-vention—because it most closely simulates the controlled laboratory conditions instituted in experimental research. Although ethnographic research cannot control what oc-curs in natural settings, ideal case selection tries to control contamination of an intervention's results by selecting for study a case in which problems are not expected to occur.

Cross Reference: See Book 1, Chapter 4, for more information on experimental research designs

Selection to Describe Variation or Patterns Across Multiple Cases or Sites, or to Approach Representativeness

Definition: Comparable cases are those selected because each exemplifies as closely as possible specific characteristics of interest to the research

Comparable case selection. Ethnographers usually cannot set up experimental conditions that permit them to estab-lish multiple—and exactly identical—cases in which to study specific activities, events, or people. However, they *can* look for multiple—and quite similar—cases in which they can study the degree to which structures, patterns, or themes in which they are interested are stable or even exist across multiple settings or people. Sometimes, the cases can be matched quite closely, particularly when the cases to be studied are individuals or identical innovative programs.

During their professional lifetimes, researchers often choose to study a single kind of phenomenon over time, with different populations, and in varied settings. These studies can be termed comparable case studies if their results are systematically compared. Similarly, a researcher may choose a site primarily because it is similar—or com-parable—to one that he or she, or another researcher, had studied previously and because the researcher wishes to explore the topic of the first study in more detail or in different ways. Multiple site ethnographies also are consid-ered to be comparable case studies; in such studies, one or a group of researchers attempts to study the same phenomenon simultaneously in similar settings—or at least to make clear what the differences among settings are, to the extent that they are dissimilar. LeCompte's (1974, 1978) "Learning to Work" study, described in Books 1 and 5, is such a study. Another early example was the series of ethnographic studies exploring what happened in schools undergoing racial desegregation in the United States during the late 1960s and the 1970s. These studies, under the direction of an anthropologist, Murray Wax, all focused on the same phenomenon: the impact of racial desegregation on patterns of social interaction and conflict among teachers and students and within communities. They used similar research strategies and asked similar research questions. However, although most were conducted in high schools, each study was conducted by a different researcher, and the sites differed widely; they even were in different regions of the country, a factor that considerably affected the context for interracial conflict (Holland, Eisenhart, & Harding, 1976; Schofield, 1982; Wax, 1979).

In other instances, ethnographers can conduct an ethnology, or a secondary analysis of separate ethnographic studies, done in different sites, by different ethnographers, or even at different time periods. In such cases, the data sought are reports of studies that address a topic of interest to the researcher but do so in slightly different ways, with slightly different populations, or under somewhat different circumstances. The task of the ethnographer, then, is to analyze the impact of these differences on the subject under investigation. The process is analogous to a series of controlled experiments in which the researcher varies a different factor in the experiment each time it is performed so as to assess varied influences on the results. This process is sometimes termed a meta-analysis.

Quota sampling. Quota sampling is not probabilistic, but it does attempt to select representatives from all known sectors or categories within a population. It requires that either the major characteristics of the population or the population characteristics salient to the research question be identified. Researchers then select a certain number—or quota—of individuals representing each of these characteristics for their study. For example, because researchers interested in voting behavior know that gender, ethnicity, age, educational level, and income affect how people vote, they generally select for study people who represent all combinations of those five variables. Similarly, researchers seeking to explore the variation within a population need to include representatives—or quotas—from all relevant segments of that population in their sample.

Quota sampling is particularly useful in the early stages of research because it can help researchers identify the full range of behavior, attitudes, and opinions within a population without having to elicit information from every single member. For this reason, it is an appropriate strategy for identifying people to participate in focus groups and in the semistructured interviews that are a precursor to developing an ethnographic survey.

Cross Reference:
See Book 3, Chapter 2, on focused group interviews

EXAMPLE 10.3 ━━●━━●━━

USING QUOTA SAMPLING TO STUDY SEXUAL RISK BEHAVIORS IN MAURITIUS

Quota sampling was used in Mauritius to define the range of variation in life histories and sexual risk behaviors. The researchers hypothesized that sexual risk varied by ethnicity and gender. In selecting respondents for semistructured interviewing, the following selection frame was used:

Cross Reference:
See Chapter 7, in this book, for more discussion of the role of quota sampling in semistructured interviewing

Ethnicity	Male	Female
Hindu	10	30
Muslim	10	30
Christian/Creole	10	30

━━●━━●━━

Quota sampling is not a very accurate way to represent the percentages of demographic or attitudinal characteristics of a group, but it is a very important strategy for capturing the range of cultural variation.

If the population is known to be skewed, so that some groups are considerably larger than others, the quotas can be "weighted"; this means that researchers might select a larger quota from those specific categories within the population that have more members. Alternatively, if some segments of the population are considered to be more relevant to the research question than others, then overselecting might be done for those groups to recruit more study participants from them and ensure that the researchers fully understand the parameters or dynamics of those groups.

Targeted selection. Targeted selection is a strategy that allows researchers to approximate a process of selecting from an entire universe of units or people, even when the size or characteristics of the universe itself are unknown. In this way, it, like quota sampling (see above), begins to approximate the precision of probabilistic sampling, which we discuss later in this chapter. Targeted sampling is possible only when researchers have access to multiple sources of secondary data describing the population of interest; these help to ensure that the major divisions or categories of the study population can be identified and members selected systematically from each (Watters & Biernacki, 1989). Secondary data sources usually include such information as crime rates; arrests for reasons relevant to the research topic; information about buildings and residences (e.g., abandoned or boarded-up buildings, or those scheduled for demolition, any of which could be geographic locations useful for recruiting participants in urban drug use studies); police records; health and social service data; ethnographic observations; behavioral monitoring data; or any other information relevant to the study. Once these data are

Definition: Targeted selection uses multiple sources of data to identify high-priority areas from which a group of study units can be selected

Cross Reference: See Book 4, Singer's chapter on hidden populations, and this book, Chapter 9 for further discussion of the uses of multiple sources of data for targeted sampling purposes

available, they are triangulated to create geographically based targeted sampling areas.

EXAMPLE 10.4   ━●◆●━●◆━

TARGETED SELECTION OF INJECTION DRUG USERS

Based on estimates from the Hartford City Health Department, somewhere between 7,000 and 12,000 injection drug users reside in the city of Hartford, Connecticut. Because many are homeless, residing with friends, moving from house to house of family members or friends, living in shelters, or living on the streets, these people are difficult to locate and cannot be enumerated. For research purposes, the universe of this population is unknown. Street outreach programs and ethnographic research, however, suggested that such people, however many there were, would be concentrated in several neighborhoods of the city.

Because the city of Hartford collects data on arrests of drug users, drug sellers, and prostitutes; types of crimes (e.g., muggings, prostitution, burglaries, car thefts); housing conditions; child abuse referrals; infant mortality; and a variety of other issues, these data could be aggregated and defined as measures of "exposure to risk." Working together, and with the help of city agencies, the Institute for Community Research and the Hispanic Health Council aggregated, organized, and mapped these risk exposure data by neighborhoods characterized by high, moderate, and low levels of risk exposure. Highest-risk neighborhoods were then targeted as locations where participants for an intervention study could be recruited and enrolled. Such a system of ranking neighborhoods by levels of risk exposure also permitted the researchers to do weighted quota sampling for each risk category.

━●◆●━●◆━

APPROACHES TO SAMPLING
IN ETHNOGRAPHIC RESEARCH

Up to now, we have been discussing procedures for selecting participants for study from populations defined on the basis of specific criteria of interest to the researcher. Ethnographers initially use unstructured and semistructured observations and interviews with criterion-based groups to explore initial research questions and narrow the focus of their studies.

Once they have studied these smaller groups in depth, they then determine whether or not what they found with the small groups also pertains to the entire population. For this purpose, ethnographic surveys (discussed earlier in this chapter) using probabilistically selected samples are necessary. As we noted at the beginning of this chapter, samples are small groups taken from a larger group; probabilistic or semiprobabilistic sampling procedures are designed to ensure that the characteristics of the small group very closely match those of the larger group that it is to represent.

Probabilistic samples must be constructed very carefully, because their purpose is to represent more conveniently a larger universe of units or members. If they are not representative, researchers cannot make **generalizations** about the population as a whole with any degree of confidence. Researchers might want to make some statements about all three-wheel drivers in the capital city of Sri Lanka based on what they learned about such drivers recruited for their sample. As we shall indicate later in this chapter and in Chapter 11, if their sample were poorly constructed, it could lead to inaccurate generalizations, as well as to research whose results are invalid.

Definition: Generalization is the process of making inferences about a larger population based on research results obtained from a sample

Several of the approaches we have described as criterion-based selection are not based on statistical probability; rather, they are concerned with other ways of achieving representation or ability to represent the entire population. Targeted sampling and certain types of chain referral selection are efforts to approximate probability or statistical sampling. They are used when it is not possible to meet all of the conditions of probability sampling as described below.

The Forms of Probabilistic Sampling

Social science researchers use two kinds of probabilistic sampling: systematic sampling and random sampling. There are many texts that give elaborate details on procedures for sampling; we have listed them as additional resources at the end of this chapter. Here, we simply describe briefly the most common procedures.

Systematic sampling. Systematic sampling is the most commonly used kind of sampling because its requirements are not as stringent and more often can be met in field research conditions.

How to Create a Systematic Sample

To create a systematic sample, researchers first decide *what* they want to sample and then determine *how many* such units will be necessary for the study. For example, researchers interested in the smoking behavior of college students might select a nearby college and determine that they can administer surveys to half of the student body of 662 students. They then create an appropriate *sampling interval,* or "*n*," calculated by dividing the actual or estimated population size by the desired sample size. Since the smoking study will sample half of the students, the sampling interval is 2. Researchers then select every "*n*th" (or second) member from a list of the entire population for their sample. In the smoking study, researchers could use a directory that lists all of the students' names, choosing for their sample every second student on the list. If they surveyed 25% of the students, their sampling interval would be 4, and they would choose every fourth student on the list.

Systematic sampling does not require that every single unit to be sampled be identified in advance and placed on a list. In fact, most systematic studies of naturally occurring behavior such as social interactions—which cannot be enumerated and listed—use systematic sampling. Researchers studying three-wheel drivers in Sri Lanka, for example, might decide upon a sampling interval of 5 minutes for their observations at stops and stands, recording every 5 minutes whatever behaviors occur. In a more structured fashion, researchers studying instruction in a theater arts program could, for example, decide to focus on the speeches or lines that students deliver in their practice sessions. Knowing that practice sessions occur not only in formal classes but also in small classroom groups, the hallways, and even on the the playground, the researchers could follow a group of theater students for a week, videotaping their interactions throughout the school day. Reviewing the videotapes, they then could use a sampling interval of 3 to record every third instance of a speech or line delivery.

A limitation of systematic sampling is that sampling intervals arbitrarily ignore any confounding variation or fluctuation in the population or research context. For example, if the college population described above included a large number of students from Vietnam, where very common names are Ngoc and Nguyen, sampling every second student name from an alphabetical list of surnames might result in an overrepresentation of Vietnamese, whose smoking behavior could differ from students from other ethnic groups. If the week that researchers chose for videotaping theater students occurred just before a major theatrical production at the school—so that students were practicing intensely for their performances—or if they chose to follow students who were most active as performers, rather than as stage crew or set designers, they would be more likely to observe line delivery than if they had chosen a more normal week or a more varied group of students.

Cross Reference: See Book 3, Chapter 1, for systematic sampling in the audiovisual recording of ethnographic observations

Random sampling. Random sampling is the most commonly mentioned and best understood form of probablistic sampling, although it is not the most commonly used. Simple random sampling requires that

- The characteristics of the entire population be known in advance
- Every member or unit in the population be identified and placed on a numbered list from the first member to the last
- Each member or unit in the population be available to the researcher for study

These requirements exist because simple random sampling ensures that each member of the population has the same chance as any other member to be included in the sample; thus, researchers using such sampling procedures can be certain that their samples exactly replicate the characteristics of the population from which they are drawn. Simple random samples, then, enable researchers to make valid generalizations about populations because no underlying irregularities or factors (as described above for systematic sampling) confound the degree to which samples match populations.

How to Construct a Simple Random Sample

To construct a simple random sample, researchers first decide upon the size of the sample they need, and they select a sampling interval that, when it divides the population, will generate the desired number of people for the sample. Then, they obtain a table of random numbers, available from computer programs or in statistics textbooks, and choose a number at random from it. The researchers begin sampling by finding the number in their population list that corresponds to the number chosen from the random number table. They then use their sampling interval to choose subsequent numbers from the random number table. Selecting random numbers involves counting down the column of random numbers by the sampling interval—by 2, in the case of the college students. They select for their sample those members of the population whose numbers on the list match the random numbers selected from the random number table. The numbers in random number tables usually contain far more digits than the size of the researchers' population, so researchers must first note the number of digits in the total size of the population (three, in the case of the 662 students enrolled in the college described above); they use only the three right-hand digits of each random number. For example, if the first number in the table chosen were 29384132, the researchers would divide it into 29384 and 132; the first person selected for their sample would be Person #132. This whole process can be simplified by using a computer program to select a population using a program that applies a random number table to a list read into the computer—if such a program is available to the researchers.

Variations on Simple Random and Systematic Sampling

If the populations in which researchers are interested contain distinct subgroups or are clustered in specific groups, researchers may decide to use variations of random or systematic sampling. These sampling procedures are called *stratified sampling* and *cluster sampling*.

Stratified sampling. **Stratified sampling** involves identifying significant segments or groups within a population and then sampling separately from each segment. Studies of the

 Definition: Stratified sampling involves sampling separately from each previously identified segment of a population

sexual attitudes of urban, suburban, and rural boys and girls, for example, could be done with a stratified sample in which separate lists of urban, suburban, and rural boys and girls were created, and then systematic or random samples drawn separately from each. *Stratified sampling facilitates comparisons; it also ensures balanced representation in the sample of segments within the population.* Stratified sampling is particularly useful when some population segments are much larger than others. For example, Native Americans constitute a tiny percentage of public school enrollments in the United States; they tend to be missed by ordinary systematic or random sampling procedures. Researchers who really want to include Native American schoolchildren in their samples use stratified sampling procedures; often, they will weight their samples so that a larger percentage of Native American students is included than of other ethnic groups, just to make sure that this very small but very diverse group is represented adequately.

Key point

Cluster sampling. **Cluster sampling** involves identifying the natural groups or settings in which a population can be found, listing the groups or settings, and sampling these groups or settings, rather than sampling a list of individuals. The units of analysis, then, become all of the individuals found within the specific clusters in the sample. Cluster sampling is especially useful for populations whose groupings are stable, such as children in *classrooms,* households in *neighborhoods,* or patients in *residential treatment facilities.* Researchers can create a sample of classrooms, neighborhoods, or treatment facilities and then study all students, residents, or patients in the selected units.

Definition: Cluster sampling involves identifying and sampling from natural groups or settings rather than individuals

USING A STRATIFIED CLUSTER SAMPLING DESIGN TO STUDY COMPLIANCE WITH REQUIREMENTS FOR IDENTIFYING LANGUAGE MINORITY STUDENTS

In 1984, LeCompte and her staff at the Houston Public School District were required to monitor whether or not teachers were properly testing and screening Latino and immigrant students for services to students who did not yet speak English. LeCompte's staff suggested examining the records of a simple random sample of all 232,000 students in the school district. This procedure was feasible because the school district maintained a comprehensive list of all students and their addresses. However, only 35% of the students in the district were potential language minority students; sampling the remaining 65% of the enrollment would have wasted resources and not answered the research question. Furthermore, language minority students tended to be clustered in specific neighborhoods. Therefore, LeCompte designed a stratified cluster sampling procedure in which the district's schools were divided into two strata: schools whose enrollments had more than 50% Latino and immigrant students, and schools whose enrollments had fewer than 50% Latino and immigrant students. Her staff selected a 50% sample of the schools whose enrollments were more than half Latino and immigrant, reasoning that these were the schools where, if problems in screening existed, the greatest number of students would be excluded from needed instruction. They then examined a 20% systematic sample of student folders by selecting every fifth student folder, to determine if children at those schools had been properly tested and assigned to appropriate instruction.

━●━●━●

The procedure just described maximized the *saturation* of the sample; that is, it focused on schools in which the largest percentage of target students were likely to be found. It also permitted the researchers to make valid generalizations about practices in those schools most heavily affected by Latino immigration. LeCompte decided to concentrate efforts in those schools, saving schools where fewer students might be at risk for later monitoring when more resources for research were available.

EXAMPLE 10.6 ➤•➤•➤

SAMPLING THREE-WHEEL[2] DRIVERS IN SRI LANKA

In Sri Lanka as well as in other Southeast Asian locations, the three-wheeled vehicles that drivers use are a major source of public transportation. The vehicles and their drivers provide an important link in the commercial sex trade, maintaining connections between commercial sex workers, their clients, and the locations in which sexual exchanges take place. Three-wheel drivers must register their vehicles with the municipality, at which point they are assigned to "stops"—locations where they can park their vehicles and wait for customers. The stop locations are known, and even though the registration lists are not up to date, every three-wheel driver must register, and every driver is assigned to a stop. The lists provide a general idea of large, medium-sized, and smaller stops, but a complete list of drivers at each stop can be obtained only through enumeration at that stop.

In a study of sexual risk among drivers of three-wheeled vehicles, a team of Sri Lankan and North American researchers mapped the locations of three-wheel driver stops. Ethnographic interviews with the drivers enabled the researchers to differentiate stops by size and by estimated proportion of drivers engaged in the sex trade. Based on these stratification criteria, a sample of stops was chosen for more in-depth exploration and formal enumeration of the three-wheel drivers assigned to the stop. A random sample of drivers stratified by age was then chosen for ethnographic surveying.

Cross-Sectional, Trend, Cohort, and Panel Studies

Most samples are constructed for cross-sectional studies. These are studies that take place at one point in time, and whose results apply only to that time period. Sometimes, however, researchers want to look at events or phenomena longitudinally, or over time. For these purposes, trend, cohort, or panel studies are useful, although they are more expensive, can be difficult to execute, and may require considerable follow-up.

Trend studies. Trend studies are the simplest to implement; in them, a researcher simply replicates a study several times over a designated period of time. LeCompte, for example, could have monitored the same set of schools every year for 5 years to see whether or not compliance practices changed over time. Trend studies have weaknesses, however, because conditions within the settings sampled, and even the people within those settings, will change over time. For example, the influx of immigrants and Latinos to many of the schools sampled could have ceased. This would make compliance data districtwide inaccurate, because the most heavily affected schools no longer fell into the sampling frame.

Cohort studies. Cohort studies eliminate some of these difficulties. Cohort studies define the population of interest and then study groups with those characteristics at designated intervals over time. LeCompte could have designated "schools in which more than 50% of the enrolled children were Latino or immigrants" to be the sampling frame of interest, and then selected for study each year only those schools in the district with more than 50% Latino or immigrant enrollment, whether or not they were in the original study. Cohort studies permit distinctions between historical influences and ordinary life-cycle or developmental influences, but, like trend studies, they suffer from the disadvantage that settings and populations again can differ over time from the original settings and populations.

Cross Reference: See Book 1, Chapter 4, for a discussion of different types of quantitative research designs

Panel studies. Panel studies eliminate all of these disadvantages. Panel studies select a specific sample or group of people or units and then follow the same group over time. If LeCompte had instituted a panel study, she would have followed for successive monitoring only the students whose folders were examined in the first study. Doing so would mean that she would have had to locate these students each year, regardless of whether they had transferred to different schools within the district (a not insurmountable problem) or moved away from Houston (a serious logistical problem, indeed!). In addition, panel studies suffer from attrition; panel members move away, die, or refuse to continue participation, thus changing the composition of the sample in ways that the researcher must explain. Panel studies are particularly useful for studies of illness, health, and educational attainment. Panel studies, for example, determined that the percentage of people ever completing a high school education in the United States was much higher than data from high schools indicated, because only by following people over time could it be determined that many people completed their high school degrees through informal means or in adult education programs decades after they left high school. Studies of the progression of HIV/AIDS and treatment of patients with heart disease also have been greatly facilitated by using panel designs.

REQUIREMENTS FOR AND CAUTIONS ABOUT THE USE OF SAMPLES

What Researchers Need in Order to Draw a Sample

- A precise definition of the population and sampling units
- Familiarity with the community or research setting
- Knowledge of the population's characteristics

A Precise Definition of the Population and Sampling Units

Definition, itemization, and enumeration of the population are critical to any form of probabilistic sampling, especially in exploratory or ethnographic surveying, where the universe or population is known but the individual units or members have not been itemized or listed for purposes of sample selection. In some settings—for example, schools, public housing projects, clinics, or labor unions—a complete listing of membership is available. In many cases, however, such lists do not exist. Researchers must create them by identifying all members of the population and then counting them.

Enumeration involves visiting, or observing and listing, each unit or member of a population. In a demographic study of neighborhoods in Hartford, Connecticut, for example, staff of five community-based organizations enumerated every residential unit on a set of city blocks randomly selected from sets of blocks ranked by density of population in each one of 13 residential neighborhoods. The enumeration involved visiting each building and residential unit on the designated blocks to determine whether it was occupied; how many people lived in it; and what their self-identified, primary ethnic/racial category was. On the basis of this enumeration procedure, a random sample (see our discussion of random sampling later in this chapter) of residences on each designated block was chosen. The previously mentioned study of three-wheel drivers in Sri Lanka involved enumerating three-wheel drivers at a random sample of stops or stands, categorized or stratified by size and their level of involvement in the sex trade, which in turn was determined by previous ethnographic observation and interviews.

Locating people or units so they can be listed, however, assumes that they are part of a known or defined and locatable population. As we have pointed out, it may be impossible to establish a precise population of naturally occurring behavior, or to create precise definitions of unknown, hidden, or hard-to-reach populations. For this reason, ethnographic researchers attempt to approximate precision by imposing on the study group a set of researcher-defined geographic boundaries and inclusion/exclusion criteria.

By researcher-defined geographic boundaries, we mean that the researcher designates as members of the target group those who live, or on specified occasions are found, within specified borders of place or time. For example, the population of three-wheel drivers was defined as those who frequented specified stops or stands; the population of village-level nurses investigated by researcher Ramachandar (see Chapter 5) included all village-level nurses within a particular region; the population studied by the theater arts researchers was defined as all performances and line deliveries uttered within a specified week.

By inclusion and exclusion criteria, we mean specific traits, behaviors, or other qualifying features that define the individual as someone of interest to the researcher. In the study of the three-wheel drivers, drivers who had no connection with the sex trade, for example, were not included in the study.

Decisions defining these boundaries are arbitrary, in that they are made by the researchers, but they are not artificial. Rather, they stem from careful prior fieldwork, which generates descriptions of observable behavior, cultural meanings, beliefs, values, expectations, and shared understandings; information about how target group members identify themselves; specific social scenes, including locations, settings, and socially defined occasions and events—all of which mark group activities. The selection strategies described above impose boundaries for purposes of recruiting study participants, but they also retain sufficient flexibility that researchers can change the inclusion rules based on new information. This need for flexibility reflects the constant tension ethnographers experience between the desire for researcher control of all aspects of the research project and the reality of constant confrontations with and feedback from the field.

Familiarity With the Community or Research Setting

Familiarity with the community or research setting is important in helping the researcher determine whether to draw a simple random sample or to stratify the sampling frame so as to appropriately capture the range of variation within the population. It also helps to determine how big the sample should be. For example, if researchers want to collect data from a single ethnic group in a multiethnic neighborhood, a simple random sample will not guarantee that the target group will be included, especially if the target group is very small or segregated. Ethnicity often influences where people live in a neighborhood; a simple random sample of an otherwise multiethnic neighborhood might miss the one block on which the target population resides.

EXAMPLE 10.7

SAMPLING HOUSEHOLD UNITS IN A MULTIETHNIC NEIGHBORHOOD

The Asylum Hill neighborhood in Hartford, Connecticut, is the most diverse of 15 urban neighborhoods, including 14 major ethnic groups. However, analysis of census block clusters shows that the neighborhood as a whole is highly segregated, with Latinos living on some blocks in rental housing, African Americans on other blocks in private and condominium housing. West Indian/Caribbean, African, and European American residents live on still other blocks. To obtain a representative sample of households, researchers had to use a stratified cluster sample, in which a list was created that organized blocks by ethnic distribution and ranked blocks by density of inhabitants. The ranked list was then grouped into blocks with high, medium, and low densities of inhabitants. Household units in these blocks were enumerated, and a random sample of household units weighted by density of block was chosen for face-to-face surveying. Interviewers were told to return up to eight times to be sure to interview every household on the sample list (Berg, 1992).

Knowledge of Population Characteristics:
Problems of Bias and Representativeness

We have already indicated that researchers who sample must take care to make sure that their samples accurately represent the populations from which they are drawn, or, if this is impossible, that researchers account for any lack of representativeness and describe why it exists in the study.

 Definition: Bias is any influence or factor that distorts research results in a particular direction

Lack of representation introduces **bias** into a study. Certain kinds of lack of representativeness in samples are not under the control of researchers. Bias introduced because of sample error, for example, exists simply because samples are not the entire population; each sample drawn from a population will vary slightly, even when the most rigorous mathematical procedures are used in the sampling procedure.

 Definition: Sampling bias exists when sample characteristics do not match population characteristics because some segment of the population was not sampled

Other forms of unrepresentativeness, however, are the responsibility of researchers to minimize. The most important of these is **sampling bias.** Sampling bias is not a major concern in preliminary or exploratory studies that focus on identifying relevant cultural domains and the range of good strategies for such studies. The objective of such research is to reach the *informational saturation point,* that is, the point at which additional data collection, including interviews and observations, produces no new information about cultural domains, subdomains, or factors. This is the point at which "sufficient redundancy" (Trotter & Schensul, 1998) is reached—when patterns of response begin to repeat themselves and generate no new information.

EXAMPLE 10.8

INTERVIEWING AGENCY STAFF ON DRUG USE OF ADOLESCENTS

In a study of transitions in drug use among adolescents from "gateway drugs" (marijuana, alcohol, and cigarettes) to "hard drugs" (cocaine, heroin, and pills), researchers at the Institute for Community Research in Hartford decided to interview some members of the staffs of youth-service agencies in the area. The first person interviewed reported that for the most part, young users were accessing alcohol and marijuana, but as far as he knew, most others used nothing at all. These data did not conform to other sources of information about young drug users, so researchers went on to interview four other front-line youth workers from different parts of the city. They all reported the same information, confirming that use of both alcohol and marijuana was widespread and that young people in the city were not using other drugs. The research staff determined that there was no further need to interview additional agency staff because the same information would be forthcoming. Instead, they decided to interview young people directly about their drug use patterns.

EXAMPLE 10.9

INTERVIEWING FACTORY FLOOR SUPERVISORS ON OPPORTUNITIES FOR SOCIAL INTERACTION BETWEEN UNMARRIED MEN AND WOMEN

Factory floor supervisors are key gatekeepers for researchers desiring to access factory workers in Mauritius, Sri Lanka, and other parts of Southeast Asia. They also are responsible for supervising their workers and monitoring their activities throughout the course of the workday. Researchers in both countries interested in opportunities for engagement between male and female factory workers decided to interview several factory floor supervisors known to be friendly toward workers about the availability of these opportunities. Interviewers made lists of opportunities that included formal social events during the work year, union meetings, lunchrooms, bus stops, and factory courtyards. After several interviews in which no new opportunities were listed, researchers decided that they had interviewed to saturation and were not likely to expand the list by continuing to interview factory floor supervisors.

Saturation, or sufficient redundancy, generates a universe of domains, subdomains, and factors, but it does not tell us about the distribution of information about these domains and subdomains within the varied segments of the population. When researchers want to determine the extent to which particular characteristics; behaviors; and ways of viewing domains, factors, or practices characterize members of the entire population, then it is crucial to achieve representativeness in samples—and that requires elimination of as much sampling bias as possible. Considerations in eliminating sampling bias include the degree to which researchers

- Define the target group precisely for purposes of the research
- Take care to collect data from a broad range of locations
- Eliminate categorical prejudices
- Find those segments of the target group that are hidden
- Ensure the accessibility—or ease of recruiting for participation—of all segments of the population, even if they are not hidden

It is easy to understand how lack of definitional precision regarding the target population could bias sampling; for example, investigations into the HIV/AIDS epidemic missed both women and heterosexual males in their early stages because North American and European researchers did not think such groups were susceptible to the disease and therefore did not include them in studies. Categorical prejudices have the same biasing effect on samples; they are the product of various forms of societal discrimination that affect who is included in, and who is excluded from, research studies. Studies of educational levels in many developing nations often were inflated, for example, because the low educational levels of girls were not reported; since only the education of boys was considered important, girls often were left out of accounting procedures. Similarly, most medical research has been conducted with male populations; researchers have justified this practice on the grounds that "women's physiology is too complex," and used male-only studies as an allegedly simpler, although biased, alternative.

Similarly, sampling bias can result if researchers collect data from limited, rather than a broad range of, locations. Samples drawn from institutionalized populations will not, for example, accurately reflect behaviors of noninstitutionalized individuals. Although annual studies in the United States show that drug use among 12th-grade students is declining, such studies do not include in their samples students of the same age who have dropped out of school, and among whom drug use may be considerably higher. The asthma patients least likely to follow medical instructions for control of their condition are those who do not attend clinics—which are convenient sites in which to recruit participants in studies of illness. Thus, a study of change in asthma-related behaviors that focused on clinic patients would produce results generalizable only to clinic users, not to the entire population of asthma sufferers.

Finally, samples can be biased because they do not include people who are inaccessible, either because they come from segments of the population that are widely dispersed from mainstream segments, because contacting and recruiting them might be dangerous either for them or for the researchers, or because social taboos or customs surround them with obstacles to researcher access. People who have health problems for which they may be socially isolated in some societies (such as tuberculosis, leprosy, or AIDS), or whose sexual preferences are socially stigmatized, fall into this category. Studies of computer use and Internet access among schoolteachers in the United States, for example, tend to suggest high rates of usage; however, most such studies do not include isolated or rural communities. McLennan (1997) found that teachers from very rural schools who participated in a heavily funded—and widely publicized—effort to encourage teachers to use the Internet in their instruction not only did not use the Internet, but without exception, could not get on-line access to the Internet or even to electronic mail at their schools because the schools lacked sufficient equipment, telephone lines, or service providers in the area.

Segments of the population who live in dangerous areas are not likely to be sampled because of the risk to interviewers who must contact them; similarly, Muslim women in *purdah,* who are forbidden to interact with outsiders, particularly men who are not members of their family, will be omitted from samples either because no record of their existence is available or because there is no way to meet with them to elicit information.

How Big Should a Sample Be?

Although we feel that it is far from the most important aspect of research design, among the first questions novice researchers ask is, "How big should my sample be?" This can be a difficult question to answer, especially when the size of the target population is unknown. How many homeless youth, for example, should be interviewed to represent a total population (of unknown size!) of homeless youth in San Francisco? How many preadolescents would be adequate to assess the impact of an arts program on children not identified as artistic or creative (from the entire universe of children not so identified by conventional tests)? The answers to such questions do not lie in simple formulae. Rather, they can be found in explorations of population characteristics, researcher logistics, and objectives of the investigation. Among the things researchers need to consider in selecting an appropriate size for their sample are the following:

- How much variability or diversity exists within the population
- Which kind of statistics the researcher plans to use and what level of significance is sought
- How generous the resources available to the researcher are

One simple rule of thumb is that the sample should be large enough to maximize variability within the group. This means that a sample size of 400 is not only needed to represent variability, but also to perform most common statistical procedures (Bernard, 1995, p. 79). However, as the discussion below indicates, this is far too simple a rubric.

In general, sample size is related to known heterogeneity in the target population: The greater the heterogeneity, the larger the sample needed to be representative of all diversity within the population. If the characteristics of a population are completely unknown, then sampling is inappropriate because it might miss significant components of the population. On the other hand, if the characteristics of the population are completely shared—that is, little or no variability exists in the population, then a single individual would suffice for the study. Such a situation exists hypothetically in the Human Genome Project, because the objective of the project is simply to identify all human genes, and all humans possess the same number and kinds of genes.

Resources also affect sampling. There may be no time, money, or personnel to study a sample of 400 people. In Book 1, we detail how researchers should design their studies around their available resources and in line with logistical, definitional, and conceptual criteria. Logistical criteria pertain to the time, money, distance traveled, and communication processes needed to recruit and track members of a sample. Definitional criteria refer to how the group will be bounded and who will be included in it; for example, eligibility for inclusion in a study measuring the energy expenditures of children may be bounded by age and eth-

Cross Reference: See Book 1, Chapters 4 and 5, for more information about designing research

nicity. However, who is actually included in the sample may be defined by how far the children live from the researcher. Conceptual criteria refer to whether enough members of the target population can actually be found. A study of injection drug users' risk behavior in a small suburban Connecticut town might be important, but it also might be impossible to find a large enough group of drug users in the town to make the study worthwhile—not only because of the town's size, but because social taboos might cause the target population to be hidden. Researchers, and especially ethnographers, must temper their enthusiasm and match their sampling procedures to field realities and the capacities of their time lines and budgets.

Cross Reference: See Chapter 9, in this book, for further information on statistical procedures used in ethnographically informed quantitative research

Finally, researchers need to consider the statistical procedures they plan to use for their analysis. Sometimes, these procedures are mandated by specific funding sources; other times, they are required to answer research questions. In any case, most statistical procedures other than simple descriptive statistics such as percentages, means, modes, and distributions require balance among the units or categories in the population studied as well as a minimum number of cases in each category or cell to be implemented. Researchers should know enough about the characteristics of their sample and of the variables they are using for analytic purposes to be able to select from among statistical procedures.

Arriving at the appropriate representative sample size depends on the charactistics of the population in question, the resources available for accumulating the sample, and the size of the phenomena to be detected (cf. Bernard, 1995, p. 74). Representativeness depends on the probability value (to what extent are your sample statistics incorrect), and the confidence level (how incorrect a sample statistic actually is). Significance at the .01 level with a 10% confidence level means that 99% (100% − .001) of the time, the statistic for the variable is correct to within 10% of the true value of the variable. Studies employ power analysis when prespecified comparisons between groups are the object of study. Readers are referred to Sudman (1976) and Jaeger (1984) for more information on power calculations which determine the sample size necessary to ensure representativeness.

SUMMARY

In this chapter, we have addressed the principal issues involved in selecting and sampling people and units for ethnographic studies. We also have begun to address areas in which studies can be biased or that cause invalid inferences to be made. In the final chapter of this book, we discuss important issues of reliability and validity in ethnographic research.

NOTES

1. Reputational selection and chain referrals often are called network sampling (because they amass study groups made up of the network of friends, family, or contacts possessed by key individuals), or snowball sampling (because the study group starts with a single individual and grows incrementally, as a snowball grows while rolling down a snow-covered hill).

2. Three wheels are human-powered taxis, part bicycle and part cart. They are often called pedicabs.

11

VALIDITY AND RELIABILITY IN ETHNOGRAPHIC RESEARCH

Cross
Reference:
See Book 1,
Chapter 3, for a
discussion of
positivism and
experimental design

In this chapter, we address the principal criteria for judging the quality of research. Conventional criteria for reliability and validity derive from positivism and the requirements for experimental research. They define **reliability** as the stability of research results and their ability to be replicated by other researchers, and **validity** as a measure both of whether or not researchers have actually discovered what they claim to have found, and of the extent to which what they have learned can be applied to other populations. The recent scientific literature has been full of highly publicized studies whose claims proved unreliable because they could not be repeated by other scientists or because the methods used to conduct the studies were so unusual that they could be used nowhere else. Attempts to create cold fusion and to clone animals are just a few examples. Invalid research is that which is rejected because the people studied reject its results as untrue for them, or the research was judged to be inaccurate because it omitted important aspects of the population or setting. Other studies may be valid but not very useful simply because the results are

Definition:
Reliability
refers to replicability
of research results
over time, different
sites and
populations, and
with different
researchers

Definition:
Validity is the
degree to which
researchers actually
have discovered
what they think their
results show, and
how applicable the
results are to other
populations

271

applicable only to the very small group of people studied, that is, they are not generalizable.

Ethnographers have struggled for decades with positivistic criteria for reliability and validity, because the methods, field conditions, and objectives of ethnographic research do not lend themselves to the same kinds of detachment and control over practice that are possible in clinical studies, experimental and epidemiological research, and even standardized surveys and demographic research. All of the latter have procedures for controlling sources of bias and disruption in the field; they also focus on maintaining researcher detachment from participants in the study—something that is nearly impossible for ethnographers, given their long-term, intimate relationships with participants.

Some ethnographers have ignored this epistemological struggle, arguing that rules for validity and especially for reliability simply do not apply to ethnography. Others, claiming that different research paradigms require different standards for quality, have designed alternatives to reliability and validity that they feel are more appropriate for ethnography (see Eisenhart & Howe, 1992, for a review of this issue; also see Lather, 1986; Lincoln, 1990; Smith, 1990). These include "credibility," "goodness," "believability," and "catalytic validity," or the capacity of research not only to help researchers and participants understand each other better, but to transform their lives and work toward elimination of social oppression (Lather & Smithies, 1997; Whyte, 1991). Still others have adopted a middle ground, adapting, translating, and modifying positivistic rules to make them appropriate for ethnographic practice and attending also to the special qualities of ethnographic research and its impact on both researchers and participants (LeCompte & Goetz, 1982; LeCompte & Preissle, 1993, Schensul, S., 1985). This last approach is the one with which we feel most comfortable, because we believe that the *qual-*

ity of investigation must be of paramount concern in any scientific endeavor—including ethnographic research.

We begin this discussion by noting several characteristics of ethnography that affect its ability to conform to traditional definitions of reliability and validity. We use both the conventional terminology to describe these threats to validity and reliability, and descriptions that we feel portray their origins more accurately. None of them, in our opinion, compromises the credibility, usefulness, or truth value of ethnographic research, nor diminishes the rigor of the knowledge that ethnography creates. Below, we list two of the principal ways in which ethnography deviates from more controlled and standardized forms of research.

Cross Reference: Book 1, Chapters 1, 2, and 4, present a detailed description of differences between ethnography and other common approaches to social science research

> ### Why Ethnography Diverges From Standard Canons for Validity and Reliability
>
> - Ethnography's most important form of data collection is participant observation, in which researchers themselves are the "instrument."
> - Ethnographers cannot impose rigid laboratory controls on their studies because their focus is the natural flow of human events over time.

The Researcher as Instrument

In ethnographic research, the researcher is the primary instrument of data collection. As we describe in Book 5, all information collected in a study is filtered through the perceptual apparatus and subjective opinions of the researcher. Such filtering is true to some extent of all research, but it is especially salient in ethnographic research, where who researchers are; their stance toward the people or organizations studied; their agendas for the research project; and whatever personal, professional, or disciplinary biases and perspectives that researchers bring to the field have the potential for affecting research questions, data collection and analysis, and interpretation of results.

Lack of Control Over Field Conditions

In ethnographic research, researchers lack the kind of control over the conditions of research that characterizes clinical, experimental, or even cross-sectional survey or epidemiologic research. Ethnographers must always be open to surprises—sometimes unpleasant ones—when expected events fail to occur, unexpected events *do* occur, and virtually everything one hoped to find in the field turns up missing or gone awry. In addition to the fact that ethnographers study a continual flow of events whose instances can never be replicated, such "messy" field conditions are exactly what make ethnographic results unreliable, in the traditional research sense. However, as we shall point out, this lack of replicability does not affect the value of ethnographic results and, in fact, can be accommodated for by careful explication of field conditions, researcher actions, and methods for data collection and analysis. In this chapter, we discuss issues of validity and reliability and address how they are considered in ethnographic research.

THE TYPES OF VALIDITY AND RELIABILITY

There are several kinds of validity and reliability, all of which affect the extent to which research is judged credible and of high quality. In general, validity is concerned with accuracy and dependability of instruments and observations (Krueger, 1988, p. 41), and with the degree to which results obtained by researchers make sense to and are shared by the people studied and can be generalized to other populations (cf. Goetz & LeCompte, 1984, p. 210). **Internal validity** refers to the extent to which scientific observations

and measurements—such as surveys and interviews—
authentically represent the reality in which the people studied live—as they define it—or the degree to which the
responses obtained from respondents are a valid reflection
of how those respondents felt and thought about the topic
(Krueger, 1988). Construct validity, another form of internal validity, pertains more specifically to instruments such
as tests, questionnaires, and interview guides, although it is
also relevant to the questions researchers ask in interviews.
It involves the degree to which the questions or measures
used really assess what they are assumed to measure. For
example, lack of construct validity can be found in the
standardized tests used in the United States to assess all
prebaccalaureate educational programs regardless of their
content; because such tests actually measure only proficiency in reading, writing, and mathematics, they lack construct validity for programs in the fine arts, for example,
which are designed to teach proficiency in the arts. External
validity refers to the degree to which such representations
can be applied to other groups.

Reliability is concerned with whether the research results
can be replicated by another researcher using the same
methods. Internal reliability refers to the degree to which
other researchers would match previously generated constructs with a particular data set in the same way as did the
researcher who originally compiled it. External reliability
addresses whether or not independent researchers would
discover the same phenomena or generate the same constructs as an original researcher if they did studies in the
same or similar settings (cf. Goetz & LeCompte, 1984,
p. 210). We have alluded to many of these issues in our
discussions of researcher subjectivities; sampling procedures; instrument development; and data collection, analysis, and interpretation; these are found in Books 1, 3, 4, 5,
and 6, and in Chapter 9 of this book. In this chapter, we will

Definition:
Internal validity
refers to the
corespondence
beween measures
and the reality of
the field situation

Definition:
Construct
validity refers to
whether instruments
measure what they
are assumed to
measure

Definition:
External
validity refers to
the applicability
of representations
to other groups

Definition:
Internal
reliability refers
to the match
between constructs
and a data set

Definition:
External
reliability refers
to the comparability
of results in repeat
studies using the
same methods

provide a more detailed discussion of the principal concerns that ethnographers have about validity and reliability and how they are addressed.

VALIDITY

Most methodologists agree that validity is a major strength of ethnographic research. Establishing validity requires researchers to assess whether constructs devised by researchers represent or measure the categories of human experience. It also calls for determining the extent to which conclusions effectively represent empirical reality—within and outside of the original study site. In the pages that follow, we discuss these issues in terms of both internal and external validity.

Internal Validity

It is easy to understand why ethnography has high internal validity, because ethnographers live with groups for a long period of time, getting to know people well and allowing for both continuous data analysis and opportunities to refine constructs in ways that ensure a match between scientific categories and participant realities. Ethnographers have time to learn the language, specialized word usage, and speech patterns of informants so that interviews can be phrased close to or in the actual language of the informant. In much the same way, because participant observation is conducted in natural settings, it reflects the reality of informant life experiences better than the contrived, manipulated, or controlled settings common to experimental and quasi-experimental research. Finally, as we note in Books 2, 5, and 6, analysis and interpretation of ethnographic data incorporate self-monitoring and -reflection, which require ethnographers to expose their own actions and interpretations to constant introspection, and all phases of research activity to continual questioning and reevaluation. All of these features contribute to the degree to which ethnographers can make sense of the world in which the people studied live, and do so in ways that make sense to those people themselves.

Notwithstanding these strengths, questions of validity still arise in ethnographic research, although they differ at various stages of the research process. Questions of validity with reference to selecting and interviewing key informants are quite different from those pertaining to the development and implementation of an ethnographic survey. In exploratory or semistructured phases of a study, researchers expect that different respondents will produce different answers to the same question; indeed, because exploratory research involves a search for variation, it may be preferable that respondents produce different responses so that the researchers can gain a complete understanding of the range of responses within the target population. It can be quite a long time between initial data collection and the point at which an ethnographer finally develops a cultural portrait that establishes consistent patterns and makes sense. For these reasons, the concept of validity, critical to all scientific research, means one thing when applied to certain stages in ethnographic data and another with reference to data collected in positivistically informed and experimental studies. Another aspect of validity that is often ignored is that it also depends on the appropriateness of the research design, both for the context of the study and for the research question for which it is being used. For example, if researchers plan to use a data collection method (e.g., a group interview) that requires forms of interaction or ways of divulging and communicating information deemed inappropriate in the culture or context of the research, the results will not be valid.

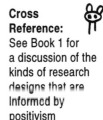

Cross Reference: See Book 1 for a discussion of the kinds of research designs that are informed by positivism

EXAMPLE 11.1 ━•━•━

CONDUCTING MIXED- AND SAME-GENDER FOCUS GROUPS ON
MALE-FEMALE RELATIONSHIPS WITH YOUNG SRI LANKAN ADULTS

Research on sexuality and relationships among youth and young adults in an urban
area of Sri Lanka showed that the sexual vocabularies of young men were very well
developed. On the other hand, the vocabularies of young women were extremely
limited, and young women were very reluctant to discuss issues related to sexuality
even in the context of a face-to-face interview with a Sri Lankan interviewer of the
same gender. Researchers Stephen and Jean Schensul, Tudor Silva, Bonnie Nastasi,
and Chellia Sivayoganathan debated the feasibility of joint discussions. Focus groups
with youth suggested that it would be problematic to hold such discussions in mixed
groups.

Consequently, the group intervention that was conducted following the formative
research phase of the study was offered separately to groups of young men and
women. The young women's intervention was held behind closed doors that were
guarded by another female researcher to make sure that no men overheard the
discussion. Only after achieving some comfort with the topics of "relationships,"
"reproductive health," and "sexuality" did young women agree to discuss and solve
dilemmas related to sexual decision making in a mixed group. After these problem-
solving sessions, both women and men requested that joint meetings be held much
earlier in the intervention. Interventionists' careful attention to the protection of
women's privacy in the early stages of the intervention led to further developments
in this sensitive cultural area later on. Premature mixing of the groups would have
resulted in the loss of data and participants, thus jeopardizing the internal validity of
the study.

━•━•━

Threats to Internal Validity

The following are the major threats to internal validity
in ethnographic research, and some ways of preventing
them.

Threats to Internal Validity

- Cultural scenes studied by ethnographers are not stable over time; people studied grow up, move, and die, especially given the long duration of many ethnographic studies.
- Participants can withhold information or lie; what they say and do is affected by their perceptions of who researchers are, what they want to know, and how and with whom they interact in the community.
- Some components of the population or setting may be omitted from the study.
- Researchers can report what turn out to be false or premature conclusions.

Cultural scenes and their inhabitants undergo change. These threats to internal validity are commonly referred to as problems having to do with *history, maturation,* and *mortality* (Campbell & Stanley, 1963). History refers to changes over time in the overall social scene. Maturation refers to progressive development in individuals. Mortality refers to losses or gains in the group that the researcher is studying because of death or moves, or because the respondent drops out of the study. All of these issues are serious concerns for positivistically informed researchers, who try to control all aspects of the study, including the passage of time and the attrition of subjects. However, the effect of these issues is exactly the kind of thing that ethnographers investigate. *They are concerned with separating what remains constant* **Key point** *in a culture or group from what is subject to change.* They document the effects of history by documenting historical changes. Maturation is not a concern in exploratory research; and in much ethnographic research, maturation is considered to be not only a normal part of human life, but also a very interesting topic for research in itself. Ethnographers use their prolonged presence, exposure to multiple contexts in the field, and indigenous definitions of the progress of individual development or maturation to help them sort out the implications of history and maturation in their studies. Maturation does become a concern for ethnographers when they are conducting semistructured or definitional research and ethnographic surveys. It is addressed in these instances by conducting interviews and observations within a specified time period. Ethnographers also consider mortality to be a normal aspect of human life that is unproblematic in exploratory or descriptive research, whose objective is obtaining new information on a topic. If key informants or data sources disappear, they simply find other sources of information. Mortality does become an issue when units or individuals are being used to observe changes over time. Losing sufficient cases between a first interview or observation and the second can influence the outcome of an intervention or the prediction of future behavior—that is, it might be difficult to distinguish the results of the intervention or actual changes in people's attitudes and behaviors from changes attributable to the loss of specific individuals. *The best strategy for preventing threats because of mortality is to allocate sufficient time and resources—and sample widely enough—to minimize attrition or the loss of cases.*

 Key point

Participants can give false or misleading information in the researcher's presence. This threat to internal validity is commonly referred to as the impact of *observer effects.* It derives from the fact that people tend to act differently when they know they are being watched than when they are unobserved. Observer effects are a problem in any research, but because ethnographers are preeminently observers, they find such effects to be serious indeed. Key to reduction of observer effects in ethnography is the degree of trust and comfort that informants and people in the community feel with the researcher and the degree to which the researcher does or does not influence the normal flow of behavior or information in the setting. Sometimes, what people in the study think about researchers depends on their past relationships with other researchers; they may not trust a present researcher because a previous one mistreated them.

Ethnographers generally go to considerable lengths to enhance their own comfort level and respondents' trust levels, including arranging a comfortable setting, offering food or other social activities, assisting with transportation and other aspects of daily life, using a translator if required, and drawing on the support of respected community members to reassure participants of researcher dependability.

In more structured kinds of data collection, such as ethnographic interviews and observations, ethnographers try to consider (and control to the extent possible), a variety of factors so as to minimize observer effects:

Cross Reference: See Book 2, Chapters 4 and 5, and Book 3, Chapter 2, for more information on creating a high level of trust in ethnographic research

- The familiarity and comfort level that respondents have with the researcher
- The length of time the researcher has been in the field
- What the participants think about the researcher
- The gender of the researcher in relation to participants and the topic
- Whether or not the topic is one that participants will readily discuss in public, with strangers, or at all

Ethnographers can engage in a number of strategies to enhance internal validity and reduce observer effects in their interviews. They can take care to

- Pilot test the questions to make sure that participants understand them
- Ensure that people feel comfortable in the interview setting
- Ensure that members of the field research team are people whom respondents trust or with whom they feel comfortable
- Situate the interview in an appropriate location
- Clarify any ambiguity in questions
- Test research results with participants for interpretive comments before they are published or disseminated

How participants relate to one another may be simultaneously influenced by, and independent of, the presence of the researcher. In addition to the effect of observers on participants in ethnographic field settings, observer effects may include the potential influence of participants on one another. Communities and groups have their own interaction dynamics that operate independently of the researcher's presence, even though they ultimately have an effect on what the researcher observes. If researchers introduce topics that are controversial, interaction among informants or between the researcher and informants can become so charged that members in a group discussion or event may behave in an uncomfortable or atypical way, become obtrusive, or even leave. In such cases, the researcher should change the topic, end the discussion, or create other transitions.

Another important aspect of observer effects that can distort the internal validity of the data is the use of inappropriate or unfamiliar questions, language derived from the researcher perspective, or terminology and jargon from theoretical frameworks and concepts that have little direct relevance to the participants in the study. The effect is as if the researcher were speaking a language foreign to the community. Internal validity is enhanced if researchers first develop deep knowledge of the cultural context; fully understand the research used to design the study; use focus groups to generate and check questions and domains before developing more structured interviews and observations; and then pilot test observations to make sure that they are observing behavior relevant to the research questions and interview questions for comprehension, cultural coherence, and acceptability.

Furthermore, as Goetz and LeCompte (1984, p. 224) note, researchers must guard the instruments they use and the constructs they create from their own ethnocentrisms and disciplinary and personal biases. This can be facilitated by the process of introspection and "disciplined subjectivity" that we describe in Books 5 and 6, and by triangulating initial impressions and all sources of data with other sources in the setting, as well as by seeking out data from comparable studies in other settings.

Careful execution of methods can enhance the likelihood that multiple researchers in a single study will agree on what they observe; this kind of interobserver agreement is one of the best indicators of internal validity. Some useful procedures for enhancing such agreement include the following:

- Obtaining verbatim accounts from respondents
- Taking careful fieldnotes and recording discrepancies among different sets of observations
- Making use of teams of researchers and striving for high levels of interrater reliability across sites or situations in coding fieldnotes
- Using field consultants and key informants to verify observations and serve as a reality check for the principal investigator's initial conclusions
- Considering results in light of other researchers' findings
- Using electronic or mechanical devices such as videocameras and tape recorders to record data

Segments of the population or setting may be omitted from the study. Threats to validity stemming from omissions of population or context segments are called *selection* and *regression* effects. As we noted in Chapter 10, incomplete representation of the population or selection (sampling) bias can affect internal validity by distorting research results in favor of the group that *is* represented. Although ethnographers may not always be able to obtain a representative sample of participants from the target population of concern, exactly who *is* represented should be established and reasons for omissions presented. Prior ethnographic research will help ethnographers to identify all of the sectors to be represented and enrolled in the study or sought and interviewed in the field. *We recommend obtaining demographic data from all key informants and participants in the early stages of the research process so that membership in the sample can be matched against the target population.*

Key point

Researchers may arrive at false or misleading conclusions. Conventional researchers refer to this threat as the possibility for *spurious conclusions.* It is not too difficult during the enthusiasm of early fieldwork for ethnographers to jump to premature conclusions based on insufficient data. During initial fieldwork phases, researchers notice unusual, controversial, and surface patterns that recur most frequently. As we note in Book 6, the first individuals with whom the researcher establishes relationships may be atypical and not represent community perspectives accurately. Ethnographers can correct this problem by corroborating results over time, testing associations between independent and dependent variable domains over time, conducting interviews with multiple groups so as to check results from each against the other, seeking indigenous explanations for causality or historical sequences, and observing causal sequences in field settings. This is especially important when the researchers' observations of events and why they happen do not correspond to local residents' interpretations of cause and effect.

COMPETING EXPLANATIONS FOR "TROUBLE" IN A SCHOOL DISTRICT

Both witchcraft and failure to conform to culturally appropriate patterns of reverence for nature and for other human beings are common explanations for why "things go wrong" in the Navajo Nation. In the school district in which LeCompte worked, these explanations for such natural disasters as floods, leaky roofs, and for human problems, such as the suicide of a popular high school student and the failing grades of a disproportionately large number of students, coexisted with more "rational" and bureaucratic explanations generated by researchers and school administrators. Both indigenous explanations and others blaming shoddy construction, an inclement weather cycle, dysfunctional families, and a bus schedule that caused many students to miss classes—and thereby fail tests—needed to be considered in setting policy for the school district.

➤●➤●➤

External Validity

External validity addresses both the extent to which the results obtained in one study also hold true for other populations, and whether or not theoretical frames, definitions, and research techniques used in one study can be applied by other researchers to comparable studies. Some researchers argue that ethnographic studies are so unique that neither their results nor their techniques can be applied anywhere else. They tend to develop idiosyncratic terminology to describe the special conditions they find in their research sites. However, these threaten the scientific value of their studies, because one of the hallmarks of good research is the extent to which it increases our knowledge of human life in general not just our knowledge of a particular small group. We, therefore, advocate a position that both recognizes the uniqueness of the cultures that ethnographers study, and also makes it possible for other researchers to make use of their results. Goetz and LeCompte (1984) advocate making sure that the results that ethnographers generate are presented in a way that makes them *comparable* to results obtained in other studies; this means using, to the extent possible, terminology and interpretations that are well known or have a history in the scientific disciplines and are clearly defined or operationalized, as described in Chapter 3 of this book. Where this is impossible, and new terms must be created, they should be carefully defined and the reasons for their use fully explained.

Goetz and LeCompte (1984) further suggest that the theories, constructs, and methods used in a study be *translatable*. This means that they must be commonly understood and well explained; as is the case with terminology or results, deviations from common practice must be explained well so that other researchers will be able to assess their value and appropriateness.

In the following box, we describe the principal threats to external validity.

Threats to External Validity

- Using concepts, instruments, or methods that are inappropriate for the group under study because they were developed for use with another, very different group (selection effects).

- Describing concepts, instruments, methods, or results used for one group in so idiosyncratic or unique a way that they cannot be used for, or applied to, any other group (construct effects).

- Failing to document unique historical experiences of groups and cultures in the study, especially if they seriously affect the results obtained in the study (history effects).

- Creating a researcher-informant relationship, or a researcher role within the community, that seriously affects the setting or results (observer effects) without carefully documenting what that relationship and its effects were.

Characteristics of the research setting may affect research results. Cross-group comparison of constructs may be invalid because of the unique historical experiences of groups and cultures in the study. Ethnic/culture, social, race, and gender composition are important factors here, but urbanization, acculturation, and other historical processes create unique conditions that the researcher should document clearly.

Furthermore, researchers may interact with the setting and people in it in ways that alter the cultural scene under study. In some cases, and especially in applied ethnographic research, this interaction is appropriate because the researcher acts in close collaboration with the community and has its approval to engage in investigations and even to introduce change. The best way to accommodate to such effects is to describe clearly all settings, setting-observer interactions, activities of the researchers, and the effects of those activities, and to conduct observations in a variety of settings and with multiple trained observers.

Construct effects can be addressed by careful prior field-work and pilot testing, especially when researchers plan to adopt or adapt instruments originally generated in a different study and for different populations. Ethnographers commonly engage in this practice; it is entirely appropriate and efficient, but only if the prior precautions described above are taken. All of these strategies provide information that allows outside readers and other researchers to assess the quality—and validity—of the research, and they also serve as a check on bias in the study at hand.

RELIABILITY

Reliability addresses whether the results of a study can be duplicated. Reliability is a lesser concern in ethnographic research, and especially in exploratory and definitional stages of the research process. Duplication of results across groups is not the desired outcome of exploratory research. Rather, the intention of these interviews is to provide exploratory information leading to theory formulation, more valid instrument development, and explanation of quantitative results. Under such conditions, finding differences is more important than finding similarities. But careful training of interviewers, team interviewing, rigorous notes and audiovisual documentation, and thought given in advance to the structure of the questions to be used in exploratory research can go a long way toward ensuring that other researchers could approximate the research process—although not necessarily the results. Using other data to confirm the results of exploratory and definitional ethnography is another way of ensuring reliability of results.

Other ways of enhancing external reliability include the following:

Cross Reference: See this book, Chapters 2 and 3, and Book 6, Chapter 1, for a discussion of what these issues are and how they affect results

- Describing clearly both the nature and the context of the researcher's relationships with the study population and the research site; researchers may see and interpret things differently depending on the position they hold in the community

- Clarifying and describing clearly who the study's key informants are, the groups that they represent, and the status positions they hold in the community in the study

- Making clear how and where observations were made

- Providing details of quota and other sampling techniques, as well as instrument construction and testing, so that readers will be able to identify and duplicate the primary sources of information for the study

- Identifying clearly the social contexts and situations of the research, including conditions under which ethnographic surveys were administered; this enhances the likelihood of replicability and permits readers to identify limitations and gaps in the data collection process that could affect results and their interpretation

- Defining concepts, constructs, domains, factors, and variables clearly (operationalizing at all levels) to avoid idiosyncratic interpretation and limited replicability; establishing interrater reliability when developing coding categories and coding text data is recommended

■ Clarifying methods and procedures for analyzing ethnographic data so that others can duplicate the work; as Goetz and LeCompte (1984) note, "because reliability depends on the potential for subsequent researchers to reconstruct original analytic strategies, only those ethnographic accounts that specify these in sufficient detail are replicable" (p. 217)

Delineating clearly all of the steps in conducting an ethnographic study, including data analysis and links to interpretation, is central to ensuring the external reliability of a study.

CONCLUDING COMMENTS

In this chapter, we have presented the most important tenets of the principal criteria for judging the quality of research results. As we noted at the beginning of this chapter, the criteria discussed in this chapter are more or less traditional ones, those most commonly known to the scientific and nonscientific public. For that reason, they also are the criteria to which the work of ethnographers is most often held accountable, and about which funding agencies, evaluators, boards of trustees, and other researchers tend to ask questions. We believe that readers of the Ethnographer's Toolkit should be familiar with them so that they will have ready answers to such queries.

We also believe that some of the more recent definitions of validity, in particular, are relevant to the work done by applied ethnographic researchers, including users of this Toolkit. Applied ethnographers quickly learn that doing work in communities means that there are few really "correct" answers to any given problem, and there is never any single, completely correct set of procedures for arriving at solutions. Rather, arriving at workable and appropriate solutions to problems requires the kind of negotiation, sharing of power, and joint decision making advocated by critical theorists and postmodern researchers. Research that can achieve this kind of shared process is, indeed, valid, both for communities and for investigators. Furthermore, research that stimulates local communities and groups to identify and solve their own problems is, indeed, "catalytic" and, in that sense, has the "catalytic validity" (Lather, 1986) we described in the introduction to this chapter. Finally, if theory, methods, analytic procedures, and results are clearly described in local context, the potential for reliability and generalizability is enhanced.

CONCLUSIONS

Ethnographers frequently face questions about the methods they use to collect, analyze, and interpret data collected in natural settings. The questions usually have to do with three major characteristics of ethnography. Ethnography is local, and the results of ethnographic research are not readily generalizable to other settings. Ethnography is conducted in naturalistic settings where researchers do not have control over what happens and must try to observe and make sense of what they see. It is not a laboratory science. Finally, ethnography is unique in the degree to which the researcher is the primary (and often the only) instrument of data collection. In this book, we have tried to show ways in which ethnography has adapted scientific procedures to suit field research with these characteristics.

Generating clear research questions and theoretical models is an important first step in increasing the rigor of ethnographic research. Linking methods to research questions and models is a second step. Building supportive relationships with people in the field is critical to good ethnography. Cross-validating findings on an ongoing basis by comparing across responses and across different types of data is another important way that ethnographers increase confidence in their results. Not all ethnographic research calls for conducting a survey. However, in this book, we have shown how important it is for ethnographers who wish to use qualitative and quantitative data in their study to consider in advance how these different forms of data can be linked and analyzed together, so that they inform each other.

Ethnography extends skills that are important components of learning, survival, and growth in any cultural or community setting—listening, questioning, observing, analyzing, and building frameworks for interpretation and prediction. Everyone has some ethnographic skills, but doing good ethnography requires the systematic application of these skills to the investigation of a research problem. One of the most important characteristics of a good ethnographer is the ability to ask questions even when the answers seem obvious.

We recognize that most ethnographers begin their research with a question. One of the most important aspects of ethnography is that researchers take the opportunity to explore the question during the early stages of research. However, we have intentionally promoted the idea of early or formative theory building because the process is so helpful in clarifying both the research question and directions for data collection and analysis. If researchers apply the modeling procedures that we have outlined in Chapters 2 and 3 of this book, we believe that they can arrive very quickly at a formative theoretical model that deepens and becomes more complex in interaction with data over the course of a study.

Computer technology has improved immeasurably the rigor of ethnographic methods. With the advent of text and specialized numerical data management programs, ethnographers can now systematize coding systems and create text data sets that are subject to scientific inquiry and critique in much the same way as are quantitative data sets. We are not far from being able to speak our interview and observational notes directly into our text-based search programs, analyze data as it is received in the field, and present the data almost immediately to our partners in the field. These technical tools—data management and analytic software, portable computers, projectors, voice-activated software, and high-speed modems—have pushed ethnographers to make more explicit their theories, methods, and analytic approaches. Thinking about these technical tools will improve the quality, validity, and reliability of community-based research even if researchers do not actually make use of the new technology.

Despite increasing sophistication in theory building, research methods, and research technology, ultimately the ethnographic enterprise depends on human interaction. Building rapport, reciprocity, and empathy are the hallmarks of ethnography because they are fundamental to the acquisition of good information and deep understanding. Technological advances in qualitative research are useful only if they reduce, or at least do not increase, the social distance between ethnographers, research participants, and research partners.

We have said that ethnography is an applied science. Ethnography takes researchers into communities, agencies, and homes to learn with the help of willing partners—those key informants or cultural experts who help researchers understand the world through their eyes. What better basis for building strong research partnerships to address the thorny problems that beset the communities and neighborhoods in which we choose to do our work.

REFERENCES

Aday, L. (1989). *Designing and conducting health surveys: A comprehensive guide.* San Francisco: Jossey-Bass.

Amarasiri de Silva, M. W. (1993). *The social and political context of community participation in primary health in a rural Sri Lankan district.* Unpublished doctoral dissertation, University of Connecticut.

Babbie, E. (1995). *The practice of survey research* (7th ed.). Belmont, CA: Wadsworth.

Bandura, A. (1979). Self-efficacy—Toward a unifying theory of behavioral change. *Psychological Review, 84,* 191-215.

Berg, M. (1992). *Rapid Sociodemographic Assessment project (RSA)* (11 monographs). Hartford, CT: Institute for Community Research.

Bernard, H. R. (1995). *Research methods in anthropology: Qualitative and quantitative approaches to ethnographic research* (2nd ed.). Walnut Creek, CA: AltaMira.

Bieleman, B., Diaz, A., Merlo, G., & Kaplan, C. H. (1993). *Lines across Europe: Nature and extent of cocaine use in Barcelona, Rotterdam and Turin.* Amsterdam: Swets & Zeitkinger.

Bingham, A. (1998). *The malaria ecosystem in southern Mexico.* Unpublished doctoral dissertation, University of Connecticut.

Bogdewic, S. P. (1992). Participant observation. In B. F. Crabtree & W. Miller (Eds.), *Doing qualitative research.* Newbury Park, CA: Sage.

Boster, J. S., & Johnson, J. C. (1989). Form or function: A comparison of expert and novice judgements of similarity among fish. *American Anthropologist, 91,* 866-889.

Campbell, D. T., & Stanley, J. C. (1963). *Experimental and quasi-experimental designs for research.* Chicago: Rand McNally.

Carley, K. (1991). *Textual analysis using maps.* Pittsburgh, PA: Carnegie Mellon University, Department of Social and Decision Sciences.

Chambers, R. (1992). Rapid but relaxed and participatory rural appraisal: Towards applications in health and nutrition. In N. S. Scrimshaw & G. R.

Gleason (Eds.), *RAP: Rapid Assessment Procedures: Qualitative method-ologies for planning and evaluation of health-related programs* (pp. 25-38). Boston: International Nutritional Foundation for Developing Countries (INDFC).

Clement, D. C., Eisenhart, M. A., & Harding, J. R. (1979). The veneer of harmony: Social-race relations in a southern desegregated school. In R. C. Rist, (Ed.), *Desegregated schools: Appraisals of an American experiment* (pp. 15-65). New York: Academic Press.

Clifford, J. (1988). *The predicament of culture: Twentieth-century ethnography, literature, and art.* Cambridge, MA: Harvard University Press.

Cumbo, K. (1998). *The meaning of books and reading in a preschool classroom: A focus on peer contexts.* Unpublished doctoral dissertation, School of Education, University of Colorado, Boulder.

DeWalt, K. M., & DeWalt, B. R., with Wayland, C. B. (1998). Participant observation. In H. R. Bernard (Ed.), *Handbook of methods in cultural anthropology.* Walnut Creek, CA: AltaMira

Diaz, A., Barruti, M., & Doncel, C. (1992). *The lines of success? Study on the nature and extent of cocaine use in Barcelona.* Barcelona: Laboratory of Sociology, ICESB.

Diaz, N. (1998). *Perception of body image among Puerto Rican pre-adolescent girls.* Paper presented at the annual meeting of the American Anthropological Association, Philadelphia, PA.

Eisenhart, M. A., & Howe, K. R. (1992). Validity in educational research. In M. D. LeCompte, W. L. Millroy, & J. Preissle (Eds.), *The handbook of qualitative research in education* (pp. 643-680). New York: Academic Press.

Ember, C. R., & Ember, M. (1998). Cross-cultural research. In H. R. Bernard (Ed.), *Handbook of methods in cultural anthropology* (pp. 647-690). Walnut Creek, CA: AltaMira.

Fink, A. (1995). *How to ask survey questions.* Thousand Oaks, CA: Sage.

Fontana, A., & Frey, J. H. (1994). Interviewing: The art of science. In N. K. Denzin & Y. S. Lincoln (Eds.), *Handbook of qualitative research* (pp. 361-377). Thousand Oaks, CA: Sage.

Fowler, F. J., Jr. (1984). *Survey research methods.* Beverly Hills, CA: Sage.

Fowler, F. J., Jr., & Mangione, T. W. (1990). *Practical sampling.* Newbury Park, CA: Sage.

Frake, C. O. (1964). How to ask for a drink in Subanum. *American Anthropologist, 66*(Pt. 2), 127-132.

Gaviria, M., Stern, G., & Schensul, S. (1982). Sociocultural factors and perinatal health in a Mexican American community. *Journal of the National Medical Association, 74,* 983-989.

Gay, L. R. (1985). *Educational evaluation and measurement: Competencies for analysis and application* (2nd ed.). Columbus, OH: Charles E. Merrill.

Gilchrist, V. (1992). Key informant interviews. In B. F. Crabtree & W. Miller (Eds.), *Doing qualitative research* (pp. 70-92). Newbury Park, CA: Sage.

Glaser, B. G., & Strauss, A. L. (1967). *The discovery of grounded theory: Strategies for qualitative research.* Chicago: Aldine.

Goetz, J. P., & LeCompte, M. D. (1984). *Ethnography and qualitative design in educational research* (1st ed.). Orlando, FL: Academic Press.

Goldin, L. R. (1996). Models of economic differentiation and cultural change. *Journal of Quantitative Anthropology, 1-2*(6), 49-74.

Goode, W. J., & Hatt, P. K. (1952). *Methods in social research*. New York: McGraw-Hill.

Goodenough, W. (1956). Componential analysis and the study of meaning. *Language, 38*, 195-216.

Guba, E. G., & Lincoln, Y. S. (1989). *Fourth generation evaluation*. Newbury Park, CA: Sage.

Harris, M. (1968). *The rise of anthropological theory*. New York: Thomas Y. Crowell.

Henry, G. T. (1990). *Practical sampling*. Newbury Park, CA: Sage.

International Center for Research on Women. (1995/1997). *Women and AIDS research program, Phase I and Phase II research report series*. Washington, DC: Author.

Jaeger, R. M. (1984). *Sampling in education and the social sciences*. New York: Longmans.

Johnson, J. C. (1990). *Selecting ethnographic informants*. Newbury Park, CA: Sage.

Johnson, J. C. (1998). Research design and research strategies. In H. R. Bernard (Ed.), *Handbook of methods in cultural anthropology* (pp. 131-172). Walnut Creek, CA: AltaMira.

Johnson, A., & Sackett, R. (1998). Direct systematic observation of behavior. In H. R. Bernard (Ed.), *Handbook of methods in cultural anthropology* (pp. 301-332). Walnut Creek, CA: AltaMira.

Kaplan, A. (1964). *The conduct of inquiry: Methodology for behavioral science*. Scranton, PA: Chandler.

Koester, S. (1996). The process of drug injection: Applying ethnography to the study of HIV risk among IDUs. In T. Rhodes & R. Hartnoll (Eds.), *AIDS, drugs and prevention: Perspectives on individual and community action* (pp. 133-148). London: Routledge & Kegan Paul.

Koester, S. R., Booth, E., & Zhang, Y. (1996). The prevalence of additional injection-related risk behaviors among injection drug users. *Journal of Acquired Immune Deficiency Syndromes and Human Retrovirology, 12*, 202-207.

Krueger, R. A. (1988). *Focus groups: A practical guide for applied research*. Newbury Park, CA: Sage.

Kuhn, T. O. (1970). *The structure of scientific revolutions*. Chicago: University of Chicago Press. (Originally published in 1962)

Laio, S. (1997). *A pilot intervention among sex workers in Hainan: Final report to WHO*. Peking Union Medical College.

Lamphere, L. (Ed.). (1992). *Structuring diversity: Ethnographic perspectives on the new immigration*. Chicago: University of Chicago Press.

Lather, P. (1986). Research as praxis. *Harvard Educational Review, 56*, 257-277.

Lather, P., & Smithies, C. (1997). *Troubling the angels: Women living with HIV/AIDS*. Boulder, CO: Westview.

LeCompte, M. D. (1974). *Institutional constraints on teacher styles and the development of student work norms*. Unpublished doctoral dissertation, University of Chicago.

LeCompte, M. D. (1978). Learning to work. *Anthropology and Education Quarterly, 9*, 22-37.

LeCompte, M. D., & Goetz, J. P. (1982). Reliability and validity in ethnographic research. *Review of Educational Research, 52*, 31-60.

LeCompte, M. D., & Preissle, J. (1993). *Ethnography and qualitative design in educational research* (2nd ed., pp. 267-277). New York: Academic Press.

Levy, R. I., & Hollan, D. W. (1998). Person-centered interviews. In H. R. Bernard (Ed.), *Handbook of methods in cultural anthropology* (pp. 333-364). Walnut Creek, CA: AltaMira.

Lincoln, Y. S. (1990). The making of a constructivist: A remembrance of transformations past. In E. Guba (Ed.), *The paradigm dialog* (pp. 67-87). Newbury Park, CA: Sage.

Lounsbury, F. G. (1964). The structural analysis of kinship semantics. In H. G. Lunt (Ed.), *Proceedings of the 9th International Congress of Linguistics* (pp. 73-93). The Hague: Mouton.

Malinowski, B. (1922). *Argonauts of the Western Pacific.* New York: E. P. Dutton.

McLennan, S. (1997). *Teachers, Internet and schools: Case studies of challenge and change.* Unpublished doctoral dissertation, School of Education, University of Colorado, Boulder.

Medina-Mora, M. E., Ortiz, A., Caudillo, C., & López, S. (1982). Inhalación deliberada de los disolventes en un grupo de menores Mexicanos. *Revista Salud Mental, 5,* 77-81.

Merton, R. K. (1967). *On theoretical sociology: Five essays old and new.* New York: Free Press.

Miles, M. B., & Huberman, A. M. (1994). Data management and analysis methods. In N. K. Denzin & Y. S. Lincoln (Eds.), *Handbook of qualitative research* (pp. 428-444). Thousand Oaks, CA: Sage.

Moore, J. (1991). *Going down to the barrio: Homeboys and homegirls change.* Philadelphia: Temple University Press.

Murdock, G. P. (1967). Ethnographic atlas: A summary. *Ethnology, 6,* 109-236.

Naroll, R., & Sipes, R. G. (1973). Standard ethnographic sample, 2nd ed. *Current Anthropology, 14,* 111-140.

Needle, R. H., Coyle, S. L., Genser, S. G., & Trotter, R. T., II. (1995). Introduction: The social network paradigm. In R. H. Needle, S. L. Coyle, S. G. Genser, & R. T. Trotter (Eds.), *Social networks, drug abuse, and HIV transmission* (NIDA Research Monograph 151, pp. 1-2). Rockville, MD: USDHHS.

Oodit, G., Bhowan, U., & Schensul, S. (1993). *A study of women admitted to hospitals with complications due to abortion.* Report submitted to the Reproductive Health Section, World Health Organization, Geneva.

Pelto, G., & Gove, S. (1992). Developing a focused ethnographic study for the WHO Acute Respiratory Infection (ARI) Control and Programme. In N. S. Scrimshaw & G. R. Gleason (Eds.), *RAP: Rapid Assessment Procedures: Qualitative methodologies for planning and evaluation of health-related programs* (pp. 215-226). Boston: International Nutritional Foundation for Developing Countries (INDFC).

Pelto, P. J., & Pelto, G. H. (1978). *Anthropological research: The structure of inquiry* (2nd ed.). Cambridge, UK: Cambridge University Press.

Reed, D. B., & Furman, G. C. (1992, April). *The 2 x 2 matrix in qualitative data analysis and theory generation.* Paper presented at the annual meeting of the American Educational Research Association, San Francisco.

Rein, M., & Schon, D. (1977). Problem setting in policy research. In C. Weiss (Ed.), *Using social policy research in public policy making.* Lexington, MA: D. C. Heath.

Romero, M., & Berg, M. (1997). *Indicators and precursors of alcohol use in preadolescent girls: A preliminary analysis.* Paper presented at the Center for Substance Abuse Prevention annual evaluation conference, Washington, DC.

Rossi, P., Wright, J., & Anderson, A. (1983). *Handbook of survey research.* San Diego, CA: Academic Press.

Schensul, D. (1998). *Participatory action research: The Summer Youth Research Institute.* Senior thesis, Columbia University, Department of Sociology.

Schensul, J., Diaz, N., & Woolley, S. (1996). *Measuring activity levels among Puerto Rican children.* Paper presented at the 2nd annual meeting of the Puerto Rican Studies Association, San Juan, PR.

Schensul, S. (1969). *The impact of industrialization on Northern Minnesotans and Southern Ugandans.* Unpublished doctoral dissertation, University of Minnesota.

Schensul, S. (1985). Science, theory and application in anthropology. *American Behavioral Scientist, 29*(2), 164-185.

Schensul, S., Eisenberg, M., Glasgow, J., & Huettner, J. (1994). Translating state data into local health programs: Targeted research for intervention planning. *American Journal of Public Health, 84,* 671-672.

Schensul, S., Oodit, G., Schensul, J., Seebuluck, S., Bhowan, U., Aukhojee, J. P., Rogobur, S., Koye Kwat, B. L., & Affock, S. (1994). *Young women, work and AIDS-related risk behavior in Mauritius.* Women and AIDS Research Program, Research Report Series, No. 2. Washington, DC: International Center for Research on Women.

Schensul, S. L., Schensul, J., & Zegarra, M. (1985). *Pediatric health and the evolution of urban communities in Lima, Peru.* Paper presented at the 1985 annual meeting of the American Anthropological Association.

Schofield, J. W. (1982). *Black and white in school: Trust, tolerance or tokenism?* New York: Praeger.

Schweizer, T. (1998). Epistemology: The nature and validation of anthropological knowledge. In H. R. Bernard (Ed.), *Handbook of methods in cultural anthropology* (pp. 39-88). Walnut Creek, CA: AltaMira.

Silva, K. T., Schensul, S. L., Schensul, J., de Silva, M. W. A., Nastasi, B. K., Sivayoganathan, C., Lewis, J., Wedisinghe, P., Ratnayake, P., Eisenberg, M., & Aponso, H. (1997). *Youth and sexual risk in Sri Lanka.* International Center for Research on Women. Washington, DC. Phase II Report Series.

Smith, J. K. (1990). Alternative research paradigms and the problem of criteria. In E. Guba (Ed.), *The paradigm dialog* (pp. 167-188). Newbury Park, CA: Sage.

Spradley, J. P. (1979). *The ethnographic interview.* New York: Holt, Rinehart & Winston.

Spradley, J. P. (1980). *Participant observation.* New York: Holt, Rinehart & Winston.

Stringer, E. T. (1996). *Action research: A handbook for practitioners.* Thousand Oaks, CA: Sage.

Sudman, S. (1976). *Applied sampling.* New York: Academic Press.

Sudman, S., & Bradburn, N. M. (1982). *Asking questions.* San Francisco: Jossey-Bass.

Trotter, R., & Schensul, J. (1998). Research methods in applied anthropology. In H. R. Bernard (Ed.), *Handbook of methods in cultural anthropology.* Walnut Creek, CA: AltaMira.

Watters, J. K., & Biernacki, P. (1989). Targeted sampling: Options for the study of hidden populations. *Social Problems, 36*(4), 17-18.

Wax, M. L. (Ed.). (1979). *Desegregated schools: An intimate portrait based on five ethnographic studies.* Unpublished report to the National Institute of Education, Files of the Editor, Social Science Institute, Washington University, St. Louis, MO.

Weller, S. (1998). Structured interviewing and questionnaire construction. In H. R. Bernard (Ed.), *Handbook of methods in cultural anthropology* (pp. 365-409). Walnut Creek, CA: AltaMira.

Weller, S. C., & Romney, A. K. (1988). *Systematic data collection.* Newbury Park, CA: Sage.

Werner, O., & Schoepfle, G. M. (1987). *Systematic fieldwork: Ethnographic analysis and data management* (Vol. 2). Newbury Park, CA: Sage.

Whyte, W. F. (Ed.). (1991). *Participatory action research.* Newbury Park, CA: Sage.

Wilson, D. S. (1998). *Fieldnotes.* Hartford, CT: Institute for Community Research.

Wolf, S. A. (1999, April). "No excuses": School reform in exemplary schools of Kentucky. In *Images of reform: The effects of a high-stakes, performance-based state assessment on curriculum, planning, and instruction.* Symposium conducted at the annual meeting of the American Educational Research Association.

Yin, R. K. (1991). *Case study research: Design and methods.* Newbury Park, CA: Sage.

ADDITIONAL RESOURCES

Supplemental materials of use to ethnographic researchers consist of specialized texts on specific research methods, and edited or authored volumes on qualitative research methods. Below are several books and monographs in each category that we recommend as useful references on essential ethnographic methods.

General Texts

Bernard, H. R. (1995). *Research methods in anthropology: Qualitative and quantitative approaches* (2nd ed.). Walnut Creek CA: AltaMira.

This general methods texts covers all aspects of ethnographic methods in language most lay persons can understand. Chapters address social research, reseach design, sampling, literature search, general methods and quantitative research methods. This text is one of the few sources dealing with ethnographic methods that includes detailed discussion of quantitative methods (surveys, scales and scaling, sampling, and analysis of quantitative data) based on ethnographic text data. It is one of the best general methods in the social sciences.

Overviews

Pelto P., & Pelto, G. (1978). *Anthropological methods: The structure of inquiry.* New York: Cambridge University Press.

This book is the first comprehensive text to discuss ethnographic methods from an anthropological perspective. It reviews in detail the development of midrange theory, hypothesis formulation, methods of collecting a variety of different types of ethnographic data, sampling, issues of reliability and validity, ways of analyzing, interpreting and utilizing ethnographic data in communities and other settings. For readers interested in ethnographic research based on examples from societies and cultures around the world, this is the best methods text around.

Lincoln, Y., & Denzin, N. (1994). *The handbook of qualitative research.* Thousand Oaks, CA: Sage.

This edited volume provides an overview of theoretical paradigms, qualitative methods, and approaches to qualitative research from a primarily sociological perspective. It includes work on narrative inquiry, interpretation of data, and issues of representation and voice which have heretofore been missing from methods texts.

Bernard, H. R. (1998). *Handbook of methods in cultural anthropology.* Walnut Creek, CA: AltaMira.

This edited volume provides an overview of approaches to theory building, ethnographic methods ranging from interviewing to elicitation and survey research, from an anthropological perspective. Authors have cross cultural experience which they draw upon in illustrating the uses of specific qualitative methods, and in discussions of analysis and interpretation of data. Useful chapters cover applying and presenting anthropology.

LeCompte, M. D., & Preissle, J., with Tesch, R. (1993). *Ethnography and qualitative design in educational research* (2nd ed.). San Diego, CA: Academic Press.

The first edition of this text was the first work exploring the uses and execution of ethnographic research in education.

The second edition expands on the first, focussing on the role of theory in ethnographic and qualitative research design, and providing one of the only comprehensive discussions of analysis of qualitative data. It also reviews uses of software packages for use in data analysis.

LeCompte, M. D., Millroy, W., & Preissle, J. (1992). *The handbook of qualitative research in education.* San Diego, CA: Academic Press.

This edited volume, the only compilation devoted to ethnographic and qualitative research in education, includes chapters on the range of approaches to ethnographic research from cultural anthropology to micro-ethnography and critical ethnography. Each chapter was written by authors whose own research is exemplary, and includes discussions of how the individual researchers design and implement research, using examples from their own work. Included also are chapters on subjectivity, validity, ethics, the teaching of qualitative methods, and creating ethnologies.

Methods Texts

Spradley, J. P. (1979). *The ethnographic interview.* New York: Holt, Rinehart and Winston.

Spradley, J. P. (1980). *Participant observation.* New York: Holt, Rinehart and Winston.

Both of these books provide detailed information on the conduct of indepth interviews and participant observation in community and other field settings. The author covers interview and observation techniques, behavior and rapport building in the field, ways of recording, organizing and analyzing field notes, and model development.

Glaser, B., & Strauss, A. S. (1967). *The discovery of grounded theory.* Chicago: Aldine.

This seminal text explores methods for creating substantive theory from empirical data, using a technique the authors term *constant comparison.*

Weller, S. C., & Romney, A. K. (1988). *Systematic data collection.* Newbury Park, CA: Sage.

This brief monograph covers all aspects of systematic data collection including listing, pilesort and triad sorts, consensus analysis and other approaches to cognitive mapping of culture. Groundbreaking, it translates previously unaccessible psychological approaches to understanding cognitive culture (meaning) into methods useful in ethnographic field research.

INDEX

ABOUT THE EDITORS, AUTHORS, AND ARTISTS

Stephen L. Schensul (Ph.D., University of Minnesota, 1969), is Associate Professor and Director of the Center for International Community Health Studies in the Department of Community Medicine of the University of Connecticut School of Medicine. He feels he has been transformed by his ethnographic experiences, the first of which took place in the summer of 1965 (and continued for three years) in a northern Minnesota village of 155 people considerably less than the population of the apartment house where he was born and raised in the Bronx, New York. He credits this contrast as his most cross-cultural experience. His second was more than a year among the Banyankole in southwestern Uganda. It was this experience which propelled him into the view that ethnography could be used as a tool in community development. His third experience served as post-graduate training and continuous methodological discovery in applied ethnography in the Mexican American community on the West Side of Chicago over the course of seven years. He is deeply indebted to the key

informants and community activists who played a significant role in that training. His next major experience was in
Puerto Rican and Hispanic communities in inner-city Hartford, Connecticut, where applied ethnography and community activism resulted in community-based institution-
building and program development. Finally, over the last
decade and a half, his work has focused on international
health in many countries with special focus on adolescents
and young adults and reproductive health in Mauritius and
Sri Lanka. In three decades, ethnography for S. Schensul has
meant relationships, mutual learning, and collaboration.

Jean J. Schensul is a medical/educational anthropologist.
After completing her M.A. and Ph.D. at the University of
Minnesota, she conducted intervention research in education at the Institute for Juvenile Research and Center for
New Schools in Chicago. She served as co-founder and
research director of the Hispanic Health Council in Hartford for ten years, and, since 1987, has been founder and
executive director of the Institute for Community Research,
based in Hartford, Connecticut, and dedicated to community-based partnership research. She has extensive experience in the use of ethnographic and survey research methods in the United States, Latin America, Southeast Asia,
China, and West Africa. Her substantive interests are diverse, reflecting the contributions of ethnography to health,
education, the arts, and community development. She coedited three special journal issues on applied research in
education, and policy, and, with Don Stull, a book on *Collaborative Research and Social Change: Applied Anthropology
in Action*, and has published on other topics including
substance abuse prevention, AIDS, adolescent development, chronic health problems, and the arts and commu-

nity building. She is the recipient of a number of National Institute of Health Research grants, immediate past president of the Society for Applied Anthropology, former president of the Council on Anthropology and Education, and recipient (with Stephen Schensul) of the Kimball Award for Public Policy Research in Anthropology. She is adjunct professor of anthropology at the University of Connecticut and Senior Fellow, Department of Psychology, Yale University.

Margaret D. LeCompte is Professor of Education and Sociology in the School of Education, University of Colorado at Boulder. After completing her MA and PhD at the University of Chicago, she taught at the University of Houston and the University of Cincinnati, with visiting appointments at the University of North Dakota and the Universidad de Monterrey, Mexico. She also served as Executive Director for Research and Evaluation for the Houston public schools. In addition to many articles and book chapters, she cowrote *Ethnography and Qualitative Design in Educational Research* and coedited *The Handbook of Qualitative Research in Education,* the first textbook and first handbook, respectively, on ethnographic and qualitative methods in education. As a researcher, evaluator, and consultant to school districts, museums, and universities, she has published studies of dropouts, artistic and gifted students, school reform efforts, and the impact of strip mining on the social environment of rural communities. Fluent in Spanish, she is deeply interested in the education of language and ethnic minority children. She is a past president of the Council on Anthropology and Education and served as a Peace Corps volunteer in the Somali Republic from 1965 to 1967.

Ed Johnetta Miller is a weaver/silk painter/gallery curator/quilter and Master Teaching Artist. Her work has appeared in the *New York Times* and *FiberArts Magazine* and in the Renwick Gallery of the Smithsonian, the American Crafts Museum, and Wadsworth Atheneum. She is the Director of OPUS, Inc., Co-Director of the Hartford Artisans Center, and consultant to Aid to Artisans, Ghana. She teaches workshops on weaving, silk painting, and quilting to children and adults throughout the United States.

Graciela Quiñones Rodriguez is a folk artist, carving *higueras* (gourds) and working in clay, wood, and lithographs with symbols and icons derived from Taino and other indigenous art forms. She builds *cuatros, tiples,* and other Puerto Rican folk instruments guided by the inspiration of her grandfather, Lile, and her uncle, Nando, who first introduced her to Puerto Rican cultural history and Taino culture and motifs. Her work has been exhibited in major galleries and universities throughout Connecticut, at the Bridgeport Public Library, and at the Smithsonian Institution.